RANCHERO REVOLT

The Texas Pan American Series

RANCHERO REVOLT
The Mexican Revolution in Guerrero

by Ian Jacobs

 University of Texas Press, Austin

For Jan and for my parents

Western
Americana
F
1286
J33
1982

415679

Copyright © 1982 by the University of Texas Press
All rights reserved
Printed in the United States of America
First Edition, 1982

Requests for permission to reproduce material from this work should be sent to Permissions, University of Texas Press, Box 7819, Austin, Texas 78712.

The Texas Pan American Series is published with the assistance of a revolving publication fund established by the Pan American Sulphur Company.

Library of Congress Cataloging in Publication Data

Jacobs, Ian, 1952–
  Ranchero revolt.
  (The Texas Pan American series)
  Bibliography: p.
  Includes index.
  1. Guerrero (Mexico: State)—History. 2. Land tenure—Mexico—Guerrero (State)—History. 3. Peasantry—Mexico—Guerrero (State)—History. I. Title. II. Series.
F1286.J33 1982   972'.7308   82-8601
ISBN 0-292-77026-X   AACR2

Contents

Tables, Figures, and Maps

Preface

This study began life as a doctoral dissertation on the Mexican revolution in Guerrero. I began my work hoping to document the existence of a ranchero class in Porfirian Guerrero and its participation in the revolutionary movement. The attractions of Guerrero were obvious.

First, the state's history is, relatively speaking, uncharted. Second, Guerrero's controversial role in the contemporary body politic in Mexico suggested that a study of its recent past would provide fascinating results. Moreover, this mountainous, somewhat peripheral area seemed a likely region in which to find a substantial ranchero population, and while Guerrero did not give birth to a Zapata, a Villa, or an Obregón, it was an area in which an important ranchero group, led by the Figueroa family, joined the Maderista revolution in February 1911. In addition, the Figueroas originated from the portion of the state which borders on Morelos, and their dealings with Zapata seemed likely to provide a useful point of comparison of the ranchero style of revolution with the Morelos paradigm.

The nature and quantity of the archival materials in the Secretaría de la Reforma Agraria (then the Departamento de Asuntos Agrarios y Colonización) forced me to concentrate my study of land tenure on the northern portion of the state embraced by the districts of Alarcón and Hidalgo. My study of the political origins and development of the revolution in Guerrero could not be so circumscribed, and, accordingly, it proved necessary to consider the broader issues of state politics, while nevertheless according a certain emphasis to the Figueroas and other groups in the north of the state. For the activities of the Figueroa family and the role of northern Guerrero in local politics cannot be properly understood outside the context of the wider politics of the state as a whole. The north was not always the focus of state politics, although its role was often crucial. Ideally, this study might have included more material on the municipal and regional politics of the districts of Alarcón and Hidalgo, but, unfortunately, such a study was not possible. Only in Taxco have the municipal archives been conserved, and very little material could be found in the archives of the state government in Chilpancingo.

Unfortunately, I was denied access to two private archives which might have done much to elucidate further the revolutionary history of Guerrero in general, and of the district of Hidalgo in particular. These were the private archive of Carlos Carranco Cardoso and the private papers of the Figueroa family. In the absence of these documentary sources, Dr. Arturo Figueroa Uriza's history of the revolution in Guerrero is a work of fundamental importance for events from 1911 to 1924. His *Ciudadanos en armas* is based on the family archive in his possession. It displays certain natural family biases (Dr. Figueroa Uriza is the son of General Andrés Figueroa) but, prudently used in conjunction with available documentary and newspaper sources, it is a mine of information. In particular, in using Dr. Figueroa's narrative, one needs to take account of his strong antipathy for Zapatismo.

It would have been quite impossible to complete the research for this book without the help of a considerable number of people, in Great Britain, Mexico, and the United States, who gave generously of advice and friendship. Although I can mention only some of them here, I am grateful to them all. For sound and freely offered advice I am indebted to Alan Knight, Moisés González Navarro, Alicia Orive, Beatriz Rojas Nieto, and Dudley Ankerson. Alan Knight and Geoffrey Walker read and criticized my Ph.D. dissertation, and their perceptive observations helped to make the final draft more cogent and readable. Alfonso Campos read, and corrected in some points, the section on the Porfiriato. Discussions with Malcolm Hoodless and James Murray helped crystallize some of the ideas set forth herein.

I owe a debt of gratitude to Professor Enrique Florescano and his researchers in the Departamento de Investigaciones Históricas del Instituto Nacional de Antropología e Historia for their hospitality and advice, and for allowing me free access to their bibliography of Mexican economic history. In Chilpancingo, Arquímedes Morales Carranza, rector of the Universidad Autónoma de Guerrero, and his staff, notably Lic. Salvador Camelo, offered advice and assistance and generously allowed a foreign visitor to use the facilities of their institution. In the Colegio de México, Luis Muro kindly allowed me to consult his annotated index of the Archivo Histórico de la Defensa Nacional.

My research would have been quite impossible without the help and patience of the staff of a number of libraries and archives: Biblioteca Nacional del México; Biblioteca del Colegio de México; Biblioteca del Departamento de Investigaciones Históricas del Instituto Nacional de Antropología e Historia; Hemeroteca Nacional; University Library, Cambridge; British Library; Library of Congress; Archivo de la Secretaría de la Reforma Agraria; Archivo General de la Nación; Archives Department, Biblioteca de la Universidad Nacional Autónoma de México; Instituto Nacional de Estudios Históricos de la Revolución Mexicana; Instituto de Estudios Históricos de México, Condumex, S.A.; Archivo General del Gobierno del Estado de Guerrero; United States National Archives.

Dr. J. Antonio Ortega Figueroa, in 1975 *presidente municipal* of Taxco, must be singled out for special thanks for allowing me access to the papers of the *ayuntamiento* of Taxco, and for granting me the aid of one of his policemen to clear a space in which to work. Another gracious *guerrerense*, Don Jesús Figueroa Alcocer, made me a gift of his *Crónica de la Revolución en Guerrero*, and of two bottles of the excellent wine which he now produces in Huitzuco. I greatly appreciated his hospitality and generosity.

Many others who, in one way or another, helped my work along cannot be mentioned here, but two must be singled out, for my debt to them is especially deep. David Brading, my research supervisor, was unstinting with his advice and criticism, without which this book would never have been written, and much of the credit for whatever value it has belongs to him. Finally, my wife, Janet, through her tolerance and support made a special contribution to my work for which acknowledgment here is but small thanks.

Of course, any errors of fact or interpretation are my own, and nobody else bears any responsibility for them.

The reader should note that wherever "$" is used it stands for the Mexican peso, unless qualified by the prefix "U.S."

"Many of those who sign this memorandum have been born and have grown up on the small piece of land which we possess today and which . . . we have managed to buy by dint of perseverance and sacrifices; we are satisfied at having always fulfilled our duties and obligations as citizens and taxpayers, even in the periods of armed agitation."

Smallholders of Huitzuco
in a letter to Lázaro Cárdenas,
12 May 1938

Introduction

In 1904 a naturalist, passing through Chilpancingo on his way to collect samples on the Pacific coast, made the acquaintance of Manuel Guillén, governor of Guerrero. Born in Guerrero, but educated in the United States, and an owner of estates in the valley of Mexico, the urbane Don Manuel lived alone in his capital. He explained to the visitor that he "yearned for his family, but did not dare inflict the journey [from Mexico City] on the ladies." The governor's wife and daughters were fortunate that he was so solicitous of their comfort—the seventy-mile journey from the railhead in Iguala was an arduous two days on horseback.[1]

Guerrero was a backwater in those days, but even such an isolated region was not wholly untouched by Porfirian progress. For example, in 1905 five kilometers of piping brought drinking water into Huitzuco for the first time. About the same time a brand new Municipal Palace was opened, and a clock installed in the tower of the church.[2] These modest achievements were landmarks in the anonymous history of Huitzuco. They were signs of progress, of the dynamism of a new rural middle class which was growing in numbers under the rule of President Porfirio Díaz.

The Figueroa brothers, Rómulo, Ambrosio, and Francisco, were typical members of this prospering middle class. Rómulo, born in a small ranchería not far from Huitzuco in 1863, was a man of enterprise. He owned two ranchos and operated three small businesses in Huitzuco. His brother Ambrosio was born in the town in 1869. He joined the military reserve established by Bernardo Reyes, but, instead of following a military career, left Huitzuco to manage a rice mill in Morelos. In 1908, he returned home, bought some land, and settled down to the life of a provincial farmer. His youngest brother, Francisco, was born a year later and was the intellectual of the family. After attending the local school, he studied in the Instituto Literario in Chilpancingo, returning afterwards to Huitzuco to establish his own school.[3]

The three brothers had a younger cousin, Andrés, born in Chaucingo (a small ranchería) in 1884. At the tender age of ten he was sent to Cuernavaca to obtain an education which the local schools could not offer. However, Andrés was not to follow in the scholarly footsteps of his cousin Francisco. Instead, his son tells us, he became a "genuinely *guerrerense* small farmer, who ploughs the fields in the heat of a burning sun and sows the seed in the fertile furrow, [and] also milks the cow, hunts deer, or lassos a colt among the clumps of briar in the rugged mountains."[4]

If history had not drawn them into the *bola* of the Mexican revolution, Andrés and his three cousins would, no doubt, have continued to enjoy their prosperous provincial existence. However, Rómulo, Ambrosio, and Francisco would become major figures in the history of the Mexican revolution in Guerrero. Andrés would also make a name for himself in revolutionary Mexico, but his career would take him away from his native Guerrero.

For some forty years, until the late 1960s, scholars of the Mexican revolution held to a consensus on the nature and meaning of the first great upheaval of the twentieth century. Pioneered by U.S. scholars such as Frank Tannenbaum,[5] the established view of the revolution portrayed it as a mass uprising which sought to better the lot of the Mexican peasant and worker and to drag Mexico out of a dismal past into an era of greater social justice, economic progress, and political freedom. While it was recognized that many of these goals had been but imperfectly achieved, the Mexican revolution was still the "preferred Revolution"—a non-Marxist, reasonably democratic road to economic development and political liberalization.[6]

However, in the last ten years or so, ever wider cracks have begun to appear in this impressive façade of scholarly consensus. As David Bailey has recently observed, "there is less agreement today about the nature and meaning of the Mexican Revolution than at any time since scholars first turned their attention to it more than fifty years ago."[7] A major factor which led to the crumbling of scholarly consensus was the appearance of an increasing number of local and regional studies.[8] Seen from the bottom up, from the perspective of the provincial town and the rural village, the revolution assumes an entirely different aspect.[9] No longer is there one revolution but many revolutions, each with its own motives. The grand themes of social reform and economic and political justice are reduced to more humble topics, such as "the resolution of age-old conflicts within and among local communities . . . the settlement of familial and clan disputes and struggles between rival communities over the siting of local seats of government."[10]

In the short run, the wealth of detail thrown up by the growing trend towards "microhistory"[11] is proving somewhat indigestible. Sometimes it is difficult for the historian to delineate with confidence the broader themes and trends of the revolution, with the result that the end of the old consensus has not yet been followed by the general acceptance of a new perspective. However, in the long run, local studies will surely lead to a more accurate understanding of the revolution's real import, and for the time being they add immeasurably to our understanding of the subtleties and contrasts of the revolutionary era.

The fruits of regional and local studies have already been considerable: for example, they "allow us to view the preliminary working out of novel political policies and styles that later were to be implemented nationally"; they give us a better understanding of "informal mechanisms of authority and control that frequently operate in the shadow of formal institutions"; they demonstrate the continuance of traditional methods of social control in many areas within the revolutionary apparatus.[12] Moreover, regional studies serve to point up the social composition of revolutionary groups; their goals and values; the cultural and political world views which distinguished one faction from another.[13]

The best-known regional study is, of course, John Womack's account of the Zapatista movement in Morelos,[14] which chronicles the uprising of the free village peasantry against the encroachment of the modernizing sugar plantations. Zapatismo sought to recover usurped lands and to implement a millenarian vision of village democracy which the free-wheeling northerners who emerged as winners in 1917 could neither understand nor tolerate.

Our understanding of the victors in the 1910–1917 upheaval has been deepened immeasurably by Héctor Aguilar Camín's study of Sonora between 1910 and 1970.[15] Aguilar paints a richly detailed portrait of a frontier society which, under the rule of Porfirio Díaz, experienced an unprecedented economic boom. This boom left untouched traditional centers of economic and political power such as Alamos and Hermosillo, but spurred unparalleled growth in, for example, Guaymas and Navajoa. Shifts in economic fortune, however, were not accompanied by changes in political influence—the established and aging Porfirian elite clung to power at the expense of "an old class of wealthy families who had been displaced, or believed they had, by the state oligarchy." The collapse of the modus vivendi which had allowed local oligarchies a limited autonomy and protection of their economic interests created the conditions for a revolt led by elite groups who "had ambitions for a less restricted slice of the pie" than the ruling Porfirian clique allowed them.[16]

However, the Porfirian economic boom also gave rise to a restless, free-wheeling "non-commissioned class"[17]—small farmers, petty administrators, the "miscellaneous worker, who wandered from one job to another in the frontier zone,"[18] and the like. These middle groups, men such as Obregón and Calles, "saw in the revolution . . . the opportunity to realize the aspirations of an emergent semi-rural, semi-urban lower middle class, whose enemy (and paradigm) was the big land-owner, the rich men of the Porfiriato or, as Calles at times called them, the 'wealthy bourgeois.'"[19] It was these noncommissioned elements who soon displaced the elite groups which had launched the Maderista uprising in Sonora and who shaped a style of revolution which was, in many ways, the embryo of the modern Mexican state which emerged in the 1920s and 1930s.[20] Administrative efficiency and the consolidation of state power were the watchwords of the Sonoran rebels, not social reform or economic justice.

As in Sonora, in Coahuila the Maderista revolution was launched not by peasants but by *hacendados* and middle-class groups. The seeds of revolt lay in elite factional strife and the unrest of "ranchers" and "the frustrated petty bourgeoisie." Even "agrarian unrest had a middle class tone." These circumstances gave rise to a mildly populist revolutionary regime predicated on administrative efficiency and "orderly reformism."[21]

In Chihuahua, in contrast, the revolution was launched not by disgruntled elite groups but by a coalition of "the rapidly expanding urban and rural middle class," unemployed workers, and former military colonists who had been dispossessed by the expansion of the haciendas.[22] The economic and social background to the explosion of unrest in Chihuahua was the extraordinary economic and political domination of the Terrazas clique, which did away with the autonomy of local government; corrupt and abusive municipal administration; the unemployment and hardship visited on the workers and the middle classes by the 1907 depression and the 1907–1908 drought; and the assault of the haciendas on the lands of the peasants and rancheros, and especially of the former military colonies.[23]

Emphasizing regional differences in the revolution, Friedrich Katz has shown that in Chihuahua, in marked contrast to Morelos, peasants were a minority of the population, and the revolutionary movement in the state "was not composed solely, or even predominantly, of the peasant class."[24] Indeed, the minimal participation of the peasantry was characteristic of the revolution in the north as a whole.

Another subject which regional studies have helped to illuminate is the relationship between the revolutionary leaders and their troops. One of the most intriguing fruits of Héctor Aguilar's work on Sonora is his description of the recruitment methods employed by the local revolutionary leaders. While, in Morelos, Zapata's chieftains raised guerrilla armies of peasants who fought to recover their land and who would withdraw from the fray to cultivate their fields, in Sonora the rebels did not find it necessary to offer any kind of social reforms to entice recruits—indeed, they actively defended the status quo. The Sonoran forces were a paid army whose maintenance rested on "la moral del haber."[25]

In Chihuahua, on the other hand, the Villista army fell somewhere between the extremes of Sonora and Morelos. "Villa was not a traditional peasant leader like Emiliano Zapata," and since the Chihuahuan peasantry was quite small in numbers, his soldiers had to be rewarded not with land but with a cash wage. However, this did not mean that Villa was not interested in land distribution, merely that his aims and priorities were quite different from those of Zapata. Villa's chief concern was his troops, and his aim was to settle them in military agricultural colonies when the fighting was over.[26]

A similar relationship between the military chieftains and their troops has been documented in studies of San Luis Potosí. At first, the revolution in San Luis was led and controlled, much as it was in Sonora or Coahuila, by a disgruntled section of the local elite.[27] However, in late 1912 an agrarian-based revolt broke out in the Huasteca region led by the Cedillo brothers, smallholders who had suffered harassment and encroachment by neighboring haciendas.[28] Unlike Villa, the Cedillos did not pay their troops in cash. Instead, payment was in kind.[29] However, in the wake of the Agua Prieta revolt, Saturnino Cedillo moved to reward his troops by giving them plots of land in one of ten agrarian colonies which he established. These colonists constituted, in effect, a permanent reserve on which Cedillo could call to raise an army whenever necessary.[30]

Regional studies of Veracruz and Michoacán in the two decades following the end of the military upheaval of 1910–1920 have emphasized yet another variation on the relationship between political or military power and land reform. Cedillo was, as Dudley Ankerson has observed, a leader whose origins were distinctly rural and whose ideology and methods of recruitment were reminiscent of the nineteenth-century caudillos.[31] Quite a different kind of agrarian leader was exemplified by Adalberto Tejeda, who for many years dominated the state of Veracruz in the 1920s and 1930s. Like other leaders of his type, Tejeda's background was urban. His political power was based, not on charisma, familial ties, or military prowess, but on his skillful control and manipulation of the bureaucracy, and of peasant and labor unions. Tejeda's was a modern, associational style of politics quite foreign to men like Cedillo, and poles apart from the traditional authority of peasant leaders like Zapata.[32] Similarly, in Michoacán, Francisco Múgica attempted "to find . . . allies from among peasant or labour groups by offering social reforms, more radical than those of the Sonoran triumvirate."[33]

Yucatán witnessed a similar radical reformist movement from 1922 to 1924 when the socialist Felipe Carrillo Puerto controlled the state. However, a recent study of the Carrillo Puerto regime has added an extra dimension to the portrait of the modern agrarian caudillo. While Carrillo Puerto shared many of Tejeda's and Múgica's techniques and goals, his regime employed a mixture of formal institutional mechanisms of mobilization and more traditional, informal forms of authority and control, relying on the established network of Yucatecan caciques to mobilize peasant support.[34] Indeed, one senses that just such traditional forms of authority may also have lain not far below the surface of Tejeda's organizations in Veracruz.[35]

It is one of the special virtues of local and regional studies that they afford these kinds of insights into the methods used by revolutionary leaders to mobilize support. To cite another example, Paul Friedrich's now classic study of the agrarian *cacicazgo* of Primo Tapia in Michoacán painted a subtle portrait of the mix of traditional kinship relations and violence on which the *cacicazgo* was built. Friedrich also demonstrated how the agrarian cacique functioned as an intermediary between the national revolutionary regime and the peasant villages.[36]

Another particularly revealing study of peasant mobilization and control can be found in Raymond Buve's articles on the revolution in Tlaxcala, especially valuable since they embrace a broad chronological sweep from the Porfiriato to the 1930s. Buve observes that even in such a small state as Tlaxcala, significant variations in social and economic structure determined the extent of peasant involvement in the revolution. In the north where the peon was tied closely to the hacienda, the peasantry remained passive, but elsewhere semiproletarian peasants, who alternated between working in the city and cultivating their village lands, actively participated in the revolutionary upheaval.[37] However, in the 1920s and especially in the 1930s the revolutionary regime gained ever greater control over peasant mobilization, and the interplay between local power-brokers and the national government became the basic determinant of peasant participation in the revolutionary process.[38]

Local studies are, therefore, a crucial tool for understanding the nature of peasant mobilization in the revolution. By the same token, a local perspective can be used to explain the lack of mobilization. Ronald Waterbury has used just such an approach to explain the relative lack of revolutionary activity in Oaxaca compared to neighboring Morelos. In Oaxaca the hacienda was much smaller and far less dominant than in Morelos. Commerce was far more lucrative than agriculture, and merchant interests in the cochineal trade militated against the seizure of village lands which precipitated the revolt in Morelos. Indeed, the real key to the absence of revolutionary activity in Oaxaca lay precisely in the successful retention of village lands and the proliferation of peasant smallholders.[39]

The emergence of local and regional history as an established approach to the Mexican revolution is, therefore, yielding new perspectives on the events which shaped contemporary Mexico. In some respects, as already remarked, the wealth of detail makes it difficult to reach an overall conclusion about the nature and significance of the revolution. Nevertheless certain themes and trends do emerge which were reflected in Guerrero between 1910 and 1940 and which were often constants in the revolution in other areas.

Broadly speaking, three principal themes characterized the Mexican revolution in Guerrero. The first was the relationship between local forces and the central government. The second was the fragmentation of the revolution, both geographical and generational. The third was the role of the middle sectors, and in particular of a group sorely neglected in Mexican historiography—the ranchero or smallholder.

The relationship between local forces and the center was by no means a new question in Guerrero, for it had been the central theme of the nineteenth century, just as it would be for the first three decades of the twentieth. The nineteenth century in Guerrero was the era of the cacique, the regional chieftain. Indeed, coastal Guerrero was the domain of the foremost nineteenth-century cacique, Juan Alvarez. The caciques built up their following by dispensing patronage, and themselves often looked for support to their relations with politicians at the center; but, in the last resort, predicated as it was on regional domination, *caciquismo* was the natural enemy of the centralizing forces which strove throughout the nineteenth century to forge a modern nation-state in Mexico. Although the power of the caciques was steadily undermined, especially during the last few decades of the century, the question of the relationship of the periphery to the center was by no means resolved and would become a principal theme of the revolutionary period. The revolution, in theory, stood for municipal autonomy and states' rights, but in practice it consummated the work of the nineteenth-century centralists.

There could be several variations on this theme. In Sonora the frontier tradition of self-defense was translated into resistance first to the Orozco rebellion and later to the Huerta coup. In Veracruz the relationship between Tejeda's state machine and the center was a crucial issue which eventually led to his downfall. Yet in Tlaxcala local politicians made a smoother transition by incorporating their local power bases into the national party structure. Whatever the variations, by 1940 the issue was resolved in favor of the revolutionary regime in Mexico City.

Fragmentation of the revolutionary movement in Guerrero stemmed naturally from the nineteenth-century struggle against centralization to which the rebels of 1911–1917 were heirs. Following the pattern of the caciques, revolutionary leaders staked out their territory, which formed the foundation of their strength and to which they would return in times of adversity. Fragmentation was not only geographical, however, but also generational. The older military chieftains who had waged the struggle against Díaz and Huerta, Carranza, or Zapata soon found themselves replaced by a younger breed of civilian politicians who represented the wave of the future in state politics.

Regional history has naturally tended to emphasize this fragmentation of the revolutionary movement, and in the process has done much to destroy the traditional image of the revolution as a mass uprising of the oppressed peasantry. Indeed, in some states— Chihuahua, for example—the dispossessed peasant played a minor role, while in others, such as Sonora, the participation of rural laborers was tightly controlled by a leadership concerned to maintain as far as possible the status quo. Even in central Mexico, where the peasantry constituted the great mass of the population, Oaxaca could remain relatively calm while Morelos was in constant revolutionary turmoil.

Thus at closer range the subtle relationship between land and revolution has taken on more varied hues. Agrarian radicalism, one of the basic tenets of the ideology of Mexico's revolution, is now often seen as a means of social control and political manipulation.[40] In Guerrero, too, the link between agrarian reform and political control was quite clear. Land distribution was not merely a matter of social reform—it also served to tie a new clientele (the *agrarista* or *ejidatario*) to the new revolutionary regime. If a portion of the spoils of the revolution fell to the landless peasantry, the campesino paid a price.

Furthermore, in line with this trend to place the role of the dispossessed peasantry into a new perspective, a number of regional studies have emphasized the participation, often prominent, of middle sectors in the revolution—rancheros, petty administrators, mule drivers, small-time merchants, and the like. Several studies demonstrate quite clearly the enormous growth of the middle sectors of society in northern Mexico[41] and their active participation in the revolution. In Guerrero, middle-class groups would likewise play a crucial role in the events of 1911–1917 and beyond, chief among them the rancheros of the northern portion of the state. Here the relationship between land and revolution was quite different from that in neighboring Morelos, where the communal village was locked in a life or death struggle with the hacienda.

The ranchero, until very recently, has been sadly neglected in the literature on rural Mexico. This lack of concern with the smallholder is something of a paradox, since references to this important section of rural society are not lacking in documentary sources,[42] or in travelers' accounts of nineteenth-century Mexico.[43] Moreover, in the late nineteenth century, two ground-breaking Mexican scholars described the rancho, contrasting its carefully cultivated fields with the neglected and unproductive land of the large estates.[44]

Immediately after the end of the military phase of the Mexican revolution in 1920, an American scholar, George McBride, laid some stress on the rancho's role in rural Mexico, concluding that "the rancheros are coming to exert an influence that will have to be reckoned with."[45] Ten years later the anthropologist Paul Taylor published a study of the ranchero community of Arandas in Jalisco,[46] but it would be a full thirty-five years before Luis González would publish his classic account of ranchero society in Michoacán.[47]

González showed that, in San José de Gracia, the ranchero enjoyed a *belle époque* during the three decades of the Porfiriato. The rancho emerged in San José in 1862 when the Hacienda de Cojumatlán was divided into fifty or so small lots. Division of the land continued to be the rule, and in 1901 there were about 140 farms in the parish of San José averaging 178 hectares each, while in the rest of the municipality of Jiquilpan there were 1,170 farms averaging 265 hectares.[48]

In the 1970s a number of anthropologists published accounts of ranchero communities,[49] but it was not until 1978 that another major study of the rancho appeared.[50] David Brading's history of the smallholding in Guanajuato is especially important because it documents the existence of a resilient ranchero class throughout the colonial period and into the nineteenth and twentieth centuries.[51] While the rancho in Arandas and San José may have been a creation of the late eighteenth and the nineteenth centuries, in León its historical roots went much deeper.

Finally, a recent account of the rancheros of Pisaflores, Hidalgo,[52] takes the story one step further by demonstrating the smallholders' active participation in the revolution of 1910. Neither González's rancheros in Michoacán nor Taylor's Arandas smallholders had participated in the revolutionary activity of 1910 to 1920. In Pisaflores, by contrast, the rancheros were active revolutionaries. Indeed, in the Sierra Alta de Hidalgo, the revolution amounted to little more than a factional dispute between various ranchero factions.[53]

In northern Guerrero, as in Pisaflores, the rancheros would be central figures in the Mexican revolution. Their participation in the upheavals of 1911 to 1917 stemmed from the confluence of complex social and political factors which by 1911 had created a sizable ranchero class which found its political and economic horizons restricted by the heavy hand of Porfirian policy. Ironically enough, President Díaz's enforcement of liberal land policies had bolstered the very smallholder class which would help overthrow him. Moreover, his insistence on political centralization had provided the grievance which would spur them to rebellion. That is a long story—one which begins with the political history of nineteenth-century Guerrero and ends with the triumph of centralism in the 1920s and 1930s.

RANCHERO REVOLT

1. Political Opposition in Guerrero during the Rule of Porfirio Díaz

In 1876 the revolution of Tuxtepec brought to power a *oaxaqueño* general who was to dominate the history of Mexico until 1911, when the Mexican revolution swept him from power. Porfirio Díaz was one of a generation of generals who made their military reputations in the wars of the Reform and of the Intervention, men who had little in common with the brilliant generation of Liberal politicians who dominated the political scene for the nine years from 1867 to 1876.

After the defeat of Emperor Maximilian's army at Querétaro in 1867, the civilian politicians devoted their time to passionate political debate. As a result, "the government, harassed without respite, had to spend much of its time, and some of its resources, in defending itself and attacking [its opponents]; therefore, its actions and its thoughts were concentrated on the political quarrel of the day, neglecting long-term administrative activity, and, above all, public works or development."[1] The military generation of which Díaz was a member despised the squabbling of the intellectual politicians, and while this alone can scarcely account for the revolution of Tuxtepec, it does help to explain some features of Díaz's regime, summarized in the motto "less politics and more administration."

Díaz, himself one of the great caudillos of Mexico, solved the great dilemma of that classic feature of nineteenth-century Mexican politics known as *caudillaje*. The caudillo relied, for a power base, on a series of patron-client relationships which were inherently unstable. Díaz's genius lay in the invention of a modernized *caudillaje* which resolved the problem of stability by formalizing the patron-client relationship within a centralized (or at least centralizing) political system, which retained the personalistic patron-client relationship, but gave it longer life through a system of institutionalized rewards.[2]

Thus, the Porfiriato, as Díaz's rule came to be called, was char-

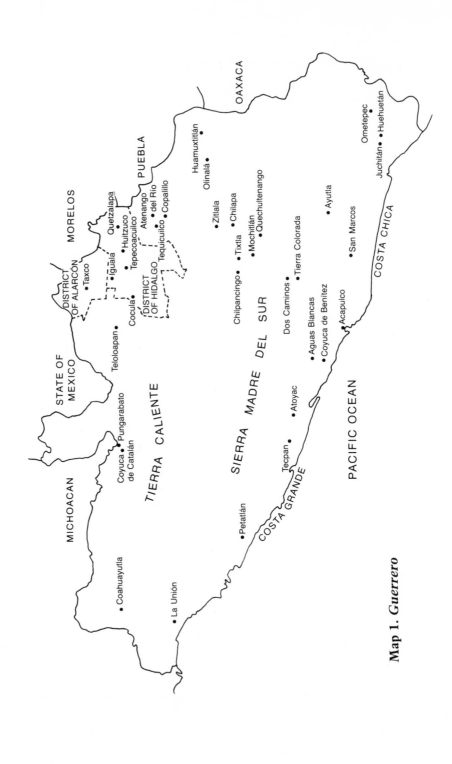

Map 1. Guerrero

acterized by a high degree of political stability, which, according to a prominent historian of the period, rested on the control of three main factors: the federal Congress, the governors of the states, and the military.[3] Control of the states was complicated by the existence, in several of them, of powerful caciques. During the wars of the Reform and of the Intervention a number of military chieftains had made themselves "the real, direct, tangible authorities of [their] region, [with] a power all the more strong and personal since [they] did everything with the authority and freedom which force, necessity, and, if need be, the law itself gave [them]."[4] Hence, there arose the larger *cacicazgos* of men such as Corona in the west, Escobedo in the north, and Díaz himself in the east, and the lesser but still more deeply rooted *cacicazgos* of Méndez, Lucas, and Bonilla in the Sierra de Puebla, Treviño and Naranjo in Nuevo León, and Fidencio Hernández in the Sierra de Ixtlán in Oaxaca.[5]

In his first period of office from 1877 to 1880, Díaz, in many cases, simply had to accept the existence of a number of powerful *cacicazgos*, such as those of Rafael Cravioto in Hidalgo, Gerónimo Treviño in Nuevo León, and Trinidad García de la Cadena in Zacatecas. The severe limitations on Díaz's power to intervene in the states in these early years is perhaps best exemplified by the case of Sonora, where the cacique, General Vicente Mariscal, was an Iglesista. Although Mariscal had opposed Porfirio's revolution of Tuxtepec, he was too strong to be removed at this stage, and Díaz had to negotiate a settlement with him. Similarly, in Oaxaca, Díaz "seemed to feel himself powerless to restore a minimum of unity and tolerance between his followers."[6]

The first successes in destroying the regional *cacicazgos* were scored by Manuel González between 1880 and 1884. In Zacatecas he ousted Trinidad García de la Cadena, and he scored a resounding success in Jalisco, where the federal commander, General Francisco Tolentino, took over the governorship and dismantled the hold of Ignacio Vallarta on the state. This was a particularly important success, "not only because [Vallarta's *cacicazgo*], like those of Puebla, Tamaulipas, Nuevo León, and Hidalgo, obstructed the action of the central government, but because the Jalisco *cacicazgo* was openly hostile to [González]."[7]

Not until 1888, when Díaz succeeded in having himself reelected, did he gain full control of the reins of power in Mexico. By then he had achieved "the position which he coveted, that of the irreplaceable man, or, more modestly, the best possibility, or the least bad, which the country had before it."[8] This consolidation of his power was achieved, on the state level, by the destruction of those *cacicazgos* which still threatened the power of the federal government, notably that of Treviño and Naranjo in Nuevo León, where Díaz succeeded in placing Bernardo Reyes in the governorship in 1885.[9] Where the local caciques represented no threat to Díaz's political control, and where they had no ambitions outside their domain, they were generally left untouched, as was the case of the Craviotos in Hidalgo.[10]

In Guerrero, Díaz faced severe political problems in subordinating the state to his control. Not least among these was the existence of a powerful *cacicazgo* of more than fifty years' standing: that of the Alvarez family on the Costa Grande. A proper understanding of the origins of the Alvarez *cacicazgo* is important for an understanding of the problems faced by Díaz in Guerrero. This story is in large part the story of the birth of the state of Guerrero itself.

Juan Alvarez was born on 27 January 1790 in Atoyac, son of an *hacendado* with a modest fortune.[11] He joined the insurgent forces of José María Morelos, and by 1821 he had emerged from the wars of Independence as "the leader of greatest prestige on the coast." Morelos had appointed Alvarez to the position of military commander of Acapulco, a post he held until 1823, and again from 1824 to 1827. A loyal follower of Vicente Guerrero, Alvarez espoused Guerrero's Liberal ideas, especially his federalism, which represented autonomy for the "South." In 1828 he supported Santa Anna's *pronunciamiento* which took Guerrero to the presidency,[12] and when Guerrero was deposed by Bustamente in 1830, Alvarez issued a manifesto in which he spoke of defending the independence of the states from encroachment by the federal executive, and, in particular, of defending the independence of the "South."[13]

Alvarez fought for Guerrero in the "War of the South," sparked off by Bustamente's coup. It was in this war, from March 1830 to February 1831, that Alvarez first found himself in conflict with Nicolás Bravo, cacique of the central region of Chilpancingo, Tixtla, and Chilapa, a centralist, and a leading figure of the Scottish-rite masons.[14] With the death of Guerrero in February 1831, Alvarez inherited much of Don Vicente's prestige and consolidated his control of the Costa Grande,[15] thus cementing the geographical basis of his rivalry with Bravo.

By 1832 both Alvarez and Bravo had carved out well-defined zones of influence. Alvarez controlled the entire Costa Grande, while Bravo held sway in the central area of the future state of Guerrero.[16] The Costa Chica was dominated, from 1830 to 1844, by an ally of Bravo, Florencio Villarreal.[17] These lines of battle remained broadly unchanged into the early 1840s, although Alvarez steadily extended his power beyond the limits of the Costa Grande.

The basis of Alvarez's power on the coast was his patron-client relationship with the *pintos* (people of mixed black and Indian blood) of the region. Don Juan's influence soon began to spread beyond the coast, however, and by the 1840s his prestige among the Indians of the Chilapa area was so great that the government was forced to call him in to negotiate an end to the caste war which broke out in Quechultenango on 19 March 1842, and rapidly spread throughout the Sierra de Chilapa as far as Tlapa, and to the Tierra Caliente as far as Cutzamala.[18] Whether or not Alvarez actually instigated the uprisings for his own ends as his enemies alleged, it is certainly true that he used them "to consolidate his personal position, but it is also true that he contributed much to improve the position of the Indians."[19]

By the mid-1840s Alvarez's power in the "South" was irresistible. In January 1845 he replaced Bravo as *comandante de la división del sur,* the supreme military chief of the area. Furthermore, he gained complete control of the Costa Chica by ousting Joaquín Rea, Villarreal's replacement as commander of that region; in the Chilapa area he supported the Indians in their land disputes and was accused by the *hacendados* of Chilapa (supported as always by Bravo) of establishing a network of "supporters and caciques."[20] Alvarez's domination of the "South" received official sanction in October 1849 with the foundation of the state of Guerrero. Formerly considered by the government in Mexico City to be virtually an outlaw (he had earned the nickname "Panther of the South"), Alvarez now became the legally recognized civil authority in the new state: he was immediately appointed provisional governor,[21] and in 1851 was elected constitutional governor. His supporters won complete control of the state Congress,[22] and his control of Guerrero remained undisputed until his death in 1867.

However, the wars of the Reform and of the Intervention saw the rise to prominence in Guerrero of a new generation of caciques who would dispute the inheritance of the *cacicazgo.* The heir designate among these new caciques was Alvarez's son, Diego, a veteran of many of his father's campaigns. His most powerful rival was Vicente Jiménez of Tixtla.[23] A third cacique, Canuto A. Neri, a native of Chilpancingo, had less prestige than either Diego Alvarez or Jiménez and generally worked in association with one or the other.

Don Juan clearly intended his son to inherit his *cacicazgo,* and on 6 May 1862 Diego duly occupied the governorship, a position he held until 1869. However, Vicente Jiménez was not disposed to concede control of the state to his rival without a struggle. Although

Diego Alvarez could rely on the support of his father in any dispute over regional dominance, Jiménez also held an ace in his hand, for while the looming crisis in Guerrero had its roots in local rivalries, it was, nevertheless, intimately related to events on the national political scene. Jiménez was a close ally of Porfirio Díaz, whose supporters were on the offensive against the administration of President Juárez. When Jiménez rebelled against Governor Alvarez in June 1867 (four months before the death of the elder Alvarez), Díaz and Ignacio Altamirano, the noted *guerrerense*, politician, and intellectual, pleaded his cause with the president. Juárez, little inclined as he was to support the independent-minded Alvarez, could scarcely countenance a Porfirista victory in Guerrero. While Jiménez tried to force Juárez's hand by presenting him with a military *fait accompli*, the president stonewalled. The best offer he would make was to send an independent figure to Guerrero as governor in order to hold new elections. Finally, Juárez had his way and a *jalisciense* general, Francisco O. Arce, was dispatched to the south to mediate between the warring factions.[24]

Arce was appointed governor on 25 January 1869, in an attempt to assert Juárez's authority and to maintain the fragile peace in Guerrero, but the imposition of Arce was not well received by the caciques of Guerrero, who clearly saw it as a restriction of their power in the state.[25] In April 1869 it was reported that "some individuals, supporters of C. General Diego Alvarez, have disturbed the public order in various points of the district of Tabares, gathering together armed men for this purpose." The authorities of the state were warned to keep a vigilant watch in order to prevent a possible revolution.[26]

A more serious rebellion took place in 1870, led by Vicente Jiménez, and supported by Canuto A. Neri. The crisis began in May 1869 when the *juez municipal* of Tixtla accused Arce of a number of violations of the state's constitution. The supporters of Jiménez in the state Congress declared Arce guilty as charged, and appointed an interim governor.[27] The hostility to Arce in Tixtla, which at that time was the state capital, was such that he was forced to abandon the city, moving first to Mexico City to consult with Juárez and then to the safety of Iguala, where the Supreme Court of Guerrero established itself and absolved the governor of the charges against him. Arce then moved his capital to Chilpancingo.[28]

Once again national political rivalries formed the backdrop to the local factional struggle. Jiménez, as in 1867, was supported by Porfirio Díaz and his allies in Congress. Juárez, who had placed Arce in the governorship in the first place, was, therefore, compelled to support him against Jiménez's machinations, supplying federal troops to shore up Arce's position. Although Canuto A. Neri defeated the federal forces advancing on Chilapa at Montealegre on 8 October 1870, on that same day Arce was able to establish a Congress composed of his supporters at Chilpancingo. Jiménez, meanwhile, had established a rival Congress in Tixtla which on 31 September 1870 declared that Arce had been deposed as governor.[29] By 8 October Arce's authority had been recognized by all the districts of the state which were not under Jiménez's control, that is, all but the district of Chilapa and part of the district of the Center.[30] In an effort to bring a swift end to the revolt, the government appointed Diego Alvarez commander of its forces in Guerrero, but the revolt dragged on until July 1871, when Jiménez was defeated at Zitlala,[31] although Jiménez's followers continued to organize their support for a subsequent attempt to take power in the state.[32]

Not discouraged by previous defeats, Jiménez and Neri rebelled again in November 1871 in favor of Porfirio Díaz's Plan de La Noria. They did not lay down their arms until October of the following year, when they accepted the amnesty offered by President Lerdo de Tejada.[33]

Alvarez's influence was still strong following his defeat of Jiménez in both the 1870 revolt and the revolution of La Noria. He returned to the governorship in 1873,[34] but Jiménez, still not content to live under the rule of his rival, saw a further opportunity to oppose him in Porfirio Díaz's revolution of Tuxtepec, having gathered a supply of arms and ammunition in order to lay claim once again to the control of Guerrero. Alvarez, as much by the same token of opposition to his rival as out of conviction, supported first Lerdo de Tejada, and then José María de Iglesias, who laid claim to the presidency after Lerdo's resignation.[35] However, the tide of war was against both Lerdo and Iglesias, both of whom were unable to halt Díaz's inexorable progress toward the Palacio Nacional. Alvarez was dragged to defeat with them in a bitter campaign whose outcome posed a series of delicate political problems for Porfirio Díaz to solve. It is worth looking quite closely at the events of 1876 and 1877, for they were the climax of the Jiménez-Alvarez rivalry. Moreover, they illustrated clearly how Díaz followed the precedent of federal intervention set by Juárez to control, or at least restrain, the warring factions in Guerrero.

By the early part of December 1876, Jiménez, with the aid of generals Rafael Cuéllar and Donato Guerra, controlled northern Guerrero and was ready to advance on Chilpancingo, and on 20 December Díaz appointed him governor of Guerrero.[36] By the end of

February 1877, Alvarez, accompanied by Canuto A. Neri, had "re-treated with his last remaining forces to the heart of the Costa Grande," where the two caciques fiercely resisted the advances of Jiménez and Cuéllar.[37] Despite his desperate military position (Jiménez's forces were even able to sack La Providencia, the ancestral home of the Alvarez family), Don Diego refused to capitulate and to recognize his arch rival as governor of the state which his father had ruled for so long. Displaying not a little cunning, Alvarez went over Jiménez's head and began negotiations with General Pedro Ogazón, Díaz's minister of war. Jiménez, suspecting a deal was being worked out behind his back, was furious at the prospect of losing his prize just when he had it within his grasp.[38]

Meanwhile, Jiménez unwittingly began to play into Alvarez's hands. First, much to Don Porfirio's displeasure, Jiménez began seizing property throughout the state to finance his operations, including property belonging to American citizens, and, to make matters worse, the U.S. consul in Acapulco was arrested, threatening a diplomatic incident.[39] Despite Don Porfirio's admonition, and denying the accusations against him in a somewhat testy tone, Jiménez pressed his campaign against the Alvarez *cacicazgo*. He purged the federal bureaucracy in the state of Alvarez's supporters and appointed his own intimates to control of the Acapulco customshouse, the major source of revenue in the state and, as such, a strategic institution of supreme importance.[40] Meanwhile, of course, he continued to prosecute his attack on Alvarez's remaining forces in the Costa Grande. One of Jiménez's aides expressed his purpose quite clearly in a letter to Díaz: "in the present struggle it is not just a matter of our regenerative cause of Tuxtepec, but of rooting out the old *cacicazgo* of Señor Alvarez, which he is trying to defend to the bitter end."[41]

By May, however, Jiménez's campaign had taken a disastrous turn for the worse. Neri had attacked Chilpancingo, and Alvarez inflicted a serious defeat on Don Vicente's forces at San Gerónimo. By the third week of the month, Jiménez was holed up in the Castillo de San Diego in Acapulco in desperate straits.[42] Clearly Díaz had to take firm action to bring the state under his control. Jiménez had not only alienated the populace of Guerrero, and threatened difficulties with the United States, but he had allowed Alvarez, a supporter of Díaz's erstwhile rivals for the presidency, to return to a position of power in the state. Díaz was confronted with the clear imperative of forging for his administration a local power base with at least a degree of loyalty to the federal government, as he recognized in a letter to Rafael Cuéllar. "It is necessary," Díaz wrote, "to strive to form a national party *which supports the federal government* and which is willing to aid it in its work of reconstruction, trying to [ensure] that its members act inspired by true patriotism, and not by the passions which wrack that state, and that they resolve to abstain from any influence which aims to revive hatred by attempting to [gain] the predominance of some faction."[43] Thus, the end of factionalism was clearly a prerequisite of any actions designed to give Díaz greater authority in Guerrero.

In order to achieve his objectives, Díaz had to juggle a number of conflicting interests. As a first step, he clearly had to recognize the balance of power in Guerrero by making concessions to Alvarez, who was now negotiating from a position of strength.[44] Second, Don Porfirio had to dispose of his old ally, Vicente Jiménez, who had become a severe liability, but to do so without suffering public humiliation at Alvarez's hands. Four months earlier Alvarez himself had provided the solution to Díaz's dilemma, suggesting to General Ogazón, by way of a compromise, that Rafael Cuéllar, a neutral outsider, "or . . . some other leader who deserves the government's confidence," be appointed governor.[45] Díaz lost no time in appointing Cuéllar, despite the vehement protests of Jiménez's son Rafael,[46] and in rallying behind the new administration influential figures throughout the state.[47] As an added precaution, Don Porfirio purged Jiménez's supporters from their posts in the federal bureaucracy in Guerrero and had his former ally's troops either disarmed or pressed into service in federal units.[48]

Don Porfirio's strategy included several other elements, however. Although Cuéllar was sent to Guerrero as an ostensibly neutral figure, he was, in reality, an instrument of Díaz's policy, a fact underlined by the appointment of Jesús Alfaro, a personal agent of Díaz, as the governor's secretary charged with much of the day-to-day running of the administration.[49] In addition, in a masterful display of political sleight of hand, Díaz began to bolster the status of Canuto A. Neri, in order to develop him as a counterweight to Alvarez. Cuéllar was instructed carefully to cultivate Neri, who was appointed to a federal military command in the state and offered a seat in Congress. Concerning the latter, Díaz explained to Neri, who modestly asserted that he did not feel himself capable of carrying out the duties of a *diputado*, that "my wishes in choosing you for the seat, are not precisely that you should actually take it, if that does not please you, but that you enjoy the honor which comes from it."[50] Díaz thus began to turn Neri into a political force in his own right, no longer dependent on Alvarez and Jiménez, a strategy not without its dangers, as Governor Cuéllar noted. However, Díaz assured him that, despite the risks, Neri's "services are absolutely necessary in Guerrero."[51] Certainly, Díaz's cultivation of Neri was a double-edged sword, for, while he proved willing to act as a counterpoise to Alvarez, he was busy furthering his own regional ambitions in the center of the state.[52]

It soon became clear that control of Guerrero was by no means easy to achieve. One reason was the continuing strength of Alvarez, as Governor Cuéllar noted: "as much as Jiménez loses in these districts, from Tixtla to the coasts, so much D[on] Diego recovers, either because his domination is deeply rooted, or because in [the districts] people scarcely know that we are coming." All this, Cuéllar noted, would render Alvarez "more demanding in negotiations."[53] Meanwhile, Alvarez's old rival, Jiménez, was by no means a spent force,[54] and even Díaz's own military commander in the state became infected by the endemic factionalism of local politics.[55] To make matters worse, Alfaro, Díaz's own appointee, was making himself ever more unpopular, and Cuéllar was compelled to dismiss him.[56]

In short, while the struggles of the past decade had left the Alvarez *cacicazgo* somewhat weakened, the emergence of Jiménez and Neri as contenders for influence in Guerrero had rendered Don Porfirio's political problems in the state still more complex. For the time being, he certainly did not feel himself strong enough to oust Alvarez from power immediately, and Don Diego returned to the governorship from 1881 to 1885. However, Díaz was not content to leave Alvarez in undisputed control of the state, and the strategy he adopted to control events in Guerrero was the same as that used by Juárez in 1869, that is, the imposition of an outsider free from the political passions which had wracked the state in the past and, perhaps more importantly, dependent on Díaz's support from the center in the absence of his own local power base. Not only did Don Porfirio borrow Juárez's strategy, but he used the same man: Francisco O. Arce, who became governor in 1885, despite opposition from a minority group in the state Congress and Alvarez's open hostility.[57] From 1885 until 1911 outsiders dominated the state, although in the final years of the Díaz dictatorship two native sons did occupy the governorship: Manuel Guillén, a long-time Porfirista, from 1904 to 1907, and Damián Flores, a member of the *científico* group, from 1907 to 1911. Díaz was to have much more success than Juárez, but would nevertheless encounter considerable resistance from the caciques of Guerrero.

The opposition to Arce made itself felt as early as the end of 1885, when a dispute erupted between the state Congress and the governor over the introduction into his administration of a number of people who were not *guerrerenses* by birth. The legislature proposed a reform of the state's constitution, which, in the words of Arce, "made the acquisition of the citizenship of this state almost impossible, deprived of their public positions all the enlightened people who were helping me in my government, and obliged me to stand down from my post on 1 January 1887, more than two years before the end of the constitutional period for which I was elected."[58]

When this maneuver failed, since the reform did not receive the necessary approval of the *ayuntamientos* of Guerrero, the Congress attacked Arce on a number of fiscal questions, for the allegedly unconstitutional means by which he sought to appoint members of the judiciary, and on a number of other matters. Arce's opponents also alleged that in eight districts of the state the *prefectos políticos* did not fulfill the constitutional requirements laid down for those holding such office (that they be citizens of Guerrero, and that they should have resided in Guerrero for at least three years).[59] Finally, Arce alleged, in return for turning a blind eye to some irregularities in the accounts of the state government, his opponents in Congress suggested an arrangement by which he would leave all "political business" to the Congress, while Arce would be given a free hand in "merely governmental matters." The governor denounced this proposal to Porfirio Díaz and the *secretario de gobernación*, and as a result the troublesome legislature was dissolved.[60]

Arce accused Diego Alvarez of inciting this opposition to his government,[61] and, while Alvarez denied this charge, there is some evidence that it was true. Certainly, it is obvious from their correspondence that relations between the two men were strained. In a letter to Mariano Ortiz de Montellano, Alvarez complained that Arce had strengthened his (Alvarez's) "unjust enemies" by placing them in positions of power in the state government. Moreover, in the same letter, Alvarez conceded that those who opposed Arce were persons "who support my humble person on account of friendship or family ties."[62]

As the time for elections for a new state Congress in December 1886 approached, Arce wrote to Alvarez in an attempt to secure his support for a less hostile legislature. Arce sent Don Diego "a list of the persons whom I have considered to form the next legislature of the state . . ." "You will observe," Arce remarked, "that some of the persons who figure as candidates are not sons of the state but if *I have paid little attention to this requisite*, it is because I have taken into account the imperious necessity of counting on trustworthy persons in the next chamber who are loyal followers of my administration and will support decidedly my noble intentions for the good of this state, and of my open-hearted policy, which is well known to you." Alvarez firmly refused to support such a slate of candidates, despite a further entreaty from Arce.[63] Despite Alvarez's opposition, Arce evidently succeeded in imposing the election of a loyal Congress, however, since Alvarez later accused him of using armed force and the influence of the *prefectos políticos* to ensure the victory of "the list published by the *Periódico Oficial*."[64]

Three conclusions may be drawn from this controversy. First, that Diego Alvarez's influence in Guerrero was still considerable, and, indeed, his cooperation was crucial to the smooth running of the state government. Second, that Arce had little or no political base of his own in Guerrero, and therefore had to import collaborators from other states to complete his team. Third, that it was precisely the presence of a group of outsiders, brought in by Arce, in positions of power in Guerrero that was one of the bones of contention between the governor and the Congress.[65]

Arce's introduction of outsiders into the government of Guerrero continued to be a source of controversy, so much so that in May 1889 the *Periódico Oficial* felt obliged to publish a statistical breakdown of the administration. Although in the judiciary only three out of nineteen officials were not *guerrerenses*, in other branches of the government outsiders formed a substantial minority. Ten of the twenty-eight *diputados* were not natives of the state, while exactly one-third of those in the executive branch fell into the same category. Of the *prefectos políticos*, almost half (six out of fourteen) were outsiders.[66]

This article was published shortly after Arce's reelection for the period 1889 to 1893. By that time Diego Alvarez was openly leading the opposition to Arce and was supporting the candidacy for the governorship of Canuto A. Neri, commander of the federal forces in Guerrero. However, Porfirio Díaz made it clear that Arce was his choice to continue as governor, and Neri was obliged to stand down.[67] Thus, while Neri had been used by Díaz as a counterweight to Alvarez in 1877 and had continued to command federal troops in Guerrero, the ambitions which he had displayed even in 1877 remained very much alive. Moreover, Neri had reestablished his alliance with Alvarez, and things would not go so smoothly for Arce when he again presented himself for reelection in December 1892. On that occasion Neri was once again his opponent.

In the month of the elections for the period 1893 to 1897 there were already reports of unrest in Guerrero. The newspaper *La Patria* reported that the names of Canuto A. Neri and Diego Alvarez had been put forward for the governorship, and that "at the same time the people of the south were incited to rise up in arms against the present governor of that federative entity."[68] Although the elections went off peacefully, it was officially reported that "a few restless individuals" had unsuccessfully tried to incite a riot.[69]

In March 1893 it was reported in the press that

> when the reelection of Señor Arce had been carried out, the defeated party [of Neri] did not accept the defeat, and continued working in a fashion hostile to the imposed order of things. It seems that lately tempers have frayed, and since the center fears a local conflagration, it has decided to call Señor Arce to the capital. . . . In public it has transpired that Señor Mariano Ortiz de Montellano is accepted by the two belligerent parties in Guerrero as a compromise, and that he will occupy, for the time being, the post of Señor Arce.[70]

Subsequent events would seem to confirm the version of the Mexico City press.

Ortiz de Montellano did, indeed, take office as interim governor on 4 April.[71] However, it soon became clear that, rather than calling new elections, which was supposed to be the role of an interim governor, Ortiz de Montellano was merely to keep the seat warm for Arce until political conditions in Guerrero allowed him to return. Therefore, to get over the constitutional problem caused by the fact that Arce had not taken office on 1 April, as article 39 of the state's constitution prescribed, this article was reformed to read as follows: "The governor will commence his constitutional period of office on 1 April; but if he cannot take possession of his office on that day, an interim governor will be appointed until the former presents himself to take the oath of office."[72] However, such a maneuver did nothing to improve the "difficult situation" of Guerrero, where there were "serious dangers of unrest."[73]

Finally, on 6 October 1893, a revolutionary plan was issued in Mezcala which declared that the interim government of Ortiz de Montellano was illegal since its only function was to call new elections. Instead, a constitutional reform had been passed which sought "to keep alive the authority of the said Señor Arce," and which was, moreover, "a violation of the law, order, and reason," since it was retroactive. The constitutional order had been broken in Guerrero, and the rebels therefore declared that: (1) they withdrew recognition of Ortiz de Montellano; (2) "the people . . . confers on Señor General

Canuto A. Neri" the governorship of Guerrero "until the decree call-ing for definitive elections is passed by Congress"; and (3) the people had taken up arms to defend itself against "any attacks which might be directed against it."[74] In a letter to Porfirio Díaz, Neri explained that "the movement was exclusively local . . . and I could not fore-see the attitude which the people were to take and . . . I have been obliged to follow them." Proof of this, Neri continued, was the fact that "I did not even use the federal forces which were under my command."[75]

Although the government claimed that Neri's revolt was of no importance, the press carried reports of the movement of large num-bers of troops to Guerrero. One report stated that, by the beginning of November, some 8,000 troops were converging on Neri from the states of Oaxaca, Puebla, Morelos, Mexico, and Michoacán, and from Acapulco. The same report put the rebel forces at 2,500 men.[76] In the absence of fully trustworthy reports, the exact scale of the revolt is difficult to calculate. Nevertheless, it is possible to determine the area affected by the revolt from the lists of those who accepted am-nesty when the revolt was over. The rebellion affected six of the fourteen districts of the state: those of Bravos, Guerrero, Tabares, Allende, Alvarez, and Aldama—that is, central Guerrero, a small section of the Costa Chica, and a small part of the Tierra Caliente. In addition, there was, apparently, a brief revolutionary outbreak in the district of Hidalgo.[77]

In view of the military forces which Díaz directed against the rebels, Neri's only hope of success was that Diego Alvarez would throw his support behind the revolt. Alvarez was, however, unwill-ing to compromise his position and on 6 November sent a circular letter to his supporters in which he stated that "I have not consid-ered it opportune to contribute to the development of [Neri's] move-ment, the real cause of which I do not know. . . . I write to you to advise you to maintain your peaceful attitude, and not to let your-selves be taken in by flattery, promises, or threats which would hurl you into the precipice."[78]

Nevertheless, by the time Alvarez issued this plea, Arce had resigned in an effort to pacify the state. On 3 November he wrote to the state legislature that "I do not wish to encourage . . . illegiti-mate and violent ambitions, nor be the motive or pretext for disturb-ing the public peace, harming the people, and alarming the repub-lic."[79] Arce's resignation was duly accepted by the Congress on 11 November.[80]

Meanwhile, politically isolated, and surrounded in Tierra Ca-liente by superior military forces, Neri was obliged to surrender. On

19 November he issued a manifesto to his supporters in which he stated that "since the objective which [the] movement set itself has been achieved, I urge you . . . to return to your homes."[81] Two days later the state Congress granted an amnesty to all rebels who surrendered within fifteen days,[82] and on 1 January 1894 a new interim governor was appointed: Antonio Mercenario, the administrator of the Huitzuco mercury mines.[83] In the ensuing elections, Mercenario, his candidacy duly endorsed by Neri himself, was elected with an impressive majority, and the crisis in Guerrero fizzled out.[84]

Neri's revolt was the last flurry of resistance by the caciques of Guerrero to the imposition of outsiders in the governorship and other key political positions in the state as agents of the central government. When Mercenario came up for reelection in December 1895, both Neri and Alvarez endorsed his candidacy.[85] The generation of caciques who won their battle honors in the wars of the Reform and of the Intervention were by now old men, unable to mount effective resistance to the encroachment of Don Porfirio's administration. Jiménez died in 1894, Neri in 1896, and Diego Alvarez three years later,[86] and with him went the remnants of the great *cacicazgo* which his father had established over seventy years before. Nevertheless, the demise of the Guerrero caciques did not by any means signify the end of opposition to the rule of Don Porfirio in the state, for dissent now rose from a radically different quarter: urban intellectuals, lawyers, schoolteachers, small landowners, and village merchants. In short, the very middle class which Porfirian economic and social policy had done so much to foster turned to bite the hand which had fed it. Their opposition focused initially on the figure of Arce's successor, Antonio Mercenario.

Mercenario has an unenviable reputation in the history of Guerrero, where he is generally regarded as the most tyrannical governor in the state's history. However, it was not until after his reelection in 1897 that public opposition to Mercenario made itself heard. In the last years of the nineteenth century, a group of young intellectuals launched a press campaign against the governor. Persecuted by the state government, these young men were forced to leave Guerrero and continue their campaign with newspapers published in Mexico City, Morelos, and Puebla. In 1900, as the December elections for governor approached, this group intensified its campaign and threw its support behind the candidacy of Lic. Rafael del Castillo Calderón,[87] a prominent *guerrerense* politician, and a native of Tierra Caliente.[88]

Although Mercenario was officially declared the victor in the December elections, popular displeasure at this reelection forced him to resign before taking office. In his place another outsider was appointed interim governor until new elections could be called: Agustín Mora, an *hacendado* from Puebla who, it was said, had no connections with Guerrero other than the goats which he purchased in Tlapa for his estates.[89] The resignation of Mercenario gave new life to the opposition. According to one newspaper report, "the liberal element has been stirred to action and is resolved to struggle through the ballot box, and to defeat, perhaps, the official candidate."[90]

Mora's appointment, however, did not soothe the populace's disquiet, particularly when it was announced that he would run for governor in the elections called for 21 April 1901.[91] Castillo Calderón was again put forward as a candidate, and mounted a campaign sufficiently vigorous to force Mora to take active measures to counter his opposition. Mora founded a newspaper, *El Heraldo del Sur*, to promote his candidacy and held a public demonstration in Chilpancingo.[92] However, such measures proved inadequate to eclipse the Castillo Calderón campaign, and more energetic methods had to be adopted: Castillo Calderón was attacked and forced to flee from Chilpancingo.[93]

Faced with increasing official harassment, the followers of Castillo Calderón attempted to fight fire with fire: on 8 April a revolutionary manifesto, drafted in Mochitlán, was issued in Atoyac. The rebels demanded the right of the people to vote freely in the coming elections and asserted that the rebels would respect all landowners, foreigners, travelers, and the populace of Guerrero in general.[94] The proclamation of the plan was followed by an uprising in the Mochitlán-Petaquillas area, led by a landowner and friend of Castillo Calderón, Anselmo Bello.[95] Although risings may have been planned in other parts of the state, this was the only area in which any armed movement got off the ground. The movement was ill-planned and doomed to failure from the start.

Nevertheless, the government's response was immediate and energetic. The Third Battalion, under the orders of Victoriano Huerta, and a force of *rurales* stationed in Puebla were dispatched to Guerrero, while the Fourteenth Battalion, stationed in Chilpancingo, advanced on the rebels.[96] The insurgents were soon dispersed and a number of them executed. Castillo Calderón himself escaped to Mexico City, where he was arrested but, through the mediation of the *diputado* for Guerrero, Manuel Guillén, was pardoned by Porfirio Díaz, who appointed him *juez de distrito* in Chihuahua, "but strictly forbade him to step foot again in Guerrero." Anselmo Bello escaped with the help of the Chilapa landowner Eucaria Apreza, but Eusebio Almonte, another prime mover in the affair, was captured in Mezcala and executed.[97] Although the military threat posed by the rebellion was minimal, it evidently was a serious political worry for the state government, which was still seeking those involved in October, six months after the rising had been quashed.[98]

The revolt of Castillo Calderón was symptomatic of the resentment of efforts by the central government to control the local political scene at the expense of native politicians, who were squeezed out of control of the state government by agents of the federal administration. Such resistance to outside interference had been evident since Francisco O. Arce had first taken office in 1869. The struggle against the subordination of state politics to the national political interest, first under Juárez, but much more so under Díaz, periodically plunged Guerrero into crisis and would constitute one of the major grievances of those who supported the Maderista revolt and took up arms in 1911.

The revolts of both Neri and Castillo Calderón are often rather vaguely referred to as precursor movements of the Mexican revolution. The case for considering Neri's rebellion a precursor movement rests on two pieces of evidence: first, it was a revolt against the reelection of Arce, and therefore, it is implied, Neri was a precursor of the anti-reelectionism of 1910; second, Julián Blanco, a revolutionary leader in 1911, participated in Neri's campaign.[99] However, neither argument is very convincing. Neri's opposition to the reelection of Arce was an expression of his local political ambitions, not of opposition to reelection in general. Indeed, Neri later supported the election of both Mercenario and Díaz. More crucially, however, the 1893 revolt was the last manifestation of the resistance of the caciques of Guerrero to the erosion of their power by Díaz, while the 1911 Maderista revolt (Julián Blanco's participation in both rebellions notwithstanding) was inspired by people of a very different kind from Alvarez, Jiménez, or Neri—civilian members of the urban and rural middle class, which had expanded noticeably under the rule of Díaz. Moreover, these very same groups, indeed, in many cases, the same individuals, were active in the 1901 movement, and Castillo Calderón himself was to be a Maderista in 1911. Since the social composition and the personnel of the Maderista movement of 1910—1911 in Guerrero bore such close resemblances to the opposition movement of Castillo Calderón, the case for considering the 1901 revolt as a a precursor of the Maderista uprising in Guerrero is quite convincing. Perhaps the most significant case of a group which supported both the Castillo Calderón movement and the Maderista revolution is that of the Figueroa family of Huitzuco, the initiators of the revolution in Guerrero.

According to family tradition, the Figueroas came to Guerrero from Cotija in Michoacán at some unknown date during the colonial period. After passing through Juliantla, near Taxco, they settled in a ranchería called Quetzalapa.[100] By the end of the nineteenth century, the family was apparently quite numerous and had spread beyond Quetzalapa to various parts of the municipality of Huitzuco. Several members of the family were people of substance in the Huitzuco area: small landowners, shopkeepers, petty entrepreneurs.[101] As the family historian has remarked, "far from opulence, [the Figueroas] had sufficient resources at their disposal to live in relative comfort; their prestige as honest, hardworking, dynamic men of good, clean habits, with a cultural level above the average, placed them in an enviable position" within their community.[102]

Several members of the family lived in Huitzuco itself, a town which, by the 1890s, exhibited two of the classic features of Porfirian Mexico: the integration of previously isolated areas into the export economy and the political penetration of peripheral regions by the central government. Huitzuco was the site of a highly profitable mercury mine (mercury was vital for the processing of silver, which Porfirian Mexico exported in large quantities) owned by no less a figure of the Porfirian establishment than Manuel Romero Rubio, the president's father-in-law. Not surprisingly, the mercury mine dominated the life of Huitzuco. The mine's administrator was "the lord and master of the region, with sweeping powers in the political as well as the social order." Moreover, he had at his command an escort of *rurales* to protect the mine and further its interests.[103] The political power of the mine administration is best exemplified by the case of Antonio Mercenario, until 1894 the administrator of the mine. He had been *prefecto político* of the district of Hidalgo for a time, and was *presidente municipal* of Huitzuco in 1888, 1892, and 1893.[104] In 1894 he left his work at the mine to occupy no less an office than that of governor of Guerrero.

The domination of local affairs by the mine and the agents of powerful political interests in Mexico City aroused the opposition of a number of people in the town and the surrounding municipality. For the mercury mine was not the only influence on the life of Huitzuco. Although, during the Reforma, Huitzuco had been a center of Conservative resistance,[105] by the late 1880s and early 1890s there was a strong liberal element in the town. An important factor in this development was the school established in 1882 by Manuel

Sáenz, a schoolteacher from Hidalgo, who remained in Huitzuco until 1887. As a result of the activities of Sáenz, Huitzuco "distinguished itself at that time by the independent and dignified spirit of its men, their love of progress, and the great civic virtues of a select group of citizens who had been formed under the influence of [Sáenz]."[106] It was, perhaps, partly the Liberal ideology which Sáenz instilled in the youth of Huitzuco which brought a group of citizens, among whom members of the Figueroa family were prominent, into conflict with the mine administration.

As early as December 1893, the struggle between the mine administration and the liberal opposition led to a bloody incident. On 10 December a correspondent reported to the *Diario del Hogar* that,

> on the sixth of this month, the president of this municipality received notice of the rape of a young girl, and on suspicion of complicity in this crime ordered the arrest of Don Pudenciano Figueroa, an eminently honest person, who, on being arrested without a written warrant and in a brutal fashion, put up some resistance. . . . For this reason, an employee of the mining business "Cruz y Anexas," belonging to Señor Romero Rubio, who also holds a position on the council, and who, at the time, was accompanying the municipal president, sent for some soldiers of the rural force which is under his orders, one might say. . . . At 1:30 P.M. on the said day the soldiers arrived at the Council building, when the accused was already in the presence of the municipal president, and the latter had accepted bail . . . so that Figueroa should not go to jail until the crime of which he was accused had been substantiated; but [the municipal president] . . . ignoring the bail, ordered Figueroa to be led to prison to put him at the disposition of the competent judge. The soldiers . . . tried to take the accused away, beating him and pushing him, and therefore, frightened by that treatment . . . he sought his salvation in flight; but he had not run thirty varas before he fell once more into the hands of his pursuers, whose blows bathed him in blood.

At this point Figueroa's brothers, Nicasio and Odilón, and his father arrived on the scene. According to the correspondent of the *Diario del Hogar*, they attempted to plead with the *rurales*, who, far from heeding their pleas, fell to beating them, too. In the ensuing struggle, Antonio Moronati, the administrator of the mine, gave the order to open fire. Pudenciano Figueroa was killed on the spot and Odilón was badly wounded.[107]

In a subsequent letter the correspondent indicated that this incident had political overtones. It took place no fewer than eleven days before the elections for the *ayuntamiento*, of which Moronati and his followers were trying to retain control. Moronati's group was, however, opposed by a group of citizens, among whom the future revolutionaries Rómulo Figueroa and Martín Vicario figured. If Moronati's intention was to intimidate his opponents, his maneuver misfired, since the opposition won a resounding victory.[108]

This is the first evidence we have of opposition to the domination of municipal politics by the mine administration. It was perhaps around the time of this incident that a fairly well defined opposition group of people of Liberal ideas formed. Among the members of this group were Francisco, Rómulo, and Ambrosio Figueroa; Martín and Félix Vicario; Fidel Fuentes; Urbano Astudillo; Irineo Robles; Miguel Tejada; Francisco de P. Castrejón; and José Castrejón Fuentes.[109] This group won control of the *ayuntamiento* of Huitzuco in 1894 and 1898, while in 1896, 1897, 1900, and 1901 Moronati's group controlled the municipal government.[110]

Thus by 1900 a group of Liberal dissidents, with a history of opposition to the penetration of Mexico City interests, had formed. When Castillo Calderón and his supporters began their campaign for the governorship in 1901, it was not surprising that this group should throw its support behind the opposition to Mora. In May 1901 the group met to discuss tactics, but the following day seven of them were arrested and the remainder forced to go into hiding. Although those arrested were released some three weeks later, when news of Castillo Calderón's rebellion reached Huitzuco several of them decided that it would be prudent to take refuge in Jojutla, Morelos, where Ambrosio Figueroa was the administrator of the rice mill of the Hacienda del Higuerón.[111] Nevertheless, despite this setback, the Figueroa group evidently resumed its political activities at a later date. In 1905 Francisco Figueroa was *presidente municpal*, and the group again won control of the *ayuntamiento* in 1910.[112]

Local struggles of the kind carried out by the Figueroas in Huitzuco laid fertile ground for the Maderista campaign of 1910–1911. However, still more crucial to the development of opposition in Guerrero was the movement of Castillo Calderón, which, in 1901, provided the first state-wide tie to link disparate local groups together. Future revolutionaries who were active in this campaign included the landowner from Chilapa, Eucaria Apreza, the lawyer-politician Salustio Carrasco Núñez, and a group in Tepecoacuilco led by the schoolteacher Gonzalo Avila Díaz.[113] These middle-class dissidents were active sympathizers of the Maderista movement, which grew out of the lingering political crisis which slowly sapped the foundations of the Porfirian regime.

Although Don Porfirio had succeeded in modernizing and stabilizing the political system known as *caudillaje,* he had not eliminated the essentially personalistic flavor of the caudillo patron-client relationship. Thus the key factor of the Porfirian political system was Díaz himself. His propagandists went to great pains to portray the continued presence of Díaz in the presidency as the necessary condition for the peace and progress which Mexico enjoyed during the Porfiriato.[114] Indeed, there was much evidence to show that Díaz's permanence in the Palacio Nacional was an essential condition of political stability and economic development. The stability of Mexico under Díaz was based on a series of alliances and friendships with the military and local political groups. These supporters owed their loyalty to Don Porfirio in person, not to any institution or party. Thus, if Díaz were to relinquish the presidency, the one link which held together the impressive unity of the governing elite would collapse like a house of cards. Moreover, who but Don Porfirio could command the prestige abroad which guaranteed the flow of foreign investment vital for Mexico's economic development? For Díaz never allowed anybody to acquire the standing necessary to replace him. Potential rivals, such as Bernardo Reyes or Manuel Romero Rubio, were firmly put down.

However, the very cult of the "necessary man" inspired in all sections of Mexican society a fear that grew as Porfirio grew older and the specter of his death loomed ever nearer. If no single person could replace Don Porfirio, then some institutional means of arranging a peaceful transition must be found. The first signs of this preoccupation came from within the governing group itself. In 1892 a group of Díaz's supporters formed the Comité Central Porfirista, out of which sprang an attempt on the part of the subsequently notorious *científicos* to organize a political party, the Unión Liberal, to prepare, in the words of Justo Sierra, "the framework of an organization in which the people may immediately be found ready and disciplined" in the event of the "fearful crisis" of Díaz's departure from the presidency.[115] Díaz himself was not unmindful of these fears, and for the 1904 elections conceived the plan of creating the office of vice-president and arranging for José Ives Limantour to occupy the office, backed by Bernardo Reyes in the Ministry of War, but this project failed because of the political antagonism between Reyes and Limantour.[116]

The public's anxiety increased as the 1910 elections approached. In that year Díaz would be eighty years old and was unlikely to survive a further full six years in office. The question of who occupied the vice-presidency thus assumed enormous importance. Many groups were dissatisfied with the unpopular incumbent, Ramón Corral, a close associate of the *científicos*. In February 1908 Díaz declared in the famous Creelman interview that he was willing to allow the free election of a truly representative government, and that he himself was ready to step down. Although few believed that Díaz would leave office, a flurry of political activity aimed at choosing a candidate for the vice-presidency broke out.[117] Late in 1908 the followers of Bernardo Reyes began to organize to promote his candidacy, but Reyes vacillated, and in November, Díaz, in no mood to brook an opposition campaign, dispatched him to exile in Europe.[118]

In late 1909 and 1910 many of Reyes's supporters passed over to the Anti-Reelectionist Center of Francisco I. Madero. Madero and his supporters had at first sought only to persuade Díaz to allow free elections for the vice-presidency. By April 1910, when the Anti-Reelectionist Convention was held in Mexico City, however, it was clear that Díaz would allow no such thing, and Madero and his followers were forced to adopt a stance of open opposition to Don Porfirio. Madero was named candidate for the presidency, and a former Reyista, Francisco Vázquez Gómez, for the vice-presidency.[119] It was the attempts made by Díaz to suppress the Maderista movement which precipitated the Mexican revolution.

Fertile ground for revolutionary agitation existed in Guerrero. Various sections of the population resented the control of important positions in local politics by outsiders who were often not responsive to the needs of the populace. This was especially true of the imposition of governors by the federal government, which thus sought to control the caciques of Guerrero, and the factional struggles which had marred the state's history. Resistance to this policy had come at first from the great military caciques themselves, but by the turn of the century the most vocal opposition came from the expanding middle-class groups in the cities and in the countryside: up-and-coming rancheros like the Figueroas, schoolteachers like Gonzalo Avila Díaz and Silvestre G. Mariscal, and landowners like Eucaria Apreza and Rafael del Castillo Calderón. By 1910 their ranks would be swollen by men such as the lawyer from Quetzalapa, Lic. Matías Chávez, and Lic. José Inocente Lugo from Tierra Caliente; the López brothers, student sons of a poet from La Unión; and the young law student Miguel F. Ortega.[120]

While on the state level prominent local political figures like

Rafael del Castillo Calderón were excluded from high political office, on the municipal level entrenched caciques excluded ambitious members of the middle class from control of municipal affairs. This was clearly the case in Huitzuco, but other examples are not hard to find. In La Unión, for instance, local affairs were dominated by the cacique Pioquinto Huato, a close friend of Porfirio Díaz, although, unlike the managers of the Huitzuco mines, a local man. In the first decade of the twentieth century, Huato's control of La Unión was contested by a group of citizens which included the López brothers, and in 1910 Héctor F. López and other members of the group were forced to flee from Guerrero when their lives were threatened.[121]

To the extent that it reflected opposition to the strong centralizing tendencies of Díaz's modernized *caudillaje*, the Maderista movement in Guerrero was traditionalist rather than revolutionary, an expression of a desire to restore the autonomy enjoyed by the state during much of the nineteenth century. Nevertheless, it was ironic that those who took up the old banner of states' rights in 1911 were, in many respects, new products of the social change wrought in the Mexican countryside by Don Porfirio's regime. Rancheros who were able to acquire land through the disentailment of communal village property, schoolteachers, lawyers and village merchants whose numbers had grown with the general economic expansion of the Porfiriato, and a small number of *hacendados* resented the restricted access to public office allotted to them by the Porfirian political system, and ultimately turned against the regime which had nurtured them. This, ultimately, was the great paradox of the Porfiriato in Guerrero. In any case, when the Maderista agent Octavio Bertrand came to Guerrero in January 1910 he found a number of discontented people who were receptive to his message.

The Maderista conspiracy, news of which Bertrand brought with him, was the fruit of a radical change in the style of political campaigning in Mexico during the years 1908 to 1910. In previous presidential elections, instructions had been sent out from Mexico City to the governors of the states, who then entrusted the implementation of their orders to the *prefectos políticos* and the *presidentes municipales*. Beginning in 1908, however, a new element was introduced: that of popular agitation. First Reyista and then Maderista propagandists traveled the cities, towns, and villages of Mexico preaching their cause. So dramatic were the effects of these opposition campaigns that the supporters of Díaz were obliged to sally out into the provinces to call out the vote for their candidate. Often for the first time, Mexico City politicians were seen electioneering in the states, and those who were discontented with the Díaz regime could look to a national party through which to make their grievances felt.[122]

There was no public campaigning in behalf of Madero in Guerrero, and consequently the shockwaves of the national political crisis were not felt as strongly there as in some other states. The first contact with local dissidents was through the lawyers José Inocente Lugo and Matías Chávez in Iguala, who operated as the agents of the Maderista organizer for the south, Alfredo Robles Domínguez.[123] Matías Chávez was a native of Quetzalapa, as were the Figueroas, and it was therefore natural that when a Maderista agent, Octavio Bertrand, arrived in Guerrero in 1910, he should be recommended to visit the dissidents of Huitzuco.

Bertrand made the first of several visits to Huitzuco on 26 January 1910. At a meeting held in the house of Andrés Figueroa it was resolved to form a political club, the Club Juan Alvarez. At this stage, only one member of the Figueroa family, Odilón (whose brother Pudenciano had been killed by *rurales* from the mercury mine in 1893), was appointed to a position on the executive committee of the club, although several members of the family were later to emerge as clear leaders of the Huitzuco group. This was the only formal political organization which Bertrand was able to form at this stage and was the only club in the state to appoint a delegate to the Anti-Reelectionist Convention held in Mexico City in April, in which Francisco I. Madero and Francisco Vázquez Gómez were adopted as candidates.[124] On subsequent visits to Guerrero, Bertrand was able to establish contact with a number of individual Maderista sympathizers, but the Huitzuco club was still the only formal organization he could establish in Guerrero.[125] Already the club showed signs of the enterprising spirit so characteristic of the Huitzuco group's role in the revolution: not content with limiting itself to local activities, the club also established contact with the Maderista Eugenio Morales in Morelos.[126]

In August Bertrand again visited Huitzuco, this time with a view to organizing an insurrection rather than legal political associations. It was at this stage that the Figueroas emerged more clearly in a leadership role. In a meeting held in the house of Rómulo Figueroa, his brother Ambrosio, who had been a member of the Second Reserve militia organized by Bernardo Reyes when he was secretary of war, and who was the only member of the club with any military training, was appointed commander of the revolutionary forces. Other members of the family were named to key positions in the military organization: Odilón was elected treasurer, and Rómulo (together with Martín Vicario, a family friend) was charged with the fund-raising activities of the rebels.[127] Thus, the Figueroas were now clearly the leading lights of the Huitzuco revolutionaries.

The next seven months were spent in organization and the gathering of arms and support. Two hundred pesos were received from Matías Chávez to help finance the organization of the revolt, and in October the Central Revolutionary Junta in Mexico City sent 50 carbines and 5,000 cartridges to the Huitzuco rebels. By this time some two hundred men in the Huitzuco–Atenango del Río area were "firmly committed to take up arms."[128] However, although the Maderista revolution began in November with the attack on the home of Aquiles Serdán in Puebla, and in January 1911 José Inocente Lugo and Matías Chávez were arrested for their revolutionary activities, the Huitzuco conspirators hesitated actually to declare themselves in rebellion. It was decided to send one of their number to the north to interview Madero and ask for more money and munitions. On his return on 22 February, however, the emissary brought only a copy of the plan of San Luis Potosí and a manifesto issued by Pascual Orozoco.[129]

Meanwhile, other groups unsuccessfully attempted to stage revolts in Guerrero. On 12 December 1910, Delfino Castro Alvarado, at the instigation of the schoolteacher Gonzalo Avila Díaz, attempted to stage an uprising in Tepecoacuilco, but the revolt was nipped in the bud and those involved arrested.[130] In January 1911 two groups of students, led by Vicente J. González and Miguel F. Ortega and financed by the wealthy landowner and merchant from Chilapa Eucaria Apreza, set out from Mexico City to start rebellions in Chilapa and Ayutla. Both groups were discovered, however, and forced to flee the state before their uprising could get off the ground.[131]

It was obvious that the pace of events in Guerrero was picking up, and the Figueroas could not long delay action, since it was becoming clear that the authorities had wind of the conspiracy in Huitzuco. So, on 24 February some thirty men gathered on the Cerro de San Lucas near the town, and the next day set out for Atenango del Río, attracting recruits en route from various villages in the area. In Atenango the funds of the government offices were seized, and from there the rebels set out for the ranchero communities of Chaucingo and Quetzalapa, passing through Rómulo Figueroa's own Rancho de Tequicuilco to collect more recruits from among his tenants.

On the last day of February 1911 some sixty or seventy revolutionaries entered Huitzuco. "All those who composed this small rebel force were farming people . . . they were magnificent shots, most of them rancheros, fond of hunting, who knew perfectly how to use their guns." Moreover, not only were the insurgents of the same social background as the Figueroas who led the group, but, to judge by their surnames, close to half were actually blood relations. Five were members of the Figueroa family itself, while no fewer than thirteen or fourteen came from the Castrejón clan of Quetzalapa and Chaucingo, a family related to the Figueroas since colonial times.[132]

Barely half an hour after their arrival, the rebels received news that some 150 to 200 government troops under the command of Captain Manuel Arroyo Limón were advancing on the town. Not the least bit disconcerted, the rebels barricaded themselves at strategic points and prepared to face the enemy advance. A battle lasting several hours ensued, until the rebels, short of ammunition and outnumbered, withdrew under cover of darkness.[133] Thus the Figueroas, although no longer the only active Maderistas in the state, had fired the first shots in the revolution in Guerrero. This simple priority gave them justification for claiming the leadership of the Maderista movement in the state.

Thus, the Mexican revolution had been launched in the former domains of Juan Alvarez. The basic grievance which sparked the uprising was no transitory eruption of discontent, but rather another manifestation of local resistance to progressive centralization and the emergence of a national state which sought to ride roughshod over the state's autonomy. Yet this is only part of the story. The men who now confronted the Porfirian establishment were certainly not the old military caciques of Guerrero who for so long had resisted the steady march of centralization. For, already in 1901, lawyers, teachers, urban intellectuals, schoolteachers, small landowners, and village traders had begun to figure in the opposition, which was now overwhelmingly civilian in character. Thus, as early as the turn of the century, a new opposition constituency had emerged, a constituency which, ironically enough, was the creation of the social and economic forces which the regime of Díaz had stimulated. We turn, therefore, to the question of the nature of the rural society of Porfirian Guerrero to discover the social origins of the 1910 revolutionaries.

2. Economy and Society in Northern Guerrero: 1876–1911

Politically, the keynote of the Porfiriato was centralization. The federal government progressively gained more and more control of the levers of power and made considerable inroads into the states' autonomy. On the economic front, the counterpart of political centralization was an ever increasing modernization of the economy, as the years 1876 to 1911 saw an economic development unprecedented in the country's history. The principal instrument and, at the same time, the symbol of this modernization was the railway: Mexico's incipient rail network grew from only 640 kilometers in 1876 to 19,280 in 1910.[1] The new network served areas which produced agricultural cash crops and minerals for export and ran from these areas northward to the border with the United States, or to the ports of Mexico's Atlantic and Pacific coasts (Veracruz, Tampico, Manzanillo, etc.),[2] creating the conditions for an economic boom based on exports of primary materials to the industrial centers of North America and Europe. The results were indeed striking: the value of exports increased sixfold from 1877 to 1911.[3] The railways also brought considerable change in the internal economy of Mexico. Previously isolated and self-sufficient local markets were integrated into the wider national and, indeed, international economy, stimulating an expansion of commerce, industry, and agriculture,[4] often with quite spectacular results. Small villages were transformed almost overnight into important industrial and agricultural centers when the railway passed through them. Such was the case of Torreón, whose population grew from 23,190 in 1900 to 43,382 in 1910, and of Gómez Palacio, whose population rocketed from 7,680 in 1900 to 42,846 in 1910.[5]

Such rapid commercialization of the economy imposed considerable social strains on Mexico, particularly where it undermined the traditional structure of rural society. From the start, the construction of the railways was accompanied by landgrabs on the part of latifundists who saw the opportunity to profit from the economic expansion of the Porfiriato by producing crops more profitable than maize and other staples.[6] For example, in Morelos the railway brought a rapid growth of the export-oriented sugar haciendas, which intensified the traditional assault on the land of the independent village.[7] The disastrous impact of modernization was also apparent in Sonora, where "massive unfusions of foreign capital dislocated certain traditional sectors of society, thus provoking rural rebellions against the forces or agents of development during the late Porfiriato."[8] Similarly, in Naranja, Michoacán, a Spanish company deprived the village of much of its communal land, and many villagers were forced to work in the Tierra Caliente, or even to emigrate to the United States. "They were cast into a large, impersonal labor market . . . of the efficient, large-scale maize haciendas and sugar-plantations, producing for the national and international markets."[9] In such areas, at least, the Mexican revolution took the form of a reaction against a rapidly modernizing society, an attempt to restore a real or imaginary past.

For a time the ever increasing momentum of economic expansion seemed to know no bounds, but in 1905 the export boom, on which the economic prosperity of the Porfiriato rested, began to falter. From 1905 to 1911 the volume of exports grew by 37%, while Mexico's capacity to import grew by only 13%, so that Mexico had to produce more and more exports in order to buy the imports which the country needed, creating a serious "external imbalance toward the end of the Porfiriato."[10] Thus by 1910 the Mexican economy, which had previously seemed to be expanding at a rapid pace, was gripped by a severe crisis, and the very foundations of the Porfirian economic "miracle" were called into question.

While this was undoubtedly a period of rapid growth, the economic development of the Porfiriato was not spread evenly throughout the country. The areas which benefited most were those in the center like Morelos and parts of the coastal fringe, where tropical cash crops such as sugar, tobacco, and coffee could be produced; the cattle regions of the north which shipped their livestock to the United States; and parts of the north like the Laguna which, favored by cheap transport offered by the railways, were able to export cotton or other cash crops.[11] Areas which were rendered inaccessible by the terrain or lack of railways received few of the fruits of the economic development of the Porfiriato, since here the production of cash crops for export, or the extraction of any but precious metals (where the ore was rich enough to cover the high transport costs), was uneconomic.[12] In such areas modernization went ahead slowly, or was barely perceptible, and the dislocation of society was, presumably, less severe. Guerrero was one such region, for while like other states it felt the political impact of the Porfirian regime, and while its neighbor Morelos became a classic case of the rapid modernization of a traditional society, Guerrero—except for small regions such as the coastal fringe and parts of the north bordering on the states of Morelos and Mexico—could produce few cash crops since the rugged terrain made transport difficult and costly.

Guerrero is a predominantly mountainous state which divides into three geographically distinct regions: (1) the Coastal Zone, which is traditionally further divided into the Costa Grande (the area which lies to the west of Acapulco) and the Costa Chica (the remainder of the coast which lies east of Acapulco), which extends up to 500 meters above sea level; (2) the Tierra Caliente, aptly named for its searing temperatures, a more or less flat area which lies in the basin of the River Balsas, mostly between 200 and 400 meters above sea level, although it includes the pine forested mountainous region which separates the Balsas from the Coastal Zone; (3) the Sierra Zone, which covers the remainder of the state, and whose climate is varied because of the rugged topography.[13]

The state displayed relatively few signs of the spectacular economic growth which was one of Porfirio Díaz's major achievements. Guerrero was a predominantly agricultural economy, and by far the most important crop was maize, produced mainly for consumption in local markets.[14] The production of cash crops was largely restricted to the coast, portions of the Tierra Caliente, and parts of northern Guerrero. On the coast, rice, coffee, tobacco, cotton, and copra were important crops; in the north, sugar production expanded during the years of Díaz's rule; while in the Tierra Caliente, sesame seed was of some importance.[15] Guerrero's copra and sesame seed were consumed locally in the vegetable oil and soap factories of Acapulco and Iguala, as well as in a number of small factories in the Tierra Caliente and on the coast.[16] These were often little more than cottage industries, for the state's industrial base was narrow. The oldest industry was textile manufacture. A cotton textile factory had operated in Coyuca de Benítez, on the Costa Grande, since 1842, and another opened in Atoyac in 1888.[17] However, by the turn of the century only one was in operation, and its production was extremely limited.[18] Another industry based on the processing of local agricultural products was tobacco manufacture, although, here again, production was small and rather irregular.[19] Nevertheless, a limited

Map 2. *Districts of Alarcón and Hidalgo*

degree of modernization did occur during the Porfiriato in the northern portion of the state with which we are principally concerned: the districts of Hidalgo and Alarcón.

These two districts are situated in the northernmost part of the Sierra Zone of Guerrero, the mountains here being a branch of the Nevado de Toluca range.[20] The districts, which border on the states of Mexico, Morelos, and Puebla, differ topographically in some respects. Although generally mountainous, the district of Hidalgo includes the fertile valleys of Iguala and Cocula, while Alarcón is more mountainous and rather less suited to agriculture, although some flat and more fertile land is located in the municipality of Tetipac. Hidalgo is a hot semi-arid region, situated for the most part at 700 to 1,400 meters above sea level, with extreme elevations of 400 to 2,500 meters. By contrast, Alarcón is cooler, with adequate seasonal rainfall in the north, but rather dry to the south, and lies at between 1,000 and 2,200 meters.[21] The district of Hidalgo was divided for administrative purposes into four municipalities: Cocula, Huitzuco, Iguala, and Tepecoacuilco, while Alarcón was composed of two municipalities: Taxco and Tetipac.[22]

This was an area which at the time of the Conquest was part of the Aztec empire. Taxco el Viejo had a military governor, and Tepecoacuilco, with its Aztec garrison, was a tribute-collecting center for a large area. Particularly around Iguala, a rich farming area, there was a large Indian population which declined dramatically during the sixteenth and early seventeenth centuries, reflecting the demographic trend in New Spain as a whole.[23] Except for a few of the larger towns, the population remained solidly Indian into the eighteenth century. The district of Hidalgo had rather more inhabitants who were not classified as Indian than did Alarcón. Huitzuco was a mixture of Indians and *castas*, while in Tepecoacuilco few pure Indians remained, most inhabitants being of mixed race. In Iguala, although the population was still largely Indian, there were still some whites. These three towns apart, Mayanalán, Tuxpan, Nochipala, Tlaxmalac, and Cocula were all inhabited by "pure" Indians. The Taxco area was still more heavily Indian. Although Taxco itself had some non-Indian inhabitants in 1780, as did Tehuilotepec and Acamixtla, the four *cuadrillas* of Tehuilotepec, together with no fewer than thirteen pueblos, appear to have been entirely Indian.[24] During the nineteenth century the Indian element of the population declined in importance, if one may judge by the number of individuals who spoke Indian languages (admittedly a rather crude criterion). By 1900 there were only 589 speakers of Indian languages in the district of Hidalgo, compared to 31,132 Spanish speakers. In the district of Alarcón, by contrast, Indian influence was somewhat more noticeable: there were 2,085 speakers of Indian languages, as against 32,077 Spanish speakers.[25] Nevertheless, despite some remnants of its Indian background, this was a principally mestizo region by the turn of the century.

While the available evidence indicates a shift in the ethnic makeup of the area, other indicators show that by the 1900s this remained a predominantly rural and agricultural society, just as it had been in colonial days. Northern Guerrero was densely populated: in 1910 the population of the district of Alarcón was 38,739, a density

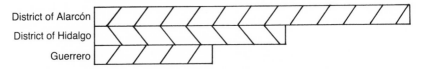

Figure 1. *Population Density, 1910: Districts of Alarcón and Hidalgo Compared to Average for Guerrero*

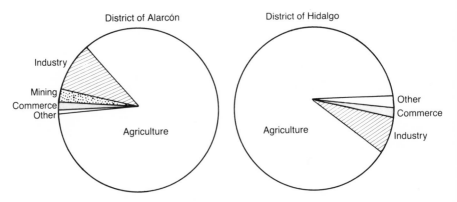

Figure 2. *Economically Active Population by Sector, 1910*

of 23.9 inhabitants per square kilometer. Hidalgo's population of 35,542 gave a density of 13.2 per square kilometer, less than in Alarcón, but still comfortably above the average of 9.1 for the state as a whole.[26] The population in both districts was predominately rural. Defining the urban population as that of any town of more than 4,000 inhabitants, Alarcón was entirely rural, while in Hidalgo only 23.6% of the populace resided in an urban center, that is, in Iguala.[27] Such figures are rather misleading, however. While Iguala was one of the largest cities of Guerrero and, along with Acapulco, the main industrial center of the state, it was estimated in 1922 that 80% of the town's population lived from agriculture, while 5% made their living from commerce, and the remaining 15% worked in industry, the professions, or muledriving.[28] In terms of its occupational structure, therefore, Iguala was little more than a large village.

In both districts the great majority of the population worked in agriculture. In Hidalgo 10,070 individuals, or 89% of the economically active population, were in the agricultural sector. Other sectors were of little importance: industry employed only 6% and commerce as little as 2%. Alarcón presented little variation on this overall picture: 10,149 (86% of the economically active population) worked in the agricultural sector, while only 8% worked in industry (presumably mostly in processing ores from the mines of Taxco), 3% in mining, and 2% in commerce.[29]

The key to the economy of both districts was the production of maize, but there were significant differences in the pattern of production. The volume of production in Hidalgo over the period 1893 to 1907 (an average of 353,682 hectoliters per year) was considerably larger than that of Alarcón, which averaged only 36,683 hectoliters, a mere 10% of the production of the neighboring district. Since the population of both districts was approximately the same, it is clear that Hidalgo produced a much larger marketable surplus. In fact, Hidalgo was the major maize-producing area of Guerrero, from 1893 to 1907 providing 25% of the state's maize.[30] In 1905, a year of crop failures and rising prices throughout Guerrero, Hidalgo produced 52% of the state's maize and supplied areas where the staple grain was scarce.[31]

The disparity in the volume of maize production was not the only feature which distinguished agriculture in the district of Hidalgo from Alarcón, for cash crops played a much more significant role in Hidalgo. Hidalgo's major cash crops were sesame seed (the best quality in all Guerrero, which found a ready market in Mexico City),[32] rice, and sugar. The district's sesame output accounted for 12% of Guerrero's production of this crop, its rice for 16%, and its sugar for no less than 70% in the years 1901 to 1907. In contrast, partly because of its unfavorable terrain and climate, but also because of its inferior communications, the district of Alarcón could produce no cash crops of any significance. Sugar production, which had been of some importance before the turn of the century, was soon dwarfed by the rise of the district of Hidalgo as the principal sugar-producing area of Guerrero. More important in Alarcón was the less refined hard brown sugar called *panocha*. Thus while Alarcón had an average yearly output of only 49,313 kilos of sugar from 1893 to 1907, its *panocha* production averaged 141,955 kilos, nearly three times more, while Hidalgo, in contrast, produced negligible amounts of the inferior-quality brown sugar. Although Alarcón also produced small quantities of coffee, its agricultural sector was geared much less toward producing a marketable surplus than was the case in Hidalgo, where the agricultural sector was much more market oriented.

Despite the fact that Guerrero was peripheral to the economic development of the Porfiriato, it was not completely untouched by the economic boom of the three decades leading up to the revolution. Modernization in Guerrero was sporadic, and was concentrated almost exclusively in the northern portion of the state, and especially in the district of Hidalgo. The principal stimulus to modernization was that symbol of Porfirian economic progress, the railway. The north was the only part of the state which was touched by the expansion of the rail network, and this alone gave the area considerable strategic importance in the economy of Guerrero. The poor communications from which Guerrero suffered were a preoccupation of the Porfirian governors, and of more than a few of their revolutionary successors. In 1907 Governor Damián Flores remarked that "it is proverbial that the state generally lacks means of communication, and this is indeed so, as far as mule tracks and cart roads are concerned, for to this very day little has been done in this field, despite its importance for the development of commerce, agriculture, and mining."[33] A study carried out in 1887 of the benefits of the proposed construction of a new road from Mexico City to Acapulco noted that from Cuernavaca to Acapulco the cultivation of sugarcane and other crops was severely circumscribed by the lack of cheap transport, a factor which confined production to quantities needed to satisfy local markets.[34]

The opening of the Balsas railway was, therefore, an event of great importance for Guerrero, and opened the prospect of a degree of integration into the export economy for the districts of Alarcón and Hidalgo at least, but the railway fell far short of the original plan to connect Acapulco and Chilpancingo with Mexico City, since construction stopped after only 103 kilometers had been completed on the Guerrero stretch.[35] The failure to carry through the original project was partially compensated for by the construction of a cart road to connect Chilpancingo with the railhead at Iguala. Construction began in 1906 and employed as many as 1,500 men. The road was opened in 1910.[36]

The construction of the railway, albeit in truncated form, spurred a wave of optimistic speculation about the economic future of the state. On 1 March 1899 Governor Antonio Mercenario reported that the completion of the railway as far as Iguala had led to an influx of capitalists to the principal districts of the state to invest in mining and agriculture,[37] but the governor's vision of a new era of economic progress proved to be based more on optimism than on fact. The railway was not, after all, to bring about the dramatic economic transformation in the state's economy which many had hoped for.

Nevertheless, in the north of the state certain sectors of the economy did respond to the stimulus provided by the construction of the railway. One example was sugar, which became an important crop in the district of Hidalgo around the turn of the century, when the railway reached the sugar land around Cocula and Atlixtac. The statistics speak for themselves: from 1893 to 1907 Hidalgo produced an average of 666,671 kilos of sugar annually, but by 1904 production had topped 1,000,000, and in 1907 the yield reached the giddy heights of 2,300,000 kilos.

Another striking result of the construction of the railway was the rapid rise of Iguala as an important commercial center, a significant shift in the commercial balance of northern Guerrero, and, indeed, of the state as a whole. Iguala had previously been of little commercial importance and had been overshadowed by nearby Tepecoacuilco, which since Aztec times had been one of the principal commercial centers of Guerrero and the center of supply, not only for its immediate area, but also for regions as far-flung as Tlapa and the Tierra Caliente. However, when the railway bypassed Tepecoacuilco, the principal merchant houses of the town transferred their business to Iguala. The population of Iguala was swelled by immigrants from Huitzuco, Taxco, and Teloloapan, in addition to those from Tepecoacuilco itself.[38] While the decline of commerce in Tepecoacuilco could be seen as early as June 1900, in Iguala, in contrast, "a firm [commercial] movement" was noted, and "important transactions" were taking place.[39] In 1911 the *presidente municipal* of Tepecoacuilco observed that traders now came from as far afield as Chilapa to trade at the railhead in Iguala.[40] It was, perhaps, no accident that Tepecoacuilco, which had suffered such a radical decline in its status and economic well-being, should have been a center of Maderista agitation in the winter of 1910.

The rise of Iguala as a regional commercial center was accompanied by an expansion in the town's soap and vegetable oil industry in the late 1890s. Soap had been manufactured in Tepecoacuilco and Iguala as early as 1859,[41] but by the 1890s Iguala and Acapulco had dominated the soap and vegetable oil industry in the state. Iguala's soap industry was expanded in 1895 when the landowner Alberto Rivera, who already operated a vegetable oil factory, established a soap plant equipped "with the most modern machinery."[42] By the turn of the century there were a number of small oil and soap factories in the town which used as their raw material the sesame seed produced in the district of Hidalgo and the Tierra Caliente.[43]

However, of the various instances of the sporadic modernization which northern Guerrero experienced during the Porfiriato, none was to have a more crucial bearing on the future of the state than the development of mercury mining in Huitzuco, albeit for its political consequences rather than for its purely economic significance. The mines, first discovered in 1870, were, on a small scale, a classic example of the integration of a remote region into the international export market. Still more importantly, however, the mines were owned by Manuel Romero Rubio, father-in-law of President Díaz, and patron of the group of young men later known as the *científicos*. Work on the mines was first begun in 1874 by a company called Urriza, Thébénet, y Arnais, whose first mine was "Nananche," and toward the end of the same year the company began to exploit a second mine. From 1879, however, the production of the mines declined, the company ran into financial difficulties, and in 1885 Ing. Luis Saulny, in partnership with Romero Rubio, bought the assets of Compañía Urriza, Thébénet, y Arnais, as well as the "Gambetta" mine owned by Francisco Azcárate and Partners since 1875. In addition, Saulny staked a claim to three more mines, with the result that, by the end of the year, he and Romero Rubio controlled nearly all the mines and ore-processing plants in Huitzuco. By 1889 twenty-two mines were being worked by various companies, although Romero Rubio's "Minas Unidas de Cinabrio Cruz y Anexas" was by far the most important.[44] The production of the Huitzuco mines from 1886 to 1896 totaled 993,108 kilos of refined mercury,[45] an output which, while it certainly yielded a healthy profit, nevertheless represented a mere drop in the ocean of Mexico's total mercury consumption.[46] Moreover, production in Huitzuco was only feasible as long as mercury prices remained high. Activity fluctuated with prices and finally stopped before 1910, although production resumed in 1916, stimulated by the high prices of the First World War. By then, however, the mines were worked by *buscones*, rather than by commercial businesses.[47]

While Huitzuco enjoyed a moderate boom as long as mercury prices in the world market remained high, the stagnation of mining in Taxco illustrated the sporadic nature of Porifirian modernization in northern Guerrero. Taxco was the traditional mining capital of the area, and since the early days of the Spanish colony, mining had been an important sector of the economy of the district of Alarcón. Cortés had begun work on the mines in Taxco in 1522. However, mining in Taxco had always been characterized by alternate bonanzas and slumps, the most famous of the bonanzas being that of José de la Borda in the mid eighteenth century.[48] Despite periodic slumps in the mining industry, Taxco dominated the fragile economy of the region. Even in 1780, when mining was at a low ebb, and commerce was consequently suffering, Taxco and the nearby town of Tehuilotepec were the principal markets for the product of no fewer than ten pueblos, and the four *cuadrillas* of Tehuilotepec depended entirely on selling their produce or their services in Tehuilotepec and Taxco.[49]

By the late nineteenth century Taxco's mining industry was suffering from chronic stagnation. In 1889 it was reported that only one *hacienda de beneficio* was in operation, and that it relied entirely on the ore taken to it by the *buscones*, who supplied about twenty-two or twenty-three tons per week.[50] In 1890 an American mining engineer noted that all the mines of the Taxco district were worked by *buscones*, who were obliged to hand over one-quarter of their finds to the mine owner and sold the remainder to the highest bidder. As a consequence of this inefficient system, production had fallen to thirty tons of ore per week, which yielded, at the most, 120 ounces of silver per ton, or 3,600 ounces per week.[51]

Despite the generally depressed nature of the industry in the latter part of the century, production in Taxco seems to have revived somewhat in the 1890s. In 1893 the Compañía Beneficiadora de Metales en Taxco established a modern processing plant, capable of refining twenty tons of silver in a single day.[52] Expanded production required an increase in processing capacity, and in 1899 four *haciendas de beneficio* were operating in Taxco itself, and two in nearby Dolores.[53] However, this modest revival proved to be only temporary, and by 1903 Taxco had plunged into another of its periodic slumps: only two mines were being worked, although another two were being readied for production.[54] By the following year no fewer than forty-eight mines in Taxco lay completely idle.[55]

Thus, even in areas where mining was of some importance, the uncertain nature of the industry meant that nowhere could a town live from mining alone. Taxco, one scholar noted, "has not lived from the unstable mining industry for centuries," and the economy of Huitzuco had been established "on a firm basis of agriculture and livestock raising since before the revolution of 1910." For Guerrero was a state in which mining was of marginal importance by the turn of the century, "because of its lack of railway communications, and therefore [the mines] were worked more or less intensely as dictated by the changes in the price of metals, insofar as they [made] it possible to pay the high costs of transport."[56]

In short, the Porfirian economic "miracle" had only a modest impact on Guerrero. Where its influence was felt, it was partial and localized (in the town of Iguala, the sugar lands round Cocula, or the mines at Huitzuco), and the greater part of the state can only have been dimly aware of the kind of dramatic changes which destroyed the very roots of traditional society in neighboring Morelos. Of course, it is possible that other areas of government policy may have effected considerable changes, or stirred much resentment. There is some indication, for example, that Porfirian tax policies (particularly the imposition of a personal head tax and a tax on the wholesale maize trade) may have been extremely unpopular, but evidence here is scanty.[57] Insofar as the sporadic modernization which occurred in the northern reaches of the state made any contribution to the gestation of the revolution in Guerrero, one can speculate that an atmosphere of modest prosperity and economic expansion must surely have contributed to the emergence of the rural middle-class groups who figured so large in the events of 1911, for such was the case in San José de Gracia (Michoacán) and in Pisaflores (Hildalgo).[58] Nevertheless, general economic forces alone could not have triggered the florescence of ranchero society in northern Guerrero without important changes in the pattern of landholding brought about by the Porfirian regime.

New TEXAS

The University of Texas Press presents
this book for review and requests that
you send two clippings of your notice.

RANCHERO REVOLT

The Mexican Revolution in Guerrero

Ian Jacobs

February 5, 1983

$25.00

"...an excellent study...one of a select group... that is reshaping our understanding of the Revolution."

—William B. Taylor

IAN JACOBS CHALLENGES THE COMMON characterization of the Mexican Revolution as the revolt of the oppressed masses against the conservative regime of Porfirio Díaz. In this important work of revisionist history, he portrays the crucial role of small landowners--rancheros--in the Revolution and its final victory.

OPPOSING THE POPULIST INTERPRETATION favored by historians, Jacobs' work stresses the inherently conservative tendencies at work in the Revolution. This is a major contribution to a new trend of local and regional studies which are transforming much of the conventional wisdom about modern Mexico.

University of Texas Press

P.O. Box 7819, Austin, Texas 78712

3. Rancho and Community in Northern Guerrero in the Porfiriato

Discussions of rural Mexico before the revolution usually recognize three basic forms of land tenure: the communal Indian village, the small property or rancho, and the hacienda or large estate. Of the three only the communal village was thoroughly indigenous, having its origins in pre-Conquest Indian society. The hacienda, although perhaps presaged by the estates of individual nobles in Aztec Mexico, was basically a Spanish institution which blossomed in the sixteenth and seventeenth centuries.[1] The history of the rancho, however, is more obscure. Small Spanish-owned properties certainly existed in the seventeenth century, although often under constant pressure from the encroaching haciendas. François Chevalier has concluded that

> the small unencumbered rancho of our day is a relatively recent phenomenon, dating from the end of the eighteenth century at the earliest and usually from the nineteenth. It is possible that the rancho represents the old holding, or rented land, which had later split away from the big estate. If so, the ranchero would have unintentionally avenged his creole ancestors who, after having been reduced to the status of sharecroppers and tenant farmers, thus regained their independence a century or so later.[2]

Chevalier's thesis that the modern rancho dates from the second half of the eighteenth and the nineteenth centuries finds some confirmation in the cases of Michoacán, Hidalgo, and Jalisco,[3] but in Guanajuato the rancho was an important element of the rural landscape throughout the colony, and, indeed, still thrives today.[4]

The origins of the rancho in Guerrero are not clear, but the small property was certainly a well-established feature of the coun-

tryside in the state by the late nineteenth century. In a speech deliv-
ered to the state Congress on 15 March 1912, Governor José Inocente Lugo claimed that "the agrarian question which worries the
pueblos because it is the basis of their conservation does not have
serious importance in our state. . . . Fortunately . . . property is very
subdivided where cultivation is most developed."[5] Lugo, himself an
hacendado, might be accused of painting an excessively glowing
picture, but in 1918 the *ayuntamiento* of Chilpancingo wrote to
Venustiano Carranza in a similar vein, saying that there was no difficult agrarian problem in Guerrero because most *vecinos* owned
land, even if only a little.[6] One area where the small property had
certainly survived was the sierra to the east of Tierra Caliente,
where "from time immemorial, the small property has always pre-
vailed. . . . The majority of the old Indian families have their lands,
which cover, in each case, one or several hills."[7] A town where the
small property was of more recent origin was Ometepec, where a
number of mestizos were able to accumulate ranchos from communal lands disentailed by the Liberal Reform laws.[8]

In northern Guerrero, in the districts of Alarcón and Hidalgo,
there is abundant evidence that the ranchero smallholders not only
existed, but, indeed, that their numbers grew in the twenty or so
years preceding the outbreak of the revolution, a development which
had far-reaching implications for the contemporary history of the
state. This expansion of the ranchero class was closely linked to the
history of the communal village, and, in particular, to the process of
disentailment of communal land initiated by the Liberals in 1856.
An understanding of this process is central to a discussion of the
flowering of ranchero society in northern Guerrero during the
Porfiriato.

The communal Indian village was a traditional feature of the
Mexican rural scene before the Conquest. Spanish colonial legislation brought about a number of changes in the status of the communal lands, but the basic right of the Indian village to hold its land in
common was not challenged. In some areas, such as the Valley of
Mexico, the communities came under strong pressure from the haciendas during the colonial period, while in areas such as the Valley
of Oaxaca the village lands survived virtually intact.[9] Despite such
regional variations, the communities' legal right to exist was never
in doubt. The most serious threat to communal holdings came in
the nineteenth century, when Liberal legislation decreed the division of village lands into individual properties and for the first time
denied the right of communal tenure of land.

Liberal policy for the development of Mexico fell into two main categories: colonization of the underpopulated areas and the disentailment of the corporate lands of the Church and of the land-owning Indian villages. The purpose of these policies was to encourage "not the large and uncultivated possessions, nor the proud landowners who squander in the great cities the fruit of what they extort from the colonist, but rather the small productive holdings, occupied by the owner whose presence and whose vital efforts make them valuable and productive."[10] As Ponciano Arriaga noted, "it is necessary not to destroy [private] property, that would be absurd; but on the contrary, to generalize it, abolishing the old privilege, because this privilege makes rational law impossible."[11] The Liberals dreamed of a new Mexico of small independent farmers each cultivating a piece of land. In short, the aim of their colonization and disentailment policies was to create a rural bourgeoisie, as a basis for a prosperous capitalist Mexico.

For the Liberals private property was the basic tenet of political economy, and they could not conceive of the primitive communal village, which for so long had been the cornerstone of the social organization of the Mexican Indian, having any place in their new Mexico. For "corporations of this kind, and all corporations, are not the best owners of a piece of land; since experience and constant observation in all countries has demonstrated that the lands that belong to a community or corporation are condemned, if not to perpetual sterility, at least to the most careless cultivation least useful to the public."[12] Disentailment of communal lands, declared Francisco O. Arce, governor of Guerrero, in 1886, taking up a traditional Liberal theme, would cause "the property of the state to increase in value under the influence of that powerful agent, individual interest, to the benefit of which the previously sterile fertility of the land has been torn from the *main mort.*"[13]

These Liberal principles found their expression in the Lerdo Law of 25 June 1856, so called after Sebastián Lerdo de Tejada, who drafted it. The law stipulated that "the ownership of all urban and rural properties of civil and ecclesiastical corporations in the republic will be assigned to those persons who are renting them, for an amount corresponding to the rent at present paid, calculating this to be equal to a 6% annual interest."[14] Thus the communities were tarred with the same brush as the holdings of the Church, and the right of the Indian village to own its land in common was peremptorily abolished.

Scholars of the effects of the Lerdo Law generally concluded that they were disastrous for the Mexican Indian. A fairly typical view is that of Nathan Whetten:

> In the north and northwest, where the mestizo element was dominant and where the villagers were well acquainted with the institution of private property, the measure seemed to produce the desired effect, and villagers used it as a means of confirming possessions which they had long regarded as their own. In the Central Mesa and in the south, however, where the Indian element was dominant and where collective property was the only kind understood or appreciated, the measure proved to have the opposite effect. In these areas the Indians opposed and evaded the law. If they were forced to comply, some of them accepted title and then immediately transferred this to some elder of the community. Many others became the prey of unscrupulous speculators and lost their lands almost as soon as the deeds had been issued.[15]

This view has received some confirmation in the case of the central states of Mexico, Hidalgo, Morelos, and the Federal District in a study by T. G. Powell, who found that in this area the principal effects of the disentailment legislation between 1850 and 1876 were "the reduction to absolute poverty of many communities which until then had been self-sufficient, the intensification of *latifundismo* and the system of debt peonage, and the demoralization of an entire social group, the indigenous peasantry."[16] Furthermore, Powell goes on to assert, "the dictatorship of Porfirio Díaz sustained the governmental pressure against the peasantry and almost succeeded in destroying that social class, but the era of Díaz ended with a violent social revolution and not with the millennium of capitalist progress so ardently desired by the men of the Reform."[17] Thus, whether by evasion on the part of the communities or through the machinations of latifundists and speculators, the objectives of the Liberal Reformers were frustrated.

This view has, however, been disputed in the case of some parts of the state of Oaxaca by Charles Berry, who found that in the central district of the state, disentailed land "was placed in the reach of the class of citizens who the Reformers hoped would buy, thereby fulfilling the goal of creating a nation of small property owners."[18] Thus it is clear that any general assessment of the disentailment laws must take into account regional differences in their impact.

In the districts of Alarcón and Hidalgo all the evidence points to conclusions similar to those reached by Berry for Oaxaca. Northern

Guerrero divided into two distinct zones defined by the type of land tenure whch predominated in each. The first, covering the municipalities of Taxco, Tetipac (the district of Alarcón), and Huitzuco, was an area where the smallholding (which I shall define as any property of less than 2,000 hectares) and the communal village were the dominant forms of land tenure, although a few large properties did exist. The second zone, in which the hacienda overshadowed other forms of tenure, embraced the municipalities of Cocula, Iguala, and Tepecoacuilco. Nevertheless, some communal land and ranchos did exist in this area, side by side with the hacienda, which I shall define as any property of 2,000 hectares or more, a definition which will be discussed more fully in the next chapter.

In the districts of Alarcón and Hidalgo, thirty-four communities survived until the promulgation of the Reform laws: twenty in the district of Alarcón and fourteen in Hidalgo. Ten communities fell within the hacienda zone, although the number of landowning villages there must once have been larger.[19] Of the twenty-four communal villages which lay outside the hacienda zone, four were in the municipality of Huitzuco, fifteen in the jurisdiction of Taxco, and five within the municipal boundaries of Tetipac.[20] Some twenty-three communities were affected by the laws of disentailment, although nine were able to retain at least some communal land. In all, eighteen communities managed to keep in communal possession 74,699.52 hectares, and another two retained an unknown quantity of land.

The explanation of the failure ever to complete disentailment in the districts of Alarcón and Hidalgo lies partly in the fact that the process got under way rather late in this area. The first community to be affected was, evidently, Tlaxmalac, in the municipality of Huitzuco. The earliest reference to disentailment of Tlaxmalac's land is in a bill of sale for a parcel of former communal land dated 8 April 1869.[21] A circular of 1 October 1872 issued by the Secretaría de Gobernación y Justicia of Guerrero, ordering all communal land to be adjudicated as private property to those already renting it within four months, provided a further stimulus for distribution of the town's holding as three titles of adjudication dating from January 1873 bear witness.[22] However, the process could not be completed overnight. Indeed, disentailment still had not been finished in Tlaxmalac as late as 1896.[23]

No doubt application of the disentailment legislation had been hindered by the civil strife of the Reform period, by the French Intervention (northern Guerrero was, it will be recalled, something of a Conservative and Imperialist stronghold), and probably also by the

**Table 1. Communities Which Retained Communal Land in the
Districts of Alarcón and Hidalgo by 1910**

Municipality	Community	Hectares retained
Taxco	Acamixtla	15,000
Taxco	Atzala de la Asunción	2,048
Taxco	Cacalotenango*	488.40
Taxco	Coxcatlán*	2,455
Taxco	Huixtac*	4,614
Taxco	Juliantla	1,420
Taxco	Landa*	430
Taxco	San Francisco Acuitlapán	1,792.40
Taxco	San Pedro y San Felipe Chichila	4,984.60
Taxco	San Sebastián	94
Taxco	Taxco el Viejo*	1,290
Taxco	Tecalpulco*	1,492.32
Taxco	Tlamacazapa*	3,630.40
Cocula	Tecomatlán	345.70
Huitzuco	San Francisco Ozamatlán	no data
Iguala	Tuxpan*	1,644.30
Tepecoacuilco	Coacoyula	4,830
Tepecoacuilco	Maxela*	5,000
Tepecoacuilco	San Agustín Oapan	no data
Tepecoacuilco	San Miguel Tecuiciapan	23,140.40
Total		74,699.52

SOURCE: ASRA, Ramo Ejidal and Ramo Comunal.
*Communities partially affected by disentailment. Those not so marked were not
affected.

internal struggles which wracked the state in the late 1860s and the
1870s. This was certainly the case in Huitzuco, where an inspection
was carried out in 1870 with a view to disentailing the town's land.
Political circumstances prevented completion of the undertaking,
however, and Huitzuco's land was still in communal possession eight
or nine years later.[24]

In 1886 disentailment was still far from completion in Guerrero, since in that year Governor Francisco O. Arce stated that,
when he had taken office the year before, he had found a multitude
of communal lands owned by the pueblos and the *ayuntamientos*,
"contrary to the law of the Reform, promulgated thirty years ago."

Arce had therefore "paid attention to distributing these lands, adjudicating them to the poor indigenous agriculturists, who in future will find peace and the fruit of their labors in a property watered with the sweat of their brow, perfectly delimited and transmissible to their legitimate heirs."[25] Arce went on to say that he had broken the back of the task, and that, before his period of office ended in 1889, all communal land in Guerrero would be disentailed.[26]

The governor's optimism found very little justification in the facts, however. By 1886, 1,011 titles of adjudication had been issued in the district of Hidalgo to "poor agriculturists in accordance with the spirit of the . . . law." Of these, 759 had been given to residents of Tlaxmalac, 182 to *vecinos* of Cocula, and 56 and 14, respectively, to the people of Apipilulco and Atlixtac.[27] Disentailment, then, had scarcely begun in the district by 1886, since only 4 of the 14 communities in Hidalgo had been affected. The picture in the state as a whole provided scarcely more basis for the governor's optimism, since in 6 of the other 13 districts only 1,541 titles had been issued.[28] These figures somewhat understate the achievements of the government, since the district of Alarcón is not mentioned despite the fact that disentailment was certainly underway there;[29] nevertheless much clearly remained to be done.

The turn of the century still did not see the completion of the task the government had set itself, for in 1903 Governor Agustín Mora reported that, although "nearly all the lands which belonged to the indigenous communities have been distributed," the process was still not complete. As Arce had done in 1886, Mora expressed the hope that the remaining communal lands would be distributed "very shortly,"[30] but once again such optimism proved to have little justification, since in 1909 Governor Damián Flores was still declaring that "the disentailment of communal property is not finished, and it is urgent to finish it in order to avoid the disorders and disagreements to which it gives rise,"[31] a reference to the frequent disputes between communities over the boundaries of their land.

In summary, the effects of disentailment were rather slow to be felt in the districts of Alarcón and Hidalgo. The 1856 legislation does not appear to have had any significant impact until the 1880s and, in fact, was never fully implemented. Furthermore, although it has been stated that disentailment met great resistance in central Mexico,[32] in northern Guerrero one finds no hard evidence of such resistance. In fact, in some cases, disentailment of communal land was actively sought by the pueblos. In Huitzuco, for example, Pablo de Jesús, the town's representative, wrote in 1878 or 1879 to the *prefecto* of the district of Hidalgo that from time immemorial Huitzuco had owned its land in common. Political circumstances, he added, had prevented the town from applying the disentailment laws, but he now requested, "on behalf of all the Indians" of Huitzuco, that their land be parceled out in private lots.[33] Huitzuco was not alone in taking such action, since in 1869 Huixtac had made a similar request.[34] These two cases, while hardly conclusive by themselves, do tend to contradict the view that the Indians neither understood the institution of private property nor wished to own their land privately.

Despite the fact that disentailment was never completed in this area of Guerrero, it did have an important impact on the social structure of the region. One of the most important effects of the Lerdo Law was the stimulus it provided for the rise of what we might call a "new village elite" of prosperous smallholders, by providing a mechanism which allowed ambitious individuals to gain access to land not previously available on the open market. One clear example of this development was the case of Clemente Unzueta in Tlaxmalac, who was accused by some residents of the town of "employing his position as representative of the communal lands and various maneuvers to gain control of the best lands" of Tlaxmalac.[35] Whether or not it is true that Unzueta used improper methods to acquire land, it is certainly true that he acquired at least some of his holdings by perfectly legal means: by adjudication or purchase of disentailed land, through his marriage to Andrea Robles, and through concessions of national lands granted by the Federal Treasury.[36] In any case, "Clemente Unzueta was for many years up to his death, which occurred on 6 October 1915, one of the most outstanding figures in the place, in whose hands power was always held, directly or indirectly."[37] By the time of his death, Unzueta owned about 1,078 hectares of pasture and 484 hectares of *temporal*.[38]

Although it is not entirely clear whether Unzueta used devious methods to acquire his land, there were certainly cases where chicanery or deception was involved, such as that of Chaucingo and Quetzalapa. This case is especially interesting since the Figueroa family, later so influential in the state's history, were natives of these two rancherías, and at least one member of the family profited from disentailment here. Chaucingo and Quetzalapa were two rancherías formed on land purchased from the Spanish Crown in 1712 by Pedro de Ocampo of Cuernavaca.[39] The land, which later came to form a *parcialidad*, a form of communal tenure, was owned jointly by the residents of the two villages, most of whom were, in fact, members of a single extended family. At some date between 1880 and 1890, Braulio Figueroa, a former elected representative of the *parcialidad*, summoned a meeting in which he warned the *vecinos* of the danger of denunciation of their land under the provisions of the Reform Laws. In order to avert this danger he proposed that sixteen trusted individuals, eight from Chaucingo and eight from Quetzalapa, be chosen to denounce the land, on the understanding that they would act only as depositaries and would recognize the de facto rights of the *parcioneros* to their parcels of crop land. However, although the depositaries abided by the agreement for a few years, they later asserted their property rights acquired under the disentailment laws to limit other *parcioneros* to the poorer land. The latter, however, never relinquished their claim to the land of which they had been deprived, and later defended it against a claim by a Spanish land company, and in 1904 unsuccessfully attempted to achieve a new distribution of the *parcialidad.*[40]

Although in the case of Tlaxmalac, and of Chaucingo and Quetzalapa, the members of the new village elite were natives of the communities in question, this was not always the case. For example, Rómulo Figueroa, another of the Quetzalapa Figueroas, purchased a number of pieces of disentailed land in Temaxcalapa, a part of the large community of Huixtac.[41] In total, Figueroa's holdings came to around sixty-seven hectares, of which some forty-two were irrigated, the rest being pasture.

Another community where outsiders purchased disentailed land was Taxco el Viejo, where the communal land was divided in 1885. Here Juan Duplat, a resident of the city of Taxco, and Guadalupe Hernández purchased some small parcels of land from the *vecinos* of the community. Later, however, both used their footholds in the village to expand their properties by invading those of their neighbors. In this fashion Duplat acquired 438 hectares and Hernandez 283, but Taxco el Viejo recovered the invaded land when the revolution broke out.[42]

A further case of an outsider who was able to acquire former communal lands after disentailment is that of Manuel Meléndez. In 1883 the lands of the community of Tlamacazapa were disentailed, and a portion known as La Mano was adjudicated to seven individuals. Between 1884 and 1886 five of these men sold their parcels to one of the other recipients, leaving only two men as owners, and shortly after 1887 Meléndez purchased La Mano from them.[43] A plan drawn up in 1898 showed Meléndez's property to be some 850 hectares, most of it poor-quality hill land.[44]

There were few cases of the expansion of so-called haciendas as a result of the disentailment of communal lands, and where this did occur, the beneficiaries were scarcely latifundists. One example is the Hacienda de San Francisco Cuadra, which was originally an *ha-*

cienda de beneficio formed to process the ore from the mines of Taxco by a Spaniard, Francisco de la Cuadra. In the sixteenth century Cuadra's descendants stopped processing metals and planted fruit trees, coffee, and sugarcane. When Ignacio Flores purchased Cuadra in 1889, the hacienda had a mixed economy based on processing metal ore and agriculture. The hacienda also had a number of silver veins on its land, although it is not clear whether these were worked, and certainly by 1891 the cultivation of sugarcane was the most important element of Cuadra's economy. In 1903 the hacienda was purchased by a lawyer, Lic. Bernardino Ramírez, who introduced Dutch and Jersey cattle, Merino sheep, and Angora goats. To accommodate this new livestock he bought some twenty hectares of pasture from residents of Landa, which had previously been part of the communal lands of the village. In addition, he purchased from one Tomás Portillo three hectares of *temporal* and twenty of hill land which had originally belonged to the community of Cacalotenango.[45] At this stage the Hacienda de Cuadra measured 381 hectares,[46] and should probably be classified as a rancho rather than an hacienda.

Similarly modest in proportions was the Hacienda de Santa Rosa, in the municipality of Tetipac, which was carved out of the communal lands of San Andrés. Precisely how this occurred is not clear, but in 1883 Alberto Arriaga "denounced" the land of the hacienda which, he stated, he had inherited from his father, and "which is of those lands known as communal [*de común reparti-miento*]." The exact size of Santa Rosa is hard to ascertain, but if we consider that it had a capacity of one *carga*, or 200 liters, of maize, and that its value in 1883 was $960 (the Hacienda de Cuadra sold in 1891 for $1,000), it seems clear that it was by no means a latifundium.[47] In addition to Santa Rosa, Arriaga also owned two pieces of land in Chontalcuatlán, both denounced in 1884 and 1887 for a value of $80 and $20, and in addition he purchased a number of fractions of disentailed land in both Chontalcuatlán and Chimaltitlán from private owners.[48] His net worth almost certainly did not exceed $1,500—no doubt fairly typical for one of the moderately prosperous rancheros of the region.

While the rise of the new village elite led to a certain amount of concentration of land in the hands of these ambitious men, it occurred only to a limited degree. In Chontalcuatlán, for example, a number of those who received a parcel of land under the disentailment legislation later sold it, and three men (among them Alberto Arriaga) were able to form ranchos, in two cases of rather more than 1,000 hectares. Nevertheless, most *vecinos* of Chontalcuatlán retained at least a small piece of land, although some, it is true, were reduced to renting land or selling their labor for wages.[49] In only one community did the new village elite take control of all the communal lands. This was Paintla, where the village lands "were adjudicated or denounced by a very few persons, of this place, Paintla. As representatives [of the village land] they issued themselves titles to it in the year 1885 and the year 1905. These representatives took possession of the lands referred to, as well as the documents, and forbade the freedom of use to all the agriculturists who live in this place, all of whom became tenants."[50]

Far more typical than the case of Paintla is that of Chontalcuatlán, where concentration did not reach such an extreme, or that of Cacalotenango, where, apparently, the former communal lands remained divided into small properties.[51] For the new village elite were not of the same breed as the *hacendados* of Morelos, who aggressively expanded their estates at the expense of the communal lands of the villages. The new village elite were rather rancheros who found in the lands which disentailment freed from unalienable communal possession an opportunity to satisfy their ambition and to establish themselves as prominent figures in their communities. These were not the proud absentee landowners whom José María Luis Mora had criticized, but the owners of the "small and productive holdings" which he and his fellow Liberals had hoped to create in the Mexican countryside.

The kind of internal differentiation experienced by the towns and villages of northern Guerrero in the late nineteenth century was undoubtedly no isolated phenomenon. For example, the Porfiriato witnessed an identical process in Ometepec and in Pisaflores in the state of Hidalgo, and in Tepoztlán in Morelos an extremely dynamic economic elite emerged.[52] Moreover, while disentailment was the main driving force of the expansion of the ranchero class in the districts of Alarcón and Hidalgo, there were a few isolated cases which suggested that this was a class already on the move. One such case is that of Vicente Gómez, a man who, despite his humble origins, managed to acquire the haciendas Cuestiopan and La Luz, apparently by dint of sheer hard work.[53] By 1893 Gómez was producing rum from the sugarcane he cultivated on his land,[54] which totaled no more than 952 hectares, of which some 277 were irrigated.[55]

Another man who was on the rise was Crescencio Rosas of Cacahuamilpa, who acquired his land by less creditable means. In 1893 the residents of Cacahuamilpa were alarmed to find that Ing. Aurelio Almazán, who had been commissioned to survey the government-owned Estancia de Michapa, had included in his survey part of their communal lands. Fearing that Cacahuamilpa might lose this land (which had apparently already been disentailed), Rosas, "the political authority of the place," offered to buy the land in question for $3,000. Rosas and another individual, Juan Tinoco, acted as agents of the village in the purchase, and on 20 December 1894 the federal government sold the land to Cacahuamilpa for the price Rosas had offered. On 13 May 1896 President Díaz ordered that the land be distributed in individual lots in proportion to the amount paid by each individual.[56]

A census of the contributors carried out on 9 April 1897 shows that 119 individuals contributed sums ranging from $3 to $1,000 (this last sum being the contribution of Juan Tinoco). Rosas's name did not appear on the census.[57] However, despite Díaz's order, Rosas and Tinoco never gave each contributor an individual title, but instead kept the land for themselves, their relatives, and their friends, and "as Sr. Rosas was the cacique of the place and a very influential person, despite all the representations made by the *vecinos*, they could not succeed in being given the lands to which they had a right."[58]

In 1899 the story took a new turn when Rosas sold the land known as Santa Teresa and an urban lot in Cacahuamilpa to Manuel Meléndez, owner of La Mano, in order to pay off a debt which Rosas owed him. Clause 5 of the contract stated that Rosas could reclaim the land within two years if he repaid the original purchase price of $1,192.57, plus $25.87 in interest for each month which had elapsed since 20 February 1899. In short, Rosas pawned part of Cacahuamilpa's land. Although Rosas died before the two years had elapsed, Rosas's children later claimed that on 20 February 1901 (the date on which the option to redeem the land expired) they offered to pay Meléndez $1,913, but he refused to accept it. A series of court cases ensued.[59]

The Rosas family evidently won their case against Meléndez, and by 1905 had again gained control of the portion of Cacahuamilpa's land which they had appropriated. Rosas's children then sold 500 hectares to Tiburcio Melgar for around $3,000 and in addition, the Rosas were accused of having leased out Cacahuamilpa's irrigated land to Melgar for a period of two years for a further $1,000.[60] This was done to pay off the family's debts to Meléndez, debts which they claimed to have contracted in order to pay the contributions of some individuals who, although they appeared in the 1897 census as contributors, had never in fact contributed their share of the price paid to the government for the 1894 purchase. According to another informant, however, Rosas had used the money he had borrowed from Meléndez to finance the cultivation of sugar on Cacahuamil-pa's land for his own benefit.[61] Whatever the truth may have been, it seems clear that Rosas had no legal right to sell any of the land purchased by the village in 1894.

While the ranchero class probably would not have experienced such a rapid growth in its numbers without the impetus supplied by disentailment, cases such as those of Gómez and Rosas suggest that other means of upward mobility were available to impel at least some individuals into the relatively prosperous ranks of the rancheros of northern Guerrero. Moreover, the rancheros were by no means a new class created by the economic and social policies of the Porfiriato, as examples of already well established rancheros show. The Vergara family, for example, had owned the property known as El Ciruelo or Cerro Gordo since 1850 when Andrés, Francisco, and Antonio Vergara inherited it from one Marcos Díaz. By 1904 its owner was Eulogia Vergara, who in her will left the property, which covered some 400 hectares, most of it pasture, to her four children.[62]

Another case of a long-established ranchero is that of Leonardo Maldonado, who in 1837 purchased the property Santa Teresa, which in the late eighteenth century had been part of the Hacienda de Tenancingo. By 1882 Maldonado had died, leaving Santa Teresa to his widow, Francisca García, who successfully defended it against a claim that the land was a *mostrenco*, and therefore subject to confiscation. In 1895 she again defended her land against a claim that it was *terreno baldío*, and a nine-year court case ensued which confirmed García's title to her 1,667 hectares of land in Santa Teresa.[63]

While the examples cited are of ranchos situated in the district of Alarcón and the municipality of Huitzuco where the land was rather more mountainous and less suited to cultivation, the rancheros were by no means excluded from the richer land in the municipalities of Cocula, Iguala, and Tepecoacuilco. Here the rancho managed to coexist with the hacienda. One example can be found in the holdings of the Mastache family. The founder of the family's fortune was Guillermo Mastache, who, when his estate was divided among his nine heirs in 1909, left assets valued at $32,658.06, making him probably one of the wealthiest rancheros in northern Guerrero. Mastache had based his fortune on two main activities: agriculture and money-lending, for at the time of his death two loans totaling $5,500 were still owed to him, and, as for his land, most of it was located in the fertile areas around Cocula and Iguala.[64] Guillermo was not the only landowner in the family, since his son Teófilo purchased four fractions of land valued at $1,000 in 1910.[65] It is difficult to know exactly how much land the Mastache family owned in total. In the municipality of Cocula they owned between 1,000 and 2,500 hectares, and their holdings in Iguala were probably of similar magnitude.[66]

Another prosperous ranchero in the Iguala area was Enrique Pedrote, owner of a property called Xonacatla which had a rather complicated history. Between 1862 and 1869 Jacinto Díaz purchased various fractions of land with which he formed Xonacatla. He later gave part of his property to his brother Jesús, who also bought a number of small parcels of land to increase his holdings. Later, the two brothers fell out over the boundaries of their properties, and in order to extricate himself from the dispute Jesús sold his holdings to the wife of the current *prefecto político* of the district of Hidalgo. This presumably stymied his brother's case. At any rate Jesús's portion of Xonacatla changed hands again in 1902, before being purchased by Pedrote in 1905 for $400. Thus Jacinto Díaz's widow, Isabel Crespo, was legally the owner only of Rincón de Xonacatla, Jacinto's portion of the property, although she and her children never recognized the legitimacy of Pedrote's title to the remainder of Xonacatla.[67] Pedrote's portion covered an area of approximately 1,308 hectares, of which only some 60 were cultivable, while Crespo's holdings came to some 660 hectares, of which around 127 were crop land.[68] Clearly both Pedrote and Crespo were modestly prosperous farmers, fairly typical of the ranchero of northern Guerrero. In this connection, Crespo's will, drawn up in 1907, gives a tantalizing glimpse into the lifestyle of the ranchero in Porfirian Guerrero. Her three children shared a modest patrimony indeed: equal shares in Rincón de Xonacatla, ten or twelve head of cattle, and a one-room house in Iguala.[69] Nevertheless, modest as her assets were, her holdings surely placed Crespo on a plane of prosperity above that to which the peon or the average tenant could aspire.

Whether long established or a newcomer, the ranchero of northern Guerrero saw a considerable expansion in the numbers of fellow smallholders during the Porfiriato. Moreover, this flowering of ranchero society was measured not only in the pattern of land tenure, but also in an increase in ranchero participation in municipal politics. During the 1890s and the first decade of the twentieth century, a considerable number of rancheros, particularly those whom I have called the new village elite who benefited from the disentailment laws, occupied municipal office in northern Guerrero. Such was the case of a number of the members of the Figueroa family, who in 1911 would figure prominently in the Maderista revolution. Similarly, at least five members of the Mastache family held a variety of municipal offices, as did Enrique Pedrote. José María Suárez, owner of the property Mazapa, held municipal office in Cocula in 1893 and 1902, and Emilio Carranco, a small landowner in Tepecoacuilco, held elected positions on the *ayuntamiento* there in 1896, 1900, 1908, and 1911. Furthermore, like the Figueroas, some of these politically active rancheros would be Maderistas in 1910–1911. Thus Pedrote and several members of the Mastache family were acknowledged supporters of Madero in 1911, and Alejo Mastache took an active role in the revolution, fighting in the forces of Ambrosio Figueroa, as did his brother Trinidad.[70]

However, the expansion of the ranchero class was only one side of the agrarian picture in northern Guerrero. A much older form of land tenure than the private smallholding was the communal village. Although rancheros had acquired sizable areas of communal land, the decline of the villages was by no means complete, since a number managed to survive as communal landholding units. Indeed, disentailment was not the only problem which beset the communities of northern Guerrero. Recurring disputes between the villages over their land were a much older problem, and one which plagued them throughout the colonial period and the nineteenth century. Since this problem is one which is rarely discussed in the literature, it is worth devoting some attention to it here, especially since disentailment served to exacerbate it toward the end of the nineteenth century.

When the Zapatista agrarian commission arrived in Taxco in 1915, it discovered that the task that it faced was very different from that which had been expected. In Morelos the role of the commissions was to restore communal lands usurped by the haciendas, but in northern Guerrero, in the words of Enrique Peredo Reyes, a member of the commission, "the petitions from the campesinos to which we had to attend referred, in the majority of cases, to difficulties which arose between one pueblo and another over the boundaries of their lands. . . . one of the most difficult problems which arose was that which concerned boundary fixing, a problem very difficult to solve."[71] This problem of conflicts over communal lands was, as Peredo Reyes pointed out, a very old one. For example, as early as 1560 a dispute arose between the Indian towns of Tenango (now Cacalotenango) and Tetipac. Tetipac laid claim to a portion of land on which a number of Tarascan Indians who had emigrated from Michoacán had settled. The Tarascans, said the Indians of Tetipac, should pay rent to Tetipac and not to Tenango, as they had been doing up to now, but on 12 December 1562 Viceroy Luis de Velasco ruled in favor of Tenango.[72]

Disputes between the communities could often lead to violence. For example, in 1882 a dispute involving Cacalotenango,
Santo Domingo, and San Pedro y San Felipe Chichila was resolved
by an agreement reached between the representatives of the three
communities in which the state government acted as mediator. On
5 August 1882 the governor of Guerrero ordered the *prefecto político* of the district of Alarcón to give formal possession of their land
to the three villages. However, Santo Domingo resisted the agreement, and the *prefecto* was obliged to ask for an escort of federal
troops in order to carry out the possession.[73]

In 1886 Governor Arce had expressed the hope that such disputes would cease to occur when the communal lands had been disentailed, and each *vecino* of the communities had a well-defined
title to a piece of land.[74] However, in some cases the incorrect application of the disentailment laws actually exacerbated old conflicts,
as in the case of Temaxcalapa in its dispute with Teuzisapan. This
had seemingly been settled by arbitration in 1852, but the conflict
flared up again when, in 1885, the *prefecto* of the district of Aldama
(to which Teuzisapan belonged) issued titles of adjudication to seven
vecinos of Teuzisapan for the disputed land. Meanwhile, the *prefecto* of the district of Alarcón had issued titles to the same land to
residents of Temaxcalapa. At the turn of the century the governor of
Guerrero ruled in favor of Temaxcalapa, as did the Supreme Court in
a judgment of *amparo* in 1908.[75] Nevertheless, the dispute dragged
on, periodically leading to violence, until the personal intervention
of Governor Gabriel Guevara resolved it in the 1930s.[76]

Another case in which disentailment exacerbated a land dispute
was that of the villages of Oapan, Ahuehuepan, Ahuelicán, and San
Juan Tetelcingo. In 1861 San Juan made an informal arrangement
whereby it ceded part of its communal lands to the residents of
Ahuehuepan, but in 1881 this land was claimed by Oapan. The dispute was resolved when an agreement was reached by which Oapan
and San Juan would each receive half of the disputed land. San Juan
then rented its share to *vecinos* of Ahuelicán, and the residents of
Ahuehuepan thereby lost the use of land which they had previously
worked under the 1861 arrangement. Problems arose when the land
came to be disentailed, since both Ahuehuepan and Ahuelicán considered that they had a claim to it. The *prefecto* of the district of
Guerrero adjudicated the land in question to residents of Ahuelicán,
who based their claim on the fact that they had rented it since 1881.
However, the *prefecto* of the district of Hidalgo adjudicated the
same land to *vecinos* of Ahuehuepan, who based their claim to it on

the 1861 agreement. In 1891 the governor of Guerrero ruled in favor of Ahuelicán, thus solving the dispute.[77]

Cases such as those of Temaxcalapa and Teuzisapan and Ahuelicán and Ahuehuepan were evidently rather frequent, since a circular of 12 November 1897, issued by the Secretaría de Gobierno of Guerrero, remarked that numerous complaints had been received that the same piece of land had been adjudicated to two or more separate individuals, or that the correct procedure for issuing titles had not been followed.[78]

While conflicts between communal villages were quite common, disputes between landowners and the communities appear to have been less frequent and to have had less potential for violence. In part, perhaps, this was due to the fact that there appear to have been relatively few communities in the hacienda zone where the more powerful landowners had their properties, and where the best arable land was located. Some of the villages which had owned land in the hacienda zone apparently lost their land quite early. Such was the case of Mayanalán, for example, where by 1740 all but a very small part of the communal lands had been lost to surrounding landowners.[79] Some ten communities in the hacienda zone managed to retain land into the second half of the nineteenth century, however, and six of these held on to some land despite the application of the disentailment laws.[80]

Economic factors perhaps also contributed to reducing the intensity of land conflicts between private landowners and communal villages. The landowners of the districts of Alarcón and Hidalgo produced a limited range of crops mostly for the local market. Sugar haciendas, such as Atlixtac and Santa Fe Tepetlapa, were the exception, maize being by far the most important crop. The *hacendados* of northern Guerrero did not have the stimulus of a profitable export market as their neighbors in Morelos did, and their craving for land was, therefore, much less. Nevertheless, disputes between private landowners and the communities did occur. For example a conflict between the Hacienda de Cuadra and the community of Landa continued throughout most of the nineteenth century. In 1825 the Juzgado de Letras del Partido de Taxco confirmed Landa's title to the lands it had cultivated from "time immemorial," including the part claimed by Manuel Gómez, owner of Cuadra. In 1849 Landa was still involved in its dispute with Cuadra, as well as with the Hacienda de la Luz. The result of this renewed litigation was somewhat less than a total victory for Landa, since the alcalde of Taxco ruled in 1850 that, while the community's title to its land was perfectly valid,

Cuadra was to have access to the timber and water on Landa's holdings which were necessary for the processing of ore and for mining operations. Landa was specifically enjoined to refrain from taking any action which might reduce the supply of these resources for the mining industry.[81] In 1893 Diego Flores requested permission to survey the northern boundary of Cuadra (which he had purchased in 1891), thus renewing the old dispute with Landa. The examining magistrate ruled in favor of Landa, however, finding that Flores's intention was "not to restore the existing boundary markers, but to establish a new boundary line."[82]

A dispute with a still longer history was that of the Hacienda de Santa Fe Tepetlapa (originally known as the Hacienda de Zacapalco) and Coxcatlán, an Indian community near Taxco. The story began in 1767 when Pedro Zorrilla was given possession of Zacapalco. This possession was contested by Coxcatlán, however, and a protracted legal battle ensued.[83] The dispute dragged on into the nineteenth century, and became further complicated in 1888 when the owner of Santa Fe, Agustín Ponce, sold part of the disputed land to a number of individuals from Buenavista de Cuéllar,[84] perhaps by way of a maneuver to muddy the legal waters still further. Nevertheless, with the revolutionary turmoil of 1911 the Indians of Coxcatlán saw their chance to recover their land by taking the law into their own hands. On 6 September 1911 the *comisario* of Buenavista reported that

> yesterday, the Indians of Tlamacazapa and Coxcatlán, in the number of about one hundred, more or less, according to persons of reliable judgment, were in the *cuadrilla* of Palmillas Sacapalco, and I think that they will follow the line of the *camino real* toward Los Amates, because it is said that they are going about surveying their lands, and they have threatened to kill the American [owner of Santa Fe] so that he asked for help from the military garrison of Iguala, which ordered that ten soldiers stationed in this town should go [to protect him], and last night they found the American of Santa Fe, at about ten o'clock at night, because this man is very frightened. . . . and today he is in [Buenavista].[85]

The events of 1911 did not end the matter, however, and the dispute with Santa Fe was not brought to an end until the expropriation of all the hacienda's land in the 1920s and 1930s, although the conflict between Coxcatlán and the smallholders of Buenavista still continued in the 1940s.[86]

However, such disputes between landowners and the communal villages of northern Guerrero appear merely to have been the exceptions which proved the rule. At any rate, in the district of Alarcón and in the municipality of Huitzuco the communal village remained fairly strong, despite the effects of disentailment, and even in the hacienda zone some villages retained some communal land. Thus the rancheros flourished, while the communities had some success in surviving the effects of disentailment. Nevertheless, the larger holdings of the *hacendados* also played an important role in the area's economy. It is the traditional villain of the agrarian history of Mexico, the hacienda, to which we turn next.

4. The Hacienda in Northern Guerrero in the Porfiriato

The hacienda was an important part of the rural economy of Porfirian Guerrero and made its presence felt throughout the state. It is no difficult matter to unearth examples of sizable landholdings in all the geographic regions of Guerrero. In the Tierra Caliente, for example, as one traveler observed, "since the time of the Conquest most of the 'Plain' was gradually occupied by the haciendas, whose system of peonage put an end to the social life of the Indians. The extensive economy of the *hacendado* imposed impersonal methods of cultivation . . . the large areas of arable lands and the cheapness of the peon's labor guaranteed . . . good profits."[1] Also in Tierra Caliente, toward the end of the rule of Porfirio Díaz, General Cáceres, "who was able to seize the large 'disentailed' latifundium of [the] Cofradía de [Teloloapan], traveled all the region activating the division of the communities."[2]

In the center of the state the Reform legislation was also the origin of the haciendas of generals Vicente Jiménez and Francisco O. Arce, men who both rose to prominence in the Reform period, and who gained control of the lands of the valleys of Quechultenango and Mochitlán, which had belonged to the Church and to communal villages.[3] Here were classic cases of the hacienda expanding at the expense of disentailed Church estates and the Indian villages. Another major landowner in the center was Eucaria Apreza, who since 1885 had traded extensively in alcohol, sugar, and maize.[4]

In the remote sierra, General Martín Carrera formed the Hacienda de Anahuac, which his heirs sold to the American-owned Guerrero Land and Timber Company in 1912.[5] Indeed, in the years just prior to the revolution, and even for a year or so after fighting broke out, there was something of an influx of American capital into Guerrero, but generally the Americans preferred to buy land on the coast, where the sea provided relatively easy access to markets beyond the confines of the state. One of the most important landowners on the Costa Chica was Charles A. Miller, "an influential American. . . . [who] owns and operates a large ranch of some two hundred thousand acres . . . which he has devoted to the raising of live stock [sic] and cotton, and upon which . . . there are about eight thousand natives living, to whom he parcels out his land without rental and from whom he buys the cotton raised."⁶ In about 1894 Miller had married into the Reguera family, landowners who had been a dominant political force in the Ometepec area since the Wars of Independence, when they had fought on the Royalist side. By 1912, Miller's investments (excluding the value of his land) totaled U.S. $462,617.50, some 36% of it in livestock and about another 15% in machinery used to process and clean the cotton crop and a plant for the manufacture of soap. In 1921 Miller's land was valued by the government at U.S. $100,000, bringing his total investment to around U.S. $560,000 before the revolution destroyed a considerable portion of his assets.⁷

Two other Americans, Hugh and Henry Stephens, brothers who lived in Acapulco, had sizable investments in land north of Acapulco. In 1900 they purchased the Hacienda del Potrero, of some 20,000 to 30,000 acres, on which, in 1912, they had planted 5,000 coconut trees and raised 1,500 head of cattle and 100 horses. El Potrero, in which they had invested U.S. $181,240 (70% of this sum being the value of the land), yielded a net income of only about U.S. $4,000 a year, a net return on investment of only just over 2% annually. They also owned, since 1909, a half share in the Hacienda de Cacalutla which totaled around 100,000 acres, and was worth about U.S. $100,000.⁸

A number of other Americans invested in land along the coast in the first decade of the twentieth century. The Mexican Pacific Company, which had a concession to build a railway from Acapulco to Zihuatanejo, around 1907 began buying several haciendas totaling some 100,000 acres near Coyuca de Benítez, with a view to developing an export trade in copra and bananas. The company invested heavily (some U.S. $1,500,000), but the revolution stymied work on the railway, and only a small portion of the land was ever fully developed for cultivation.⁹ The Mexican Pacific Company's unhappy experience was repeated by the Washington Acapulco Company, which purchased the Hacienda Buen Suceso in 1907 and invested U.S. $40,000 in improvements, but apparently did not manage to bring the property into full production before fighting broke out in 1911.¹⁰ Other American landowners included Messrs. McCabe, Peak Bierne, and Meyer, who purchased the Hacienda Jicayán de Tovar (around 110,000 hectares) in 1909, Mrs. Herman Focke, who owned the 6,000-acre ranch San Juan near San Marcos, and Mrs. R. S. Silberberg, owner of about 100,000 acres of timber land near Ato-yac.[11] In addition, the American-owned Guerrero Trading Company owned the 190,000 hectares of the Hacienda de San Marcos, which it had purchased from the federal government in 1902.[12]

However, these Americans were relative newcomers and were not the only foreign landowners on the coast. Spaniards also had extensive estates in the area, although they were more important, and more resented, for their commercial and industrial activities than for their landholdings. The precise area of land owned by Spaniards is not known, but, as U.S. Vice Consul Pangburn noted in 1926, it is clear that

> since the first half of the nineteenth century three powerful Spanish mercantile firms (B. Fernandez y Cia. Sucrs., Alzuyeta y Cia. Sucrs. and Hermanos Fernandez y Cia. to-gether [sic] with a combination of the three firms as Alzuyeta, Fernandez, Quiros y Cia.) have practically controlled the commerce of this region. . . . [and] are large land owners. . . . [who] obliged their tenants to raise crops of their own selection (principally cotton for their cotton cloth factories) and to sell the same to them.[13]

Although the coast was set apart from the rest of the state by a sizable element of foreign landowners, there had never been any shortage of native Mexican *hacendados*. In the 1850s Manuel Orozco y Berra reported that the Galeana family owned large areas of land on the coast, and other sizable properties belonged to José Esteban Solís, José María Izazaga, Manuel Cabrera, and Lorenzo Campos. Already "ownership of the land was badly distributed; a few, almost always whites, owned large areas of land and the majority, Indians and blacks, had no lands or those which they did possess were seized from them by [the whites]." Not surprisingly, this situation had often led to racial conflict.[14]

In summary, sizable haciendas existed on the coast, where the ocean provided access to overseas markets and where local markets were sufficient to sustain a small textile industry; in the remote and sparsely populated mountain districts, where the exploitation of timber on a fairly large scale was feasible; in the fertile valleys to the east of Chilpancingo, where cities such as Chilapa, Tixtla, Tlapa, and the state capital itself provided markets (albeit modest) for the haciendas' produce; and in the valley bottom of Tierra Caliente, where sesame seed had become an important cash crop around the turn of the century.

The existence of the hacienda, therefore, cannot be ignored as a major factor in the economy of Porfirian Guerrero. Given the importance of the hacienda in the agrarian history of Mexico, and indeed of Latin America as a whole, it is at first sight surprising that no fully acceptable definition exists of the term "hacienda." This is even more perplexing for the student of nineteenth- and twentieth-century Mexico since the hacienda occupies a central position in any account of rural Mexico before the revolution.

A number of definitions have, of course, been proposed. Eric Wolf and Sidney Mintz have defined the hacienda thus: "an agricultural estate, operated by a dominant land-owner and a dependent labor force, organized to supply a small-scale market by means of scarce capital, in which the factors of production are employed not only for capital accumulation but also to support the status aspirations of the owner."[15] Thus the key variables which define the hacienda are the relationship between the owner and the labor force, the availability of capital and the size of the market, and the psychological factor of the owner's desire for social status. However, William Taylor has pointed out that this definition ill fits the hacienda as it existed in colonial Oaxaca, where the term "hacienda" designated "a mixed ranching and agricultural enterprise relying on debt peonage for permanent labor." Still another definition has been proposed in a study of coastal Peru in the colonial period: "the hacienda can be defined as an income-producing agricultural estate with a paternalistic form of social organization."[16]

In short, whichever definition one adopts as a working hypothesis for one area may not fit another. Neither size, nor labor systems, nor internal pattern of production provides fully satisfactory criteria. For the purposes of this study, no attempt will be made to resolve this old and thorny problem. Rather, a definition will be adopted which more or less satisfactorily distinguishes the hacienda from the rancho in northern Guerrero, but which might well be unacceptable in a study of any other area of Mexico. Thus any property of 2,000 hectares or more in northern Guerrero will be considered to have constituted an hacienda, and any individual who owned 2,000 hectares or more (whether in one property or in a number of smaller holdings) will, in general terms, be considered to have been an *hacendado*. Although such a definition gives rise to certain anomalies, defining as *hacendados* certain individuals who should probably be considered to have been prosperous rancheros, it conforms to reality in the sense that anyone who owned 2,000 hectares or more in the districts of Alarcón and Hidalgo possessed an unusually large area of land by local standards.

Traditional views of the hacienda depict it as a hereditary entail, which increasingly monopolized the land, and relied on feudal labor practices such as debt peonage to tie its workers to the land. In recent years this view has increasingly been called into question,[17] to the point where the view of the *hacendado* as a feudal land baron can no longer be sustained. Certainly such a view could not be applied to northern Guerrero, where there was no substantial hereditary landowning class. Nor did debt peonage or other forms of coercive labor practices predominate. Rather, rental of the land for fixed rents paid in kind was the rule, and there were probably sound economic reasons for this practice. Moreover, the hacienda here was of quite modest proportions, and there was almost certainly no strong trend toward monopoly of the land. Furthermore, if modest in extent, the haciendas were also modest in number.

If one applies my definition of the term "hacienda" to northern Guerrero in the late Porfiriato, one finds that there were four *hacendados* in the district of Alarcón, and sixteen in the district of Hidalgo. Some twenty individual properties covered 2,000 hectares or more, and thus constituted haciendas in their own right. Sixteen of these haciendas were located in the municipalities of Cocula, Iguala, and Tepecoacuilco, an area which thus clearly constituted a well-defined hacienda zone. It is worth noting that haciendas occupied a little less than twice as much land as the communal villages, and that between them the haciendas and the villages accounted for 47% of the total land area of the districts of Alarcón and Hidalgo.[18]

There was considerable variation in the amount of land held by the twenty *hacendados* of northern Guerrero. The largest and one of the most powerful landowners was Miguel Montúfar, who owned some 22,346 hectares. He was the owner of three separate haciendas, as well as a number of small properties. Rivaling Montúfar as the major landowner of the region was Alberto Rivera, owner of several estates which totaled some 19,193 hectares. Rivera also had commercial interests in Iguala. Other important *hacendados* were Emigdio Pastrana, whose Hacienda de Xilocintla was the largest single property in northern Guerrero; Febronia Gómez, who was Montúfar's stepmother and who owned some 13,832 hectares; and Rafael del Castillo Calderón, the prominent politician, whose haciendas Atzcala and El Limón covered around 11,799 hectares. A slightly smaller but more valuable estate was Atlixtac y Anexas, which was unusual in the area in that it specialized in direct cultivation of sugarcane, and which totaled about 9,357 hectares. Atlixtac belonged to an American, Thomas K. Mathewson, although ownership was later vested in a limited company.

Table 2. Owners of More Than 2,000 Hectares in the Districts of Alarcón and Hidalgo (circa 1910)

1. District of Alarcón

Landowner	Area of land owned (hectares)
Isaac Mathewson	5,476.50
Filomena Muñoz	3,592
Jesús O. Martínez	2,898
Mucio Romero	2,215.90
Total	14,182.40

2. District of Hidalgo

Landowner	Area of land owned (hectares)
Miguel Montúfar	22,346.19
Alberto Rivera	19,193
Emigdio Pastrana	14,160.17
Febronia Gómez	13,831.71
Rafael del Castillo Calderón	11,799.41
Atlixtac y Anexas S.A.	9,357.49
Manuela Mojica	6,825
Julián and Ponciano Salgado	5,200
Petra C. Vda. de Castro	3,800
Lucía Patiño Vda. de C.	3,600
Filomena Muñoz	3,592
Adela Cervantes Vda. de C.	3,310
José Ma. Montes	2,655
Francisco Fernández de la V.	2,344.50
José Nava	2,130
Diódoro Pastrana	2,072.07
Total	126,216.54

SOURCE: ASRA, Ramo Ejidal.

Below these major landowners came a number of lesser figures. Julián and Ponciano Salgado were joint owners of the 5,200 hectares of the Hacienda de Tepozonalco, while the American Isaac Mathewson's Hacienda de Santa Fe Tepetlapa covered 5,476 hectares. Manuela Mojica owned rather more land than Mathewson and the Salgados (6,825 hectares), while eleven lesser figures owned between 2,000 and 4,000 hectares. In general, there were few landowners in northern Guerrero who could really compare with their powerful neighbors in Morelos, where Luis García Pimentel, for example, owned 168,420 hectares,[19] for the land here was much less fertile. Still less do the *hacendados* of the districts of Alarcón and Hidalgo bear comparison with the powerful cattle barons of the north, who owned vast tracts of land.

In northern Guerrero land ownership was apparently quite fluid, and properties changed hands quite frequently. The case of Alberto Rivera is a good example. Although Rivera had already rented the Hacienda de Almolonga from the state government, he did not purchase his first piece of land in northern Guerrero until 1884, when he bought the haciendas Pololcingo and Palapa for $6,000. In the following year he purchased Almolonga for $2,000, and a number of additional acquisitions ensued: part of the Hacienda de Tepantlán in 1891 for $800 (Tepantlán itself had already been divided among various members of the García family) and eight fanegas of arable land near Cocula in 1907 for a price of $2,000, among others.[20] Rivera was, then, a relatively new figure on the scene in northern Guerrero. Furthermore, Rivera's estates were not destined to form a hereditary entail. His will left much of his land to finance the foundation of a school in Iguala, while his property Pololcingo was to be left for the benefit of the poor of Tepecoacuilco and Iguala. After making three minor legacies, he left his land around Iguala to his niece Teresa Rueda.[21] Thus, had the revolution not prevented the division of his estates, Rivera's holdings would have been largely devoted to charitable purposes, leaving his four heirs a rather modest inheritance.

The other principal landowner of the region had a rather longer history than Rivera; nevertheless, the majority of his holdings were of recent origin. Miguel Montúfar's father, Colonel Juan Montúfar, owned the haciendas Tierra Colorada, Sasamulco, La Mohonera, Tlayalapa, and Rincón de la Cocina, which totaled some 7,588 hectares.[22] Upon his father's death, Miguel inherited Tlayalapa (situated near Iguala) and Rincón de la Cocina: some 2,590 hectares in total.[23] Inheritance made a further contribution to Montúfar's holdings through his marriage to Catalina Cuenca, who had been bequeathed land both by her previous husband and by Manuela Gómez de Cuenca, presumably a relative by marriage.[24]

Nevertheless, the bulk of Montúfar's holdings came through his own acquisitions rather than from inheritance. Montúfar first acquired land in the district of Hidalgo in 1884, and over a period of less than three decades was to become a powerful figure in the region. In 1892 Montúfar bought the Hacienda del Tomatal, to which he later added by purchasing four adjacent pieces of land from his nephew Saturnino Martínez.[25] In 1893 Montúfar and his wife bought the Hacienda de Xalitla from Enrique C. Gudiño for $3,000,[26] and in 1899 they purchased fourteen fractions of land near Iguala from Genaro Olea. Olea was apparently beset by debt, and in 1906 also sold off his Hacienda del Zoquital to Montúfar. Olea had mortgaged El Zoquital for $25,000, and owed not only the entire principal, but also interest to the tune of $3,562.50. Incidentally, this was not Olea's only debt, since his hacienda Apango was also mortgaged, for $50,000, and likewise was sold off, in this case to an American, John B. Frisbie. Here was a classic case of a landowner, his estates mortgaged to the hilt, forced to liquidate his holdings in order to escape the stifling burden of debt.[27]

Thus, like Rivera, Montúfar and Catalina Cuenca accumulated a relatively large area of land from only 1884 onward, but the Montúfars do not appear to have had any intention of dividing their land among a number of heirs, for when his wife died, Montúfar retained control of all their holdings. In 1914 the couple's joint assets were valued at $253,298.69, of which their rural lands accounted for nearly half ($121,020). In addition, cattle (450 head) accounted for $4,500 and maize inventory (200,000 liters) for a further $6,000. The remainder of their assets consisted of urban property in Iguala and Mexico City, and money the couple had loaned to the state and federal governments.[28]

Montúfar and Rivera were by no means alone in the recency of their acquisitions. Indeed, it was the rule rather than the exception for landowners in the area to be newcomers rather than long established *hacendados*. For example, Emigdio Pastrana acquired his Hacienda de Xilocintla from Catalina Cuenca as late as 1897,[29] and Rafael del Castillo Calderón purchased his estates Atzcala and El Limón in 1894.[30] Yet again, the Salgado family bought the Hacienda de San Agustín Tepozonalco in 1885, and later the brothers Julián and Ponciano bought up the shares of other members of the family.[31] Thus it appears that the 1880s and 1890s saw a new wave of landowners come on to the scene in northern Guerrero, although the lack of evidence concerning earlier periods precludes any judgment as to whether this was part of a recurring cycle or a unique phenomenon.

A somewhat earlier cycle of land acquisition was sparked off by the disentailment of Church lands prescribed by the Liberal Reform laws. The precise results of the legislation as it applied to northern Guerrero are far from clear, but a small number of documented cases suggest that disentailment was indeed a factor in the rise of a new generation of *hacendados*. One man who benefited from disentailment was Francisco Cuenca, who "denounced" the Church-owned Hacienda de Acayahualco, a property later inherited by Manuela

Mojica.[32] In another case, Lic. José M. Cervantes, the first husband of
Febronia Gómez, claimed the property Sacacoyuca, which formerly
belonged to the parochial church of Taxco.[33] To cite one further example, a Spaniard, Pedro Cortina, acquired Tonalapa del Norte, a
Church property donated to the cult of the Virgin of Guadalupe.[34]
The evidence here, limited as it is, would seem to corroborate Frank
Tannenbaum's conclusion that disentailed Church land was usually
sold off undivided, rather than in small lots, and to some extent contributed to the concentration of land tenure.[35] Nevertheless, the contribution to monopoly of the land by large owners was relatively
minor. Manuela Mojica's total holdings were 6,825 hectares, the
largest concentration of disentailed land in the area, while disentailed land represented only 23% of the estates of Febronia Gómez.
Tonalapa del Norte, the property denounced by Pedro Cortina, probably covered little more than 500 hectares.

Another characteristic of the hacienda in the districts of Alarcón and Hidalgo was that there existed little or no peon labor, and
consequent abuses such as debt peonage and the *tienda de raya* can
have been of little or no importance. Nor was sharecropping the pre-
dominant labor system, as another scholar has stated was generally
the case in areas of central Mexico where tropical cash crops were
not produced.[36] Rather, the most important labor system in northern
Guerrero was the leasing of the land in return for a fixed rent paid in
maize. Agreements were, in some cases at least, written rather than
verbal and were for the term of one year. Some *hacendados* relied
entirely on rental for their income: for example, Alberto Rivera. In
1919 the agronomist Guillermo Bazán reported that Rivera did not
work his property Sabana Grande directly, noting that "there is no
casco de hacienda, nor has he paid wages, nor does he have any agricultural equipment or livestock." The same was true of Rivera's estates Metlapa, Palapa, and Pololcingo, and in the latter case it was
observed that the reliance on leasing the land was leading to decreas-
ing fertility due to his neglect of the property.[37]

The details of Rivera's rental arrangements can be fleshed out
somewhat by receipts for rent paid for land in Sabana Grande and
Pololcingo. Unfortunately the receipts, which cover the period 1890
to 1911 and 1919, simply state the amount paid, and do not mention
the area of land leased. However, it is clear from the sums charged
that the area of land rented by each tenant varied considerably, since
rents ranged from forty-eight *cuartillos* (about ninety-six liters) of
maize to as much as fifteen and a half *cargas* (3,100 liters). Moreover, some individuals rented several pieces of land at once: in 1907
Jesús Salgado of Sabana Grande leased three pieces of land for rents

of four, twelve and a half, and fifteen and a half *cargas* of maize.[38] In such cases, the tenant must either have sublet the land or have employed laborers. Certainly, it would not be farfetched to speculate that rental of land provided the possibility of social mobility for the enterprising tenant, although, unfortunately, no documentary evidence confirms this supposition.

In addition to receipts for rent aid, a few tenants' contracts have survived. These did not specify the amount of land rented, but simply the rent to be paid and the number of fractions of land. It was stipulated that the tenant was obliged to pay for the land in the form of good-quality maize which had been removed from the cob. Here again, rents varied widely, and one individual paid as much as ninety-seven *cargas* of maize.[39] For lack of contemporary evidence concerning the amount of land leased for a particular quantity of maize, we are compelled to extrapolate backward from evidence concerning rents charged in the years immediately following the revolution. Reports from this period indicate that rents varied from property to property, and according to the quality of the land. Thus in Tepaxtitlán, land yielding fifteen to thirty *cargas* per *yunta* (about two and a half hectares) was leased out for two to three *cargas*, while in Palapa a rent of two to four *cargas* of maize was charged for land which produced between sixteen and twenty *cargas* per hectare (see table 3). Whether the rents of the postrevolutionary period were precisely the same as those charged before 1911 is impossible to say, but it seems reasonable to assume that they were broadly comparable. Similarly, it is not possible to determine the income Rivera derived from his holdings, but he himself stated in his will that Pololcingo alone yielded 1,000 *cargas* or 200,000 liters of maize per year in rents, and over $500 from leasing grazing rights.[40] Since 200,000 liters of maize were valued at $6,000 in Catalina Cuenca's will in 1914, Pololcingo must have given Rivera a yearly income of around $6,500.[41]

Another landowner who appears to have relied solely on rental of her land was Febronia Gómez, although the earliest accounts we have of the internal operation of her properties date from 1919. By this date, at least, it is clear that she exploited none of her land directly. On Sacacoyuca she had no *casco*, no agricultural implements or livestock, and paid no wages.[42] In a report on La Mohonera, Ing. Guillermo Bazán pointed out that leasing the land was responsible for its declining fertility, since the tenant had no incentive to carry out long-term improvements as the contract was for only one year. Under these circumstances, the most a tenant might do was to manure the land.[43]

Table 3. Rents Paid for Land in the Districts of Alarcón and Hidalgo

Year	Town/Village	Rent	Yield of land rented	% of yield taken by rent
1922	Acayahualco	8–12 c/Ha.	n/d	n/d
1919	Apipilulco	30 c/5 or 6 Has.	15 c/Ha.	33–40%
1921	Cuetzala el Viejo	3 c/Ha.	5–7½ c/Ha.	40–60%
1921	Cuexcontlán	10–12 c/yunta	25–40 c/yunta	25–40%
1921	El Ejido	2 c/yunta	8–12 c/yunta	17–25%
1921	El Fraile	2 c/yunta	6–8 c/yunta	25–33%
1921	Hueymatla	2 c/yunta	10–12 c/yunta	17–20%
1923	Iguala	8–20 c/yunta	n/d	n/d
1921	Joya de Pantla	6–10 c/yunta	25–30 c/yunta	24–33%
1921	Mayanalán	3–5, or 8 c/yunta	16–20, or 30 c/yunta	19–25%, or 27%
1930	El Mogote	8 c/yunta	n/d	n/d
1919	La Mohonera	30 c/5 or 6 Has.	76 c/5 Has.	33–39%
1921	El Naranjo	3–8 c/yunta	n/d	n/d
1919	Palapa	2–4 c/Ha.	16–20 c/Ha.	13–20%
1923	Palula	7½ c/4 Has.	n/d	n/d
1919	Pololcingo	4–5 c/Ha.	12–16 c/Ha.	25–42%
1921	Rincón de la Cocina	5, 8, or 10 c/yunta	25–30 c/yunta	20–33%
1919	Sabana Grande	2–4 c/Ha.	8–15 c/Ha.	25–27%
1919	Sacacoyuca	2–4 c/Ha.	8–15 c/Ha.	25–27%
1922	Santa Cruz	3–5 c/yunta	30 c/yunta	10–17%
1921	Santa Rosa	2 c/yunta	6–8 c/yunta	25–33%
1920	Santa Teresa	6–8 c/yunta	15 c/Ha.	20–27%
1923	El Sauz	4 c/yunta	n/d	n/d
1921	Tecoacuilco	7 c/yunta	n/d	n/d
1921	Tepaxtitlán	2–3 c/yunta	15–30 c/yunta	10–13%
1921	Tepecoacuilco	10–12 c/yunta	25–40 c/yunta	30–40%
1920	Tierra Colorada	4–5 c/Ha.	15 c/Ha.	27–33%
1921	Tlapala	3, 4, or 6 c/yunta	15, 20, or 25 c/yunta	20–24%
1921	El Tomatal	3 c/Ha.	10–15 c/Ha.	20–30%
1921	Tonalapa del Norte	6–8 c/yunta	n/d	n/d
1921	Xalitla	10–20 liters/liter of sembradura	100 to 1	10–20%
1921	Xiloxintla	4–5 c/yunta	25–30 c/yunta	16–17%

SOURCE: ASRA, Ramo Ejidal.
NOTE: 1. c = *carga* (200 hectoliters). 2. Ha. = hectare. 3. *Yunta* = approximately two and a half hectares. 4. Rents were all paid in maize.

While Rivera and Gómez derived their income entirely from rental, other *hacendados* combined direct exploitation of their land with a still considerable element of rental. One such case was that of Miguel Montúfar, who raised cattle on his property Tecoacuilco, where he also produced mezcal and precious woods. Tecoacuilco had its own mezcal factory, and Montúfar had constructed a road to link this factory to Iguala.[44] He claimed to have planted eight million maguey plants on Tecoacuilco,[45] and, while it is hard to believe this figure is not exaggerated, it is clear that this estate was fairly heavily capitalized. On Xalitla Montúfar was said to have invested $25,000 in establishing a prosperous business extracting the essence of the aloe tree,[46] more than eight times the original purchase price of the estate. Montúfar (who was an engineer) prided himself on his contribution to agriculture in the district of Hidalgo and claimed to have been directly responsible for increasing the production of maize in the district after 1884. He also devised schemes to irrigate the entire area which he submitted to the Secretaría de Fomento.[47]

Nevertheless, despite fairly sizable investments in certain (presumably more profitable) crops, it is clear that Montúfar, like other landowners in the area, leased out the greater part of his land for a fixed rent paid in maize. Four lease agreements for land in El Zoquital show that, in 1909 and 1910, Alejandro Rodríguez paid a rent of thirty *cargas* of maize for 1,000 liters of *temporal*. In 1909 Ignacio Barrera paid sixty *cargas* for 2,000 liters of temporal, while in 1910 Jesús Vazquez was charged sixty *cargas* for one fanega (about five or six hectares) of *temporal*. All four contracts were for one year only and stipulated that the rent must be paid in full, even though the crops were lost.[48] Reports from the years immediately following the revolution (see table 2) suggest that rents varied quite widely from place to place. In Apipilulco in 1919 the rent was thirty *cargas* per fanega, or between 33% and 40% of the crop.[49] In Xalitla the rent was between ten and twenty liters of maize per liter capacity of land in 1921, or between 10% and 20%, given a yield of one hundred to one.[50]

Other landowners also engaged in a degree of direct cultivation: for example, Francisco Cuenca and later his heir, Manuela Mojica. Nevertheless, here again, rental still constituted a significant part of the hacienda's economy. Sugarcane was grown by Cuenca and Mojica on the Hacienda de Acayahualco until 1916, and maize on Santa Teresa until 1911, but according to one source, the cultivation of sugarcane on Acayahualco was sporadic: "if in olden times this *cuadrilla* [of Acayahualco] was known as an Hacienda, in reality it was not, because only *panocha* was made there, and this was only where [the owners] had the whim to cultivate sugarcane[;] therefore [the term "hacienda"] does not have the significance which was given to it, especially as the land was rented out at intervals."[51]

The most important employer of peon labor, and the hacienda which relied most on direct cultivation of its land, was Atlixtac, which was converted to the production of rice and sugar around 1898 by the current owner, Genaro Olea,[52] and we may speculate that perhaps it was for this investment that he contracted the debts which later forced him to sell off some of his land to Miguel Montúfar and John Frisbie. Of the two crops which Olea began to cultivate, sugarcane was by far the most important element of the hacienda's economy. Atlixtac had about 650 hectares of irrigated land for sugar production, and the cane was processed in the hacienda's own factory.[53] Significant of its partial departure from prevailing local labor practices, it was one of the few properties in the district to display the typical features of an hacienda: it had a *casco*, agricultural machinery, and resident peons.[54] Atlixtac was one of the few fruits of Porfirian modernization in northern Guerrero and was (albeit on a modest scale) the only hacienda in the area which resembled the sugar plantations of Morelos. At its peak Atlixtac totaled some 9,357 hectares.

Although Atlixtac worked nearly all its arable land itself, it did rent some land to residents of Apipilulco, La Mohonera, Tlanipatlán, and Cuetzala el Viejo.[55] In general, it seems, Atlixtac worked only that land which was more easily cultivated (flat *temporal* and irrigated land), although a small amount of irrigated land was leased out.[56] The resident peons of the hacienda lived round the *casco* in the *cuadrilla* of Atlixtac, and although the hacienda generally relied on its resident peons for labor, the lease agreements signed by its tenants did entitle the hacienda to call on them to provide labor in certain circumstances.[57] In addition, the hacienda operated a system by which it provided trusted peons with land, water, and seed, in return for which they were obliged to sell their crop to the hacienda for a previously stipulated price.[58] Thus Atlixtac combined three labor systems, but, even on such a relatively modern sugar farm, rental played an important part in its internal economy. This was probably the case in another American-owned sugar hacienda, Santa Fe Tepetlapa.[59]

In general, the rule appears to have been that maize was cultivated by means of rental, thus assuring the *hacendado* of a secure income, even on poor-quality land. The cultivation of more profitable crops like sugar was generally undertaken by the landowner, using peon labor. Given the relative importance of maize, and the small volume of the production of sugar and other cash crops during the Porfiriato, rental of the land, one can reasonably infer, must have been the most widespread labor system in northern Guerrero. This no doubt made economic sense given the precarious nature of maize cultivation on *temporal* land, and still more so on *tlacolol*. In the case of some haciendas at least, the line between profit and loss appears to have been narrow. For example, Genaro Olea was unable to make even one repayment of the interest he owed on a mortgage of his Hacienda del Zoquital over a period of three years and was forced to sell his land to pay off the debt.[60]

In the district of Alarcón, where the land was generally of poorer quality than in Hidalgo, the margin between profit and loss was probably appreciably narrower. An illustrative case is that of the Hacienda de San Vicente. In 1885 this estate was purchased by Ignacio Román, the parish priest of Tetipac, for $1,100. At this time San Vicente was an *hacienda de beneficio* where copper ore was processed, but was in a state of disrepair. Between 1885 and 1910 San Vicente changed hands no fewer than six times. By 1903 it had been converted to sugar production, and a sugar mill had been installed, although it must have been a rather primitive affair since it was driven by animals. San Vicente cannot have been a very profitable business, for while it sold for $1,500 in 1886, in 1893 it fetched only $600, and in 1903 a mere $500. The conversion from ore processing to agriculture evidently did nothing to enhance the property's profitability. Mucio Romero, a merchant from Zacualpan, who bought it in 1910, sold it yet again in 1919 to two merchants from Taxco.[61]

Another hacienda in the district of Alarcón which seems not to have been very profitable was the Hacienda de El Naranjo. In 1921 it was reported that the owners of El Naranjo had long ago ceased to work the hacienda directly and merely rented it out. The explanation for this shift from direct cultivation no doubt lay in the land's poor fertility, since El Naranjo yielded a mere 1,200 to 1,600 liters of maize per hectare.[62] An exception to the rule that the haciendas of the district of Alarcón tended to be of little value was the Hacienda de Santa Fe Tepetlapa, whose owner, Isaac Mathewson, considered it "fine sugar country."[63]

Despite the poor profitability of some haciendas, the possession of a relatively large area of land made the *hacendados* very powerful figures in northern Guerrero, if only because they controlled access to large areas of land through the rental system. Considerable numbers of tenants must have depended on the twenty *hacendados* of the districts of Alarcón and Hidalgo for land to cultivate, and the economic power of the landowners was matched by their political power. Alberto Rivera and Miguel Montúfar, for example, wielded considerable political influence.[64] Rivera was elected to the state Congress on at least five occasions, Montúfar was a state *diputado* in 1905, and his nephew Saturnino Martínez was elected to the state legislature on three occasions before 1911. On the municipal level, too, their influence could be seen. Rivera was twice *prefecto político* of the district of Hidalgo, and on at least two occasions *presidente municipal* of Iguala, while Montúfar held that office in 1902.[65]

Another landowner who enjoyed considerable political power was Emigdio Pastrana, who was "lord and master . . . of the Municipal Presidency of the Pueblo of Tepecoacuilco" on no fewer than eight occasions between 1896 and 1909.[66] Still more influential on the local political scene was Lic. Rafael del Castillo Calderón, for some twenty years a prominent figure in local political circles. Castillo Calderón was *secretario de gobierno* under Governor Arce, and several times a *diputado* in the state legislature. Finally, in 1900 and 1901 he was a candidate for the state governorship itself.[67]

The revolution which began in 1911 would destroy forever the political power of the principal landowners of northern Guerrero and in time would dismember much of their property. The immediate causes of the 1911 upheaval were political, but economic and social forces were not insignificant. For one thing, the enforcement of disentailment legislation by Porfirian governors had increased the numbers of the rural middle class, which had come to constitute the principal opposition to the Porfirian regime by the turn of the century. In this context, it was not at all surprising that the bulk of Ambrosio Figueroa's original band of rebels should have been composed of rancheros.

Other rebel groups were similarly shaped by the local pattern of land tenure. Tenants were a constituency for groups with a social program more radical than the predominantly political goals of the Huitzuco rebels. This is not surprising, for while the system of land rental adopted by the *hacendados* of northern Guerrero may have been less oppressive than the debt peonage practiced elsewhere, it could inflict considerable hardship on the tenant. For example, in the village of Santiago, not far from Taxco, in 1900 the maize crop was only about "one hundred *cargas* because the fields yielded no more than that since all the agriculturists harvested rotten maize[;] those who rented oxen and land did not immediately pay the owners of said animals and lands, for in truth they do not have enough even to get them through the year." The residents of Sochula were in a similar position. In Taxco el Viejo, however, the *vecinos* did manage to pay the rent for the hire of oxen used to work the land, despite a poor harvest.[68] Under such circumstances, rent collection must have depended on some degree of coercion, or at least the threat of coercion. One Zapatista veteran asserts that if the tenant lost the crop and could not pay the rent, Miguel Montúfar "embargoed the tenant; he left us nothing." Alberto Rivera employed similarly coercive methods of rent collection.[69]

Consequently, in the municipalities of Tepecoacuilco, Cocula, and Iguala, where the hacienda was at its strongest and leasing of the land most widespread, Zapatismo found its most receptive audience in northern Guerrero. The first revolutionary in the area to operate under the Zapatista label was Pablo Barrera of Tepecoacuilco, who called on the campesinos of the district of Hidalgo to stop paying their rents to the landowners. Thus Barrera's uprising differed from that of his allies in Morelos, where the dispossessed Indian villagers took up arms to recover lands which had once belonged to them. Barrera's movement could not draw on these deep communal roots, but, nevertheless, his cause was a popular one, as Major Odilón Figueroa reported in 1911: "Today the Comisario 1° of Sabana came to the headquarters under my command, telling me that he did not come on 2 December because he went on a commission with three or four other persons to see [Governor José Inocente Lugo] in order not to pay their rents to the owners of the land. Therefore, I ask [the governor] to admonish them severely on this matter. The man who has influenced the minds [of the people] of these *cuadrillas* is Pablo Barrera . . . who a few days ago escaped from prison."[70]

As the rule of law and order became progressively weaker in the decade 1910 to 1920, the collection of rents became ever more difficult, even for the larger and more powerful landowners. Thus in 1917 Pedro Campos, Miguel Montúfar's representative, asked the governor of Guerrero to give him the legal guarantees and support necessary to collect the rents from his employer's tenants "in a moderate proportion." Campos commented that the tenants would otherwise refuse to pay because the Zapatistas had given them parcels of land. His plea did not fall on deaf ears, since the governor ordered that Campos be afforded full protection.[71]

In the Taxco area the pattern of land tenure was quite different, as was the character of revolutionary activity. Of course, the breakdown of law and order allowed the villagers to settle old scores, but such jacqueries did not go beyond the resolution of particular disputes or grievances.[72] Nevertheless, in this area, too, Zapatismo found some support—for example, in Buenavista de Cuéllar (oddly enough, a town of smallholders who eventually turned against the Zapatistas).[73] However, Zapatismo in the Taxco area was largely an imported phenomenon, with bands raiding across the border from Morelos and the state of Mexico, a pattern which was scarcely surprising given the relative lack of agrarian grievances in the area. Elsewhere in Guerrero, too, land tenure patterns helped mold the character of revolutionary movements. The real heart of Zapatismo in the state was in Tierra Caliente, where the ethnic makeup of the population was much more markedly Indian than in northern Guerrero, and where the haciendas had occupied the fertile valley lands, leaving the Indian villagers to eke out an existence in the mountains, or to work on the estates for a miserably low wage. This situation had already led to caste warfare in the nineteenth century, and here it was that Jesús H. Salgado would recruit the peasant followers who would make him the principal Zapatista chieftain in Guerrero.

On the Costa Grande, where Silvestre G. Mariscal would be the undisputed revolutionary leader from 1911 until early 1918, the hacienda was likewise the dominant form of land tenure. Moreover, the population, a mixture of Indians and blacks, was of an ethnic stock quite distinct from that of the Indians or mestizos of the interior. No direct evidence exists of the social strata from which Mariscal drew his constituency, but since Juan Alvarez before him had relied on the landless peasantry of the coast for his support, just as Amadeo and Baldomero Vidales would in the 1920s,[74] it seems likely that Mariscal's followers were of a similar social background. Circumstantial evidence for this supposition is furnished by the violent hatred of the Spaniards which was a consistent feature of the revolution on the coast.

In addition to the Figueroas, Jesús Salgado, and Silvestre Mariscal, one other rebel leader would become a major factor in the events of 1910 to 1920. Unfortunately, little is known of the constituency of Julián Blanco, who would dominate the center of the state for several years. The population of central Guerrero had a large Indian component which in recent decades had seen the haciendas encroach on its lands, precipitating caste warfare in the 1840s. Blanco may well have drawn his support from this dispossessed Indian peasantry, but no direct evidence exists to confirm this suspicion.

Nevertheless, whatever the subsequent participation of the dispossessed in the upheavals of 1911 to 1920, the Mexican revolution in Guerrero was launched, not by landless peasants, but by relatively prosperous rancheros. The expansion of the ranchero class in northern Guerrero during the Porfiriato was accompanied by a marked increase in the political activity of the rural middle class in local and especially municipal politics. These rancheros stamped on the revolution in the north of the state a particular flavor which differed from the style of revolution found in areas like Morelos. To some degree, the revolution of 1911 erupted in Guerrero because the ranchero became, toward the end of the nineteenth century, the principal protagonist in a long drawn out struggle between the centralizing tendencies of the federal government and certain elements of the body politic in Guerrero which sought to defend their local autonomy. In short, when the Huitzuco rebels opened fire on the forces of Captain Limón on the last day of February 1911, they were defending a basically traditionalist cause. Although protagonists would come and go, the issues raised in 1911 would be a continuing theme of the state's politics for the next three decades.

5. Revolution in Guerrero: 1911–1919

Up to the end of 1910 Maderismo had been, as Dudley Ankerson has pointed out, an essentially urban middle-class movement, but Madero's attempt to base his uprising against Díaz on his urban supporters failed dismally.[1] The Maderista uprising, and the Mexican revolution as a whole, was made in the countryside. Having said this, one is bound to recognize that the Mexican countryside embraced a rural society of ineffable complexity. Not surprisingly then, the uprisings of 1910 and beyond took numerous forms and expressed innumerable grievances.

In Guerrero the Maderista revolt of 1911 was by no means a mass uprising against the Díaz regime. The revolution in the state was sparked off by a small group of conspirators in Huitzuco, the leading figures of which were all respected middle-class rancheros, shopkeepers, and the like, and most of their initial following sprang from the same rural middle-class background. True, the Huitzuco rebels established contact with a number of other small groups throughout the state, but the resulting revolutionary activity by no means constituted a large popular uprising. This goes somewhat against the grain of traditional accounts of the revolution which portray a widespread popular explosion against the Díaz regime, but is, in fact, not particularly surprising in the case of Guerrero. For the principal grievance which fueled the revolution here was the result of a lengthy historical process which might be said to have begun with the appointment of Francisco O. Arce as governor of the state. The process was consolidated by Porfirio Díaz, who succeeded in establishing the first semblance of a national state in Mexico. In Guerrero, however, this was achieved at the expense of a severe restriction of the participation of local groups in state politics, which provoked resistance, first from the state's traditional caciques, and later from the rising middle-class groups who were the instigators of the revolution in 1911.

At first sight, there might appear to be a superficial resemblance between the Huitzuco revolt and uprisings of a decidedly popular character, which, according to Alan Knight,[2] were quite widespread and like the Figueroa group espoused the cause of municipal autonomy and state's rights. However, the resemblance went no further than the similarity of slogans, for while the millenarian peasants might echo the sentiments of Cruz Chávez of Tomochic in 1892 that "no-one should interfere with them, nor bother them for anything, nor meddle in their affairs,"[3] the Figueroas had little in common with the ideology of these popular peasant movements.

The three Figueroa brothers who launched the revolution in Guerrero, like other members of the family who joined the revolutionary ranks, were products of a predominantly ranchero society, and heirs to a Liberal tradition implanted in Huitzuco by the Hidalgo schoolteacher Manuel Sáenz, who first visited Huitzuco in 1874, and returned in 1882 to establish the Escuela Particular Huitzuquense.[4] A number of those who took up arms on 28 February 1911 attended this school, among them Ambrosio and Francisco Figueroa.[5] Francisco himself became a schoolteacher, carrying on Sáenz's Liberal tradition, and was the author of a prize-winning biography of the great Mexican Liberal, Benito Juárez.[6] The two decisive elements in forming the ideology of the Figueroas were their ranchero social origin and their Liberal education. It was not unnatural that such men should later come into conflict with the Zapatistas of Morelos, who came from a completely different society, and whose agrarianism offended the Figueroas' respect for private property.

Francisco Figueroa, the ideologue of the family, considered that two main factors had been the causes of the revolution in Guerrero. The first was "the political [cause which] was the daughter of authoritarian repression and the infringement of rights, [and] may be condensed in the desire to make suffrage effective and achieve the alternation of governors, the sons of the state claiming the place in politics which outsiders had usurped." The second, "the economic cause[,] had its origins in the lack of equity in taxes and in the methods employed to collect them, especially in the case of needy people, since the wealthy were nearly always favored."[7] Particularly odious was the tyranny of "the bourgeois, inexactly called CIENTIFICOS, who had monopolized as their own possession the affairs of the government and had privilege in all great enterprises."[8]

The agrarian problem was not believed to have been a serious cause of the revolution. Francisco believed that "the land question was threatening because of the multitude of injustices which in questions of adjudication [of disentailed lands] have been committed during the old regime [of Díaz]." His government, he said, had postponed this problem by asking the people to respect private property, by withdrawing its protection from the caciques, and by "asking the landowners to show more consideration to their tenants."[9] Thus the agrarian question was largely limited to the specific problem of improper application of the disentailment laws. As for "the agrarian problem of Morelos," Figueroa wrote to Madero, "properly speaking it does not exist; and perhaps General [Ambrosio] Figueroa, who has a profound knowledge of that state, has spoken to you at length about this. The urgent thing is to solve the political problem and *give legal protection to the landowners.*"[10]

The Figueroas had a concept of the revolution which differed radically from that of Zapata and his followers. For Francisco Figueroa, the revolution's main aims were the establishment of an effective democracy and of municipal autonomy, the suppression of the office of *prefecto político,* the abolition of certain taxes which were considered to be unjust, and the reduction of the general level of taxes. In particular, it was important that the people of Guerrero recover their rightful place in the government of their state, as he declared to the state legislature: "Guerrero for the *guerrerenses,* the revolution has said with pride."[11] Figueroa found the continuing social unrest in neighboring Morelos quite unjustifiable. Referring to the attack on Huamuxtitlán, which was "scandalously sacked" by Zapata and Juan Andrew Almazán in September 1911, Figueroa demanded: "if the revolution has triumphed, if suffrage has been made effective, if taxes have been modified and order has been restored, what more do these men want?"[12]

Ambrosio Figueroa, Francisco's brother, had a similarly restricted idea of the goals of the revolution. In a manifesto dated 25 September 1911, which was issued on the occasion of his inauguration as governor of Morelos, Ambrosio wrote: "do not ask me for the solution of the difficult agrarian problem, because neither my abilities nor the time which I have available would be enough to solve it. When I took up arms *I only offered liberties;* these have been won and I will watch over them without rest."[13] The Figueroas concurred with Madero himself in believing that "there were no social problems for which a solution could not be found by honest citizens . . . who succeeded in obtaining, through the ballot box, positions of popular election."[14] The men who launched the revolution in Guerrero in 1911 were middle-class Liberals in the tradition of Juárez who had much more in common with Madero than with the Zapatistas in neighboring Morelos. It was not surprising, therefore, that, while the break between the Zapatistas and Madero came during the early phases of the revolution, the Figueroas stayed loyal to the Apostle of Mexican Democracy to the end, for he gave them the local autonomy to which they aspired.

The events of 28 February 1911 did not, then, provoke large-scale uprisings, and, in the absence of generalized unrest, Governor Damián Flores no doubt seemed justified in making light of the skirmish in Huitzuco in his annual report to Congress at the beginning of March. "At the last moment," Flores told the legislators, "the government was informed that in the *cuadrilla* of Escuchapa of the municipality of Huitzuco . . . some malefactors rose up in arms, led by Martín Vicario, Rómulo Figueroa, and Fidel Fuentes, individuals with bad records who have many times brushed with the authorities of the state." Nevertheless, Flores revealed an underlying apprehension that the possibility of political ferment in Guerrero was not, in fact, so very remote, remarking that he had ordered the *prefectos políticos* to "proceed to repress, actively and energetically, any seditious movement which may be attempted."[15]

Flores's fears were no doubt somewhat quieted since, for some time, the Figueroas gave him no more reason for concern. Pursued by two columns of government troops, and plagued by desertions which reduced their numbers almost to extinction,[16] the rebels were unable to launch any further military operations until 25 April, when they attacked the escort on the Balsas–Mexico City train.[17] Nevertheless, despite the lack of military action, by late March Ambrosio Figueroa had managed to gather a force of some 300 men.[18] Still more importantly, he had taken steps to broaden the insurrection in Guerrero. In the third week of March emissaries were sent to other parts of the districts of Alarcón and Hidalgo, to Tierra Caliente, Copalillo, Olinalá, and Chilapa.[19] This resulted in the formation of some seven rebel bands, principal among them the rising of Leovigildo Alvarez and Jesús H. Salgado in Teloloapan. Elsewhere, Laureano Astudillo rebelled in Tixtla, Pedro Ramírez and others in the district of Bravos, and Pedro de Víbar first contacted Eucaria Apreza in Chilapa and later accompanied Juan Andrew Almazán in his attach on Huamuxtitlán on 21 April.

The unrest began to spread, and by mid or late April some twenty-three rebel bands were fighting in Guerrero in five main operational zones: the northern area around Huitzuco and Atenango del Río, the Tierra Caliente from Teloloapan to Coyuca de Catalán, the Costa Grande, and the Costa Chica. The most important uprisings were those of Alvarez and Salgado; Julián Blanco, an officer in the state security forces,[20] in Dos Caminos near Chilpancingo; the followers of the wealthy landowner Eucaria Apreza in Chilapa; Enrique and Pantaleón Añorve, mestizo smallholders, in Ometepec; and Silvestre G. Mariscal, a former schoolteacher, in Atoyac.[21] While most of these groups recognized Ambrosio Figueroa as the nominal head of the Maderista revolt in Guerrero, "each leader considered himself, in principle, independent from the rest,"[22] since Figueroa's authority rested on nothing more tangible than the prestige derived from his engagement in Huitzuco against the forces of Captain Limón. This loose alliance of rebel groups planted the seeds of the fragmentation of the revolutionary ranks which began almost as soon as Porfirio Díaz had been ousted from power.

While many of these uprisings were motivated by resentment of "the despotic rule of [Guerrero's] governors who, appointed directly from Mexico City, have greatly oppressed the people through excessive taxation, and have used their office solely to become rich through their control of the courts and the state treasury,"[23] local conditions, in some cases, stamped a special character on the rebellion. In Huitzuco the domination of municipal politics by the managers of the mercury mines had been a key factor in the genesis of the revolt. In the district of La Unión, Héctor F. López and other "principal inhabitants of the region" had for some time resisted the *cacicazgo* of Pioquinto Huato, and in 1909 fell prey to active persecution from the district and state authorities when they publicly denounced abuses of governmental power.[24] An ethnic component was added to the revolt in the Tlapa area, where Cruz Dircio led "the Indians of Mixtec blood, whose hatred was centered implacably on the Spanish merchants of that town, who for many years made them victims of an iniquitous extortion."[25] Similarly, a fierce hatred of the Spaniards was one of the consistent features of the revolution on the coast. The capture of Ometepec on 19 April was followed immediately by the murder of "a prominent Spaniard," Marcelino Enríquez, a representative of the Spanish merchant houses which were so powerful in the area.[26]

The government was unable to make an effective response to the burgeoning rebellion. On the coast, by the end of the third week in April, San Marcos had fallen. All officials except the postmaster and the telegraph operator had fled from Ayutla, and as early as 11 April rebel bands were known to be camped within one or two days of Acapulco.[27] On 20 April Governor Flores decided to abandon the sinking ship, adopting as a fig leaf to cover his ignominious departure the excuse that he was obliged to go to Mexico City on business.[28] His hasty departure accelerated the decline of the Porfirian regime in the state: by the end of April, Silvestre G. Mariscal was besieging Acapulco,[29] and by early May, Julián Blanco had gathered some 1,500 men from the coast and the center of the state in readiness to attack Chilpancingo.[30] On the following day, Lic. Silvano Saavedra—who had been appointed interim governor when Flores fled—resigned, and although a replacement was appointed,[31] effective government in Guerrero had ceased.

Meanwhile, events were moving fast beyond the confines of Guerrero's mountains. By March rebel bands were active in Morelos, and, with the death of Pablo Torres Burgos, Emiliano Zapata was emerging as "Supreme Chief of the Revolutionary Movement of the South," a grandiloquent title which still, however, reflected only a limited degree of control over the Morelos insurgents. In the north the revolution's progress was taking a more organized and institutionalized form. Madero had established a provisional government in Bustillos, and Abraham González was already issuing orders as provisional governor of Chihuahua.

With the pace of revolutionary events elsewhere picking up, this was no time to dally with minor military operations in Guerrero. While Blanco, Mariscal, Añorve, Salgado, and others secured the coasts, the center, and the Tierra Caliente of the state, the rebels led by Ambrosio Figueroa had been extending their operations beyond the boundaries of Guerrero. If the Figueroas were to consolidate their position as leaders of the revolution in the south, they could not do so by limiting their operations to the obscure mountain towns of Guerrero. Their control over other rebel groups in the state was, to say the least, tenuous, and their prestige was based solely on the fact that they had fired the first shots of the revolution in Guerrero. However, Ambrosio's status as leader of the revolution in the state received some official confirmation on 17 April when, at a meeting called by Guillermo García Aragón, a Maderista agent, he was formally styled "Chief of the Liberating Army of the South," and the Huitzuco rebels were formally incorporated as the Morelos Column.[32] Thus, without consulting other rebel groups in the state, the Figueroas and their Huitzuco followers laid a firm claim to the control of the revolt in Guerrero.

The formalization of Ambrosio Figueroa's status was carried a step further when García Aragón proceeded to arrange an interview between Figueroa and Zapata in Jolalpan, Puebla, on 22 April 1911. At the initiative of Fidel Fuentes, Ambrosio's secretary, a pact was drawn up which stated that Zapata would have supreme command of all revolutionary forces operating in Morelos, while Figueroa's claim to the command of the rebels of Guerrero was likewise recognized.[33] The main point of the Pact of Jolalpan was to define clearly the spheres of influence of the two chiefs. By way of celebration of the agreements reached, it was also decided that Figueroa and Zapata should make a joint attack on Jojutla, Morelos, on 28 April.[34]

The attack on Jojutla, however, never took place, for already Zapata was mistrustful of the intentions of the Figueroa brothers. Zapata's suspicions were fueled by the knowledge that the commander of the federal garrison of Jojutla was Colonel Fausto Beltrán, an old friend of the Figueroas, who had already contacted the brothers once with a view to negotiating an armistice in Guerrero. This, together with the well-known fact of Ambrosio's friendship with a number of Morelos *hacendados*, apparently made Zapata suspicious, and he informed Figueroa that he would not take part in the attack on Jojutla. Zapata's fears deepened when the Guerrero rebels were allowed to penetrate as far as the suburbs of the town. Rumor had it that the Figueroas had connived with Beltrán and the Morelos *hacendados* to destroy Zapata's forces, or even murder Zapata himself. Zapata demanded that the attack be called off and a new conference held, but Ambrosio Figueroa refused.[35] This, strictly speaking, was a violation of the Pact of Jolalpan, since Zapata had been recognized as supreme chief of the revolution in Morelos. The fleeting unity of the two chieftains had stemmed from their mutual need for recognition and had lasted but six days.

The Figueroas had been allowed to approach Jojutla unmolested because Beltrán had instructions to inform them of the negotiations of the Díaz regime with Madero in the north, and to invite the Figueroas to negotiate an armistice in the south. Needless to say, the fact that the old dictator was anxious to negotiate with the Huitzuco rebels gave their local standing a considerable boost, for by inviting them to talks in Mexico City, Díaz bestowed on them recognition of the preeminence they claimed, even if the military and political facts did not entirely justify it. Francisco Figueroa and another *huitzuquense*, José Soto, were dispatched to Mexico City to interview Díaz. They took with them orders that their demands were to concern only local matters, in particular the appointment of a new governor in Guerrero, since the Porfirista state government had clearly collapsed. In the meantime, an armistice of twenty days was agreed upon with Beltrán, and Figueroa agreed to withdraw his forces to northern Guerrero.[36] With the armistice negotiated at Jojutla the Figueroas staked a still firmer claim to represent the entire revolutionary movement in Guerrero. Gratifyingly, the Mexico City press now began to portray them in this very light.[37]

On 3 May 1911 Francisco Figueroa and Soto, joined by Francisco de P. Castrejón Cerezo, a close friend of the Figueroas, met first with

José I. Limantour, and then with President Díaz himself. Díaz and Limantour suggested that peace could be arranged in Guerrero with the appointment of a man of honest reputation as governor, and proposed the name of the lawyer Lic. Faustino Estrada.[38] However, before reaching any agreement, Soto and Figueroa conferred with Madero by telegram. From Ciudad Juárez, Madero replied that he approved of the armistice agreed upon with Beltrán, but told the representatives of the Huitzuco rebels that "you must refrain from negotiating peace which the official representatives . . . are discussing in [Ciudad Juárez]."[39]

Despite Madero's firm order to break off further negotiations with Díaz and to refrain from entering into discussions of national issues, Figueroa returned for a second interview with the president, carrying instructions from the Huitzuco insurgents which went far beyond the purely local demands put to Díaz on 3 May. The new instructions from Huitzuco stated that "we desire that the first requisite that is imposed on the federation to sign the peace [treaty] be the immediate resignation of General Díaz, because this gentleman can never in any other way give an effective guarantee of his offers." The rebels further demanded that the city of Iguala be handed over to them by 10 May in order to secure supplies for themselves.[40] The pretensions of the Figueroas were quite clear: not only did they claim supreme authority over the revolution in Guerrero (a pretension formalized in the pact of Jolalpan and in Díaz's offer of negotiations), but they now staked a claim on the national scene by demanding the president's resignation. Needless to say, Díaz refused the Figueroas' demands.[41] However, just a week later the aging dictator acceded to Madero's insistence on his resignation and the establishment of a provisional government under Francisco León de la Barra.

Meanwhile, in Guerrero, upon the failure of negotiations with Díaz, Ambrosio Figueroa made preparations to attack Iguala, the strategic key to the entire state of Guerrero, since the city straddled all the major lines of communication. By 1 May Figueroa had assembled 2,000 troops from the districts of Alarcón and Hidalgo, the Tierra Caliente, and the states of Mexico and Morelos. The attack on the city began on 13 May, and on the following day the federal garrison surrendered,[42] thus handing Figueroa the most decisive victory achieved by the rebels in Guerrero. It was now quite impossible for the federal forces to retain any control over the state. Since 11 May rebel forces from the center and coasts commanded by Julián Blanco had threatened Chilpancingo, and the fall of Iguala precipitated the evacuation of the state capital on the following day.[43] Acapulco was now the only town in the state still in federal hands, but even there their grip was extremely shaky.[44]

Having captured the most strategically important prize in the state, the Figueroas took steps to strengthen their hold on Guerrero by calling an assembly of revolutionary chiefs in Iguala on 16 May to elect a provisional governor. In fact, the assembly was not attended by all the rebel chiefs of Guerrero, but only by those who had participated in the capture of Iguala, and five other leaders from the central region of the state: Laureano Astudillo of Tixtla, José Rueda Bravo, Manuel D. Asúnsulo, a miner originally from Chihuahua, Manuel Villegas, and Miguel Serrano. Important chiefs, such as Julián Blanco in the center, Enrique Añorve on the Costa Chica, Tomás Gómez and Silvestre G. Mariscal on the Costa Grande, were not represented. The rebels from the north of the state thus dominated the assembly, and it was not surprising that of the three candidates for the governorship, one (Francisco Figueroa) should be a brother of Ambrosio Figueroa, another (Fidel Fuentes) a close friend of the Figueroa family and a member of the original Huitzuco band, and the third (General Alfonso Miranda) an ally of the Figueroas, although a native of Morelos, rather than of Guerrero. When the choice fell on Francisco Figueroa, the brothers took a significant step toward consolidating their position in Guerrero, since they now controlled both the civilian government and the supreme military command of the revolution in the state.[45] Francisco's appointment received official sanction from Madero eight days later.[46]

The Figueroas' control of Guerrero was further strengthened with the appointment in June of Ambrosio as inspector of the *cuerpos rurales* in the state. This was an important appointment: while the troops of other rebel chiefs were disarmed in June and July, Figueroa was allowed to retain control of his red-shirted *colorados*. Moreover, of the four chiefs appointed as his subordinates, at least three were close associates of Figueroa,[47] and even when Ambrosio later became governor of Morelos, the command of the *colorados* was entrusted to his brother Rómulo and another Huitzuco revolutionary, Martín Vicario, a veteran of the campaigns against the mercury mine interests.[48] Indeed, so confident were the Figueroas of their control of Guerrero that in his seven months as provisional governor Francisco felt himself able to undertake major steps to reconstruct and promote the state's economy. Plans were drawn up and approved for a railway line from Naranjo to Taxco, while further plans were in hand to build a line from Iguala to Huitzuco, and to link the railhead at Balsas to Acapulco via the Balsas river valley.[49]

The rise of the Figueroas in the south seemed irresistible. On 9 August Madero offered Ambrosio the governorship of Morelos, where Zapata was already close to rebellion, but Figueroa hesitated to accept, no doubt fearing that his influence in Guerrero might be weakened by his absence. He expressed doubts as to the wisdom of Madero's decision to send federal troops into Morelos and had reservations concerning the loyalty of their commander, Victoriano Huerta. As for Zapata, Ambrosio wondered if it might not be wiser to negotiate rather than to send federal forces after him. His brother Francisco expressed similar doubts to Madero, adding that Ambrosio's departure could lead to serious divisions among the revolutionaries in Guerrero, divisions which, in fact, had already begun to break out. Discontent was already evident as a result of the removal of Emilio Vázquez Gómez from the Ministry of Government.[50] Indeed, unrest over the Vázquez Gómez affair could scarcely have escaped Figueroa's attention, since his brother Rómulo and cousin Odilón had both publicly protested Madero's removal of his minister.[51] However, despite their misgivings, the Figueroa brothers had overcome their doubts a month later, and on 27 September Ambrosio's appointment was ratified by the Senate.[52]

Powerful merchant and landowning interests in Morelos were behind the drive to appoint Ambrosio governor. It was well known that relations between Figueroa and Zapata were strained since the stillborn attack on Jojutla, and relations between the two rebel chiefs were further embittered when one of Ambrosio's principal lieutenants, Federico Morales, executed Zapata's close friend Gabriel Tepepa in Jojutla on 25 May 1911.[53] Thus when Zapata's enemies searched for a suitable candidate to clip the Morelos chieftain's wings, Figueroa, who was well known in the state, was an obvious choice, and as early as 17 May "a commission of prominent citizens and merchants from the evacuated cities of Morelos" had asked Ambrosio to protect them from Zapata.[54] In June the Morelos landowners, led by Ambrosio's former employers, the Ruíz de Velasco brothers, began to pressure the government to appoint Ambrosio governor.[55] The pressure to import leaders from Guerrero to put Zapata in his place continued with a petition in August from a group of *morelense* exiles in Iguala to Madero, asking him to appoint Federico Morales, the executioner of Tepepa and Ambrosio's right-hand man, chief of arms in Morelos. The group included members of prominent landowning and merchant families.[56]

Thus, with direct control of the military and governmental hierarchies in Guerrero, with powerful political support in Morelos, and with the patronage of the Madero administration in Mexico City, the Figueroas had emerged as the strongmen of the south a mere seven months after they had taken up arms in Huitzuco. However, within a matter of months the meteoric rise of the brothers from Quetzalapa would falter, and by June 1912 the persistent attacks of their enemies would culminate in their being stripped of all their military and political offices in Morelos and Guerrero.

Indeed, there were already a number of signs that the Figueroas' control over events in Guerrero was not as firm as it appeared. Although they had taken a number of steps, often unilaterally, to formalize their status as leaders of the revolution in Guerrero, their position rested fundamentally on a tacit and rather loose alliance of revolutionary chiefs. Such an alliance was likely to fall apart as soon as any chief had personal difficulties with the Figueroas or considered that he could further his ambitions by asserting his independence. For instance, in late May, when the fighting was over, the well known *guerrerense* politician and leader of the 1900–1901 revolt against Mercenario and Mora, Rafael del Castillo Calderón, returned to Guerrero and attempted to establish himself as one of the main revolutionary chiefs. On 28 May Ambrosio Figueroa telegraphed Madero that Castillo Calderón "has deposed authorities provisionally appointed by me in the district of Mina, calling himself general in chief of the forces of Michoacán and southern Guerrero."[57] Castillo Calderón was calling himself a Maderista but was in fact leading a counter-revolution, Figueroa told Madero, since he had "close links with prominent members of the *científico* party," in particular Enrique C. Creel.[58] Although Castillo Calderón feigned to surrender himself a few days later, he continued "recruiting people and propagating his politics" and General Federico Morales had to be sent to capture him.[59]

Castillo Calderón's activities were only one symptom of the underlying weakness of the Figueroas' position, which on the coast was still more delicate and potentially much more explosive, in part because of rampant factionalism among the revolutionary bands. By early June the Costa Chica was controlled by Enrique Añorve of Ometepec and his lieutenant Manuel Centurión, and the Costa Grande by Silvestre G. Mariscal. Añorve was a member of a long-influential family from Ometepec. He had recruited the villagers of Igualapa, Acatepec, and Huehuetán, who rebelled in the vain hope of recovering their communal lands which had been broken up by the disentailment laws and sold off to mestizo smallholders.[60] Mariscal was a schoolteacher from Atoyac who would dominate the Costa Grande for many years. He recruited his followers among the *pinto*

population of the Costa Grande, who were divided from their com-
patriots on the Costa Chica by a deep-rooted traditional rivalry.[61]
This rivalry, added to the ambitions of Añorve and Mariscal, was an
explosive mixture.

On 10 June the U.S. consul in Acapulco reported that "keen jealousy is said to exist between these two revolutionary leaders who
question each other's supremacy and each other's motives. This
feeling is said to be filtering down to the men and some apprehension is beginning to be felt lest it break out in a violent clash between the rival forces."[62] Fighting did indeed break out between the
two factions, on 2 June when Añorve's men entered Acapulco, and
again on 23 June.[63] Mariscal proved to be particularly troublesome,
refusing to disarm his troops as Figueroa had ordered him to do in
July, claiming that he had authorization from the Secretaría de Gobernación to retain his men. According to some reports Mariscal
was indeed receiving protection from Mexico City in the shape of
Lic. Matías Chávez, at the time *subsecretario de gobernación*, and a
candidate in the forthcoming elections for the state governorship. In
return Mariscal was promising Chávez his support in the elections.[64]
Mariscal's reluctance to disarm can probably be explained by the
fact that the coast had been garrisoned by troops loyal to Figueroa.
To disarm under these circumstances would be to surrender control
of the coast to the Huitzuco chieftain.

There was little Figueroa could do about the refusal of Mariscal
to disarm because "he feared antagonizing leaders who shoud be deposed lest the consequences be disastrous to the interests he represents in the coming elections."[65] The problem was temporarily resolved by calling Mariscal to fight the Zapatistas in Morelos.
However, at the end of November, Mariscal returned to Guerrero on
personal business and, back in his native Atoyac, attacked the forces
of Figueroa's commander on the Costa Grande, Perfecto Juárez y
Reyes, who was wounded and died on 14 January 1912. Mariscal was
subsequently arrested in Mexico City and imprisoned in Acapulco.[66]

Another revolutionary chief of considerable importance who asserted his independence from the Figueroas was Jesús H. Salgado.
Salgado, who owned land and mining interests in the Teloloapan
area,[67] rebelled in late August, but two months later began to negotiate his surrender. However, apparently encouraged by the publication of the Plan of Ayala, in which the Morelos Zapatistas formally
declared their opposition to Madero, Salgado broke off negotiations
and issued a "Proclamation to the Sons of the State of Guerrero," inviting the people of Guerrero to take up arms. The proclamation declared that the people of Guerrero had rebelled against Porfirio Díaz

in order to "destroy an odious *cacicazgo,*" but now found themselves forced to "pay . . . homage to [Ambrosio Figueroa] as cacique of the state." Moreover, echoing the Plan of Ayala, Salgado complained that those who had been "despoiled of their lands have not got them back again, despite the fact that the Plan of San Luis Potosí offered them this, and small-scale commerce and the poor people are still overwhelmed with odious taxes." Those who joined his cause were offered pay ranging from $1.00 to $1.50 per day, as well as a parcel of land,[68] a clear appeal to the landless Indian peasantry which formed his main source of support. Salgado's rebellion posed an obvious threat to the Figueroas' control of Tierra Caliente, but also raised fears of ramifications which went beyond the local factional struggles, as José Inocente Lugo pointed out. "Magonismo is a threat in our state," Lugo wrote, "because even some of the most prominent chiefs of the south have encouraged the inveterate pretensions of the Indians with respect to the revindication of the lands which belonged to the former communities, and naturally all the *vecinos* of the [Balsas region] are alarmed by the fierce attitude of that caste."[69] Thus, Salgadismo was feared not only for its potential affinity with the Zapatista movement, but also because it conjured up images of anarchy and caste warfare which had plagued the Tierra Caliente in the nineteenth century.

The tensions between the various revolutionary chiefs in Guerrero were exacerbated by the elections for state governor in November 1911. In August the American vice consul in Acapulco reported that "the various revolutionary leaders in Guerrero have become attached to different political parties in Mexico City, and if a counter revolution should arrise [*sic*], a condition of chaos would probably result from the hatred and jealousy existing amoung [*sic*] them." It was public knowledge that Ambrosio Figueroa was anxious that one of his supporters should replace his brother Francisco in the governorship, the vice consul added.[70] Indeed the Figueroas had chosen as their candidate to succeed to the governorship Martín Vicario, a member of the group which had opposed the mine administration in Huitzuco, and one of Ambrosio's most important military commanders. However, the Huitzuco group was dealt a severe blow when Vicario was narrowly defeated by José Inocente Lugo, a landowner from the Tierra Caliente who had been one of the first Maderista organizers in Guerrero.[71] The defeat was a bitter pill to swallow, and Francisco Figueroa complained to Madero, who had just been elected president, that this was an indication that he intended "to take away from [the Figueroas] the considerations which [they] have earned." This was not the case, Madero assured him, since "for me it is entirely the same if Lic. Lugo or Colonel Vicario turns out to be elected governor. All I wish is that, when the appointment depends on the local legislature of the state, it should choose the man who has the majority of votes."[72] Although Ambrosio for the time being retained the command of the military forces of Guerrero, the loss of the control of the civil government was a serious blow to the Figueroas' supremacy in the state.

However, the defeat in the November election was only the beginning of the Figueroas' troubles, since from the beginning Lugo displayed a resolute hostility toward the Huitzuco chiefs. As rebel activity began to extend throughout the state in late 1911, Lugo became increasingly critical of the Figueroas' military command. By the second week in December, Lugo told Madero, "the hordes of Salgado" were beginning to invade the district of Hidalgo, and there was a real danger of their linking up with Zapata.[73] Lugo asked Madero to send half a battalion of troops to defend the coast. Moreover, he wrote, a professional military man should be sent to direct operations in Guerrero, for if this were not done, "we will be exposed to a general conflagration, since pillage and the offer of lands is seducing the low classes of the people."[74] Lugo's criticism became more and more insistent as the military situation declined. By the second half of December, Zapatistas were operating in the Taxco region and had threatened the city itself, which had been left ungarrisoned by Major Odilón Figueroa. After this debacle Lugo told Madero that both Odilón and Rómulo Figueroa should be sent to Morelos and put under an energetic commander, since they were both incompetent.[75]

Lugo's persistent criticism was not without effect. Madero was becoming increasingly impatient with the Figueroas' inability to suppress the growing rebellion in Guerrero. "I also have information," he wrote to Ambrosio, "that in Guerrero the troops are very badly organized, since you will understand that for Salgado to have been able to recruit men and sustain himself without having had any clash with the rural forces of the state, it is because of a reprehensible neglect, since you will remember that over three weeks ago I advised you to send forces to Coyuca [de Catalán] to pursue Salgado and those forces have still not reached that region."[76] Although the military position was improved for a brief period when Salgado surrendered and licensed his troops on 14 December,[77] he rebelled yet again in January 1912, and in some quarters this renewed insurrection was blamed on enmity between Salgado and the Figueroas.[78]

The Maderista hold on northern Guerrero was loosened still further with the rebellion of Pablo Barrera, who operated in the area of Tepecoacuilco, only a few kilometers from Iguala and Huitzuco, and who was the first rebel chief in Guerrero to be authorized to operate under the Zapatista label. From December 1911 until June 1912, Barrera roamed northern Guerrero, instructing tenants not to pay their rent to the landowners and looting the property of the landowners and merchants of his native Tepecoacuilco.[79] Barrera's call to cease paying rents clearly fell on receptive ears, since a number of landowners complained that they had not been able to collect payment from their tenants. Their difficulties were compounded by the local authorities, who were sympathetic to Barrera, as Martín Vicario discovered. On 2 January Vicario had summoned the *presidente municipal* of Tepecoacuilco to the house of the *hacendado* Emigdio Pastrana and asked him to call a meeting of tenants in the municipality to inform them of their obligation to pay rents, but the *presidente* flatly refused to do so.[80]

The deteriorating military position in Guerrero, of which Barrera's revolt was but one symptom, contributed to increasing animosity between the Figueroas and Madero. By January the latter was writing to Ambrosio Figueroa that the 1,680 men stationed in Guerrero "have not given any service to the government," and far from garrisoning the state "they are conspicuous by their absence."[81] Ambrosio's political and military standing in Morelos was similarly on the wane, and on 18 January he resigned the governorship.[82] He returned immediately to Guerrero only to suffer yet another blow to his prestige: the federal general Aureliano Blanquet had been appointed his superior, depriving him of overall command of the revolutionary forces in the state, although he still retained command of his *colorados*.[83]

By February the rebellion had spread still further, prompting the government to take stronger measures. All those living outside the towns and villages of the state were ordered to move into the nearest center of population on pain of being treated "with all the rigor of the law on suspension of guarantees."[84] The deteriorating military situation and his demotion as a consequence were, it seems, the main reasons which drove Ambrosio Figueroa to order the summary execution of Salustio Carrasco Núñez on 14 February 1912, an event which became something of a *cause célèbre* at the time.

Carrasco Núñez was a young lawyer in Iguala, son of Lic. Severo Carrasco Pérez. His father was a colonel in the auxiliary forces of Guerrero and had fought against the French invaders in 1863. In addition to his military career, Carrasco Pérez had also held elected office in Sinaloa, Hidalgo, Jalisco, and Guerrero, and from 1885 to 1900 had been treasurer general of Guerrero. Salustio was, therefore, a member of a distinguished family and was himself well known in political circles in Guerrero. He had been editor of *El Eco del Sur,* a newspaper which opposed the administration of Antonio Mercenario, and had been associated with the movement of Castillo Calderón in 1900–1901. As a result, he spent some time in the prison of Belén. More recently, he had been *prefecto político* of the district of Hidalgo during the administration of Damián Flores. He was also the author of a manifesto in support of Francisco León de la Barra and Madero which had been signed by Andrés and Odilón Figueroa and was the leading light of a political group called the Puritan Democrats. In the recent gubernatorial elections he had supported the candidacy of Lic. Faustino Estrada against the Figueroas' candidate, Martín Vicario.[85]

On the evening of 13 February 1912, Carrasco Núñez was arrested in Iguala and in the early hours of the next morning was summarily executed on the orders of Ambrosio Figueroa. Ambrosio justified the execution by claiming that Carrasco Núñez was hostile to Madero's administration and sympathetic to Zapata. It was alleged that Carrasco Núñez had supplied the forces of Jesús H. Salgado with money and arms, and that he had directed the military operations of the rebel band of Ramón Bahena.[86]

It soon became clear that the execution was a serious mistake, for Ambrosio became the subject of scathing attacks in the Mexico City press, and a group of prominent *guerrerenses* resident in the capital presented a formal protest to President Madero and to the *procurador general de la república.*[87] Madero, having received this protest from "a numerous group of *guerrerenses*," suggested Figueroa should join Pascual Orozco in his campaign in the north "in order to avoid gossip,"[88] but Ambrosio flatly refused to do so until he had completed the pacification of Guerrero. Carrasco Núñez was, he remarked, a mere *tinterillo.* In a letter to Madero he added that "perhaps in the procedure against the aforesaid person there may have been some irregularity, or the requisites established by the law of suspension of guarantees were not duly fulfilled, but I am determined to make the peace in this state at the cost of blood and of as much as may be necessary." Madero, Ambrosio wrote, should not "pay attention to those who speak of the law in these moments in which one should speak only of submission or death, since the situation does not demand *tinterillos* but soldiers sufficiently energetic to solve the situation."[89] Figueroa could hardly have spoken more clearly: the execution of Carrasco Núñez was part of a desperate effort to check the Figueroas' declining fortunes in Guerrero.

However, even such vigorous actions failed to stem the tide, for a variety of reasons. One factor which was perfectly fortuitous was the disablement of Ambrosio Figueroa on 13 May 1912, when he was accidentally shot in the knee by a cousin, Julio Figueroa. The wound left him crippled and unable to resume his military duties.[90] Of more immediate importance was the continuing deterioration of the military position of the Maderista government in Guerrero,[91] which served to aggravate further the continuing feud between Ró-mulo Figueroa and Governor José I. Lugo, who was endeavoring to strip Figueroa of his military command in the state.[92] In early June Lugo finally succeeded in removing the Figueroa brothers from Guerrero. They were summoned to Mexico City, and the federal colonel Reynaldo Díaz was appointed to take over Rómulo's command. Once in the capital, it became clear that the Figueroas had fallen out of the administration's favor, and they were obliged to remain in Mexico City, since Lugo informed Madero that Jesús H. Salgado was willing to surrender, but only on condition that the Figueroas not be allowed to return to command the rural forces of Guerrero.[93] The Huitzuco chiefs were not allowed to return to the state until December, and even then they were not assigned any military command. In addition, they were ordered to live apart: Ambrosio in Chilpancingo, Rómulo in Huitzuco, and their lieutenant Martín Vicario in Acapulco.[94]

The period which opened with the battle of Huitzuco on 28 February 1911 and ended with the return of the Figueroa brothers to Guerrero in December 1912 was a crucial one in the development of the Mexican revolution in Guerrero. In the beginning, the Figueroas managed to establish a fragile hegemony over the revolutionary forces of Guerrero, a hegemony based on loose alliances and tacit recognition of their status as leaders of the Maderista movement in the state. Their power had spread to the neighboring state of Morelos, and they even became figures of some importance on the national political scene. The inherent weaknesses of the Figueroas' power soon became evident, however. Out of the mass of petty revolutionary chieftains which the uprising of 1911 cast up emerged four regional groupings which would characterize and determine the development of the revolution in Guerrero. On the Costa Grande, Silvestre G. Mariscal reigned supreme. Although he had been imprisoned in Acapulco since the killing of Perfecto Juárez y Reyes in January 1912, he still called the tune in the Atoyac area. In November 1912 Julián Radilla, Mariscal's lieutenant, rebelled on the Costa Grande and was able to operate with impunity.[95] Jesús H. Salgado had staked out his independence in Tierra Caliente as early as August 1911, and by January 1913 his men were operating in considerable numbers as far afield as the Costa Grande.[96] In the center the strongman was Julián Blanco, whose influence spread as far as the Costa Chica. Although Blanco maintained good relations with the Figueroas for some time, by June 1912 he had joined forces with their enemy Governor Lugo.[97] Finally, in the north, the Figueroas, now cut down to size, still clearly dominated the area around Iguala. In the nineteenth century the rivalry of the caciques of Guerrero had defined itself along geographical as well as political lines: Alvarez on the Costa Grande, Bravo in the center, and Florencio Villarreal and Joaquín Rea on the Costa Chica. Similarly, by the end of 1912 the revolutionary factions had aligned themselves along regional lines. In a way, the Mexican revolution in Guerrero represented the final struggle for the inheritance of the Alvarez *cacicazgo*.

These regional alignments became perfectly clear when each leader found himself compelled to define his attitude to the coup of Victoriano Huerta. From its inception the administration of Madero had been plagued by chronic unrest in the countryside and political dissent in the capital. In November 1911 Madero had ditched his vice-presidential nominee, Francisco Vázquez Gómez, a man who enjoyed considerable support in the country in general and in the revolutionary ranks in particular. Then in March 1912 one of Madero's foremost military chieftains, Pascual Orozco, supported and financed by conservative groups in Chihuahua, rebelled against his former leader. Although Orozco was defeated, ironically enough by Huerta himself, unrest persisted and undermined the foundations of Madero's regime. Finally, in February 1913 a military uprising in the capital, led by Bernardo Reyes (who died in the fighting) and Felix Díaz, a nephew of Don Porfirio, precipitated Madero's downfall. Ten days later Victoriano Huerta, with the reluctant acceptance of Felix Díaz, and the enthusiastic blessing of the American ambassador, deposed Madero and his vice-president, José María Pino Suárez (both of whom were subsequently murdered), and himself took office.

Huerta, a man with a long and distinguished military career which included the campaigns against the rebellions of Neri and Castillo Calderón in Guerrero,[98] attempted to bring some order to the increasingly chaotic political life of Mexico. As a first step, he sought the allegiance of the state governors, most of whom, with the exception of Venustiano Carranza in Coahuila, pledged their loyalty to Huerta. Among those who offered their support to the dictator was Governor Lugo of Guerrero, who had little choice but to accept the *fait accompli* in Mexico City, since he lacked military support, his two closest associates, Julián Blanco and Gertrudis G. Sánchez, being unwilling to go to his aid.[99]

Huerta's coup posed a serious problem for revolutionary leaders in Guerrero. All the main chiefs received invitations to join him in the task of pacifying Mexico, and in many cases considerations of tactics and temporary convenience outweighed any ideological or other considerations. One of the first to offer his services to Huerta was the veteran politician Rafael del Castillo Calderón. On 2 March a group of his supporters called on Huerta asking him to reverse the result of the recent elections for state governor in which Castillo Calderón had been defeated by the candidate backed by Governor Lugo.[100] Castillo Calderón was no longer the influential figure he had been, however, and Huerta could afford to ignore his plea, declaring the dissolution of the state government and appointing a new governor.[101]

At the end of February or the beginning of March, a number of revolutionary chiefs met in Atoyac to consider their attitude to Huerta. Those present included Silvestre G. Mariscal, who had been released from jail as a conciliatory gesture, Martín Vicario, formerly a lieutenant of Ambrosio Figueroa but, since his assignment to Acapulco, ever more closely allied to Mariscal, Julián Radilla, and Juan Andrew Almazán. The meeting decided to support Huerta,[102] an example followed, albeit in some cases temporarily, by Julián Blanco at Chilpancingo, Gertrudis G. Sánchez at Coyuca de Catalán, and Genaro Basabe in the Tierra Caliente.[103] The new military governor, General Manuel Zozaya, made negotiations with the revolutionaries his policy, offering to incorporate them into the regular army or pay them for the surrender of their arms. Thus, while Mariscal, Radilla, and other leaders went to Mexico City to confer with Huerta, "a sort of armed truce" existed "with uncertainty prevailing."[104]

This fragile truce was broken on 30 March when Gertrudis G. Sánchez rebelled in Coyuca de Catalán. Joined by other commanders of the *rurales* in Tierra Caliente, he moved into Michoacán, leaving the Salgadistas in undisputed command of that area.[105] Then, on 6 April Rómulo Figueroa led the northern chiefs in rebellion against Huerta, while in Chilpancingo his brother Ambrosio secretly conferred with Julián Blanco and Juan de la Luz Romero to rise up against the regime.[106] On 16 April Rómulo entered Chilapa unopposed at the head of 400 cavalry and was joined by the garrison under the command of his friend Eustorgio Vergara.[107]

Despite Rómulo's belligerent actions, Huerta and Governor Zozaya continued their policy of negotiation, although Figueroa's forces were, nevertheless, attacked when the opportunity arose. The government's hand was strong, since it had in its power Ambrosio Figueroa, now a cripple, who was unable to leave Chilpancingo.

Serapio Salceda, Rómulo's godfather, was sent to Guerrero to negotiate with him, and Ambrosio, realizing that his life was in danger, also attempted to persuade his brother to surrender. Rómulo, awaiting an opportunity to free his brother from the government's clutches, agreed to a truce and feigned willingness to negotiate.[108] Unable to obtain Ambrosio's freedom, however, and under increasing pressure from Zapatista and Huertista forces, Rómulo decided to join Gertrudis G. Sánchez in Michoacán.[109] Shortly afterwards, on 23 June, Ambrosio was executed in Iguala, along with his cousin Odilón Figueroa and other members of his staff.[110]

The Huertistas' position appeared to be very strong, since they held all the major cities and towns in the state. On 22 May they had roundly defeated Rómulo Figueroa near Iguala, and the following day the forces of General Antonio Olea entered and sacked Huitzuco itself. Later in the year, in October, Olea drove his forces through the Tierra Caliente, taking Coyuca de Catalán, and Pungarabato. On 7 October he occupied Huetamo in Michoacán, thus driving the Guerrero revolutionaries back into their own state.[111]

However, in November the tide began to turn against the Huertistas. The first blow fell in late October or November when Julián Blanco defected to the Constitutionalist cause.[112] In November fears of Mariscal's defection to the Constitutionalist cause began to be expressed, and they became more acute by mid December when he refused orders to attack Blanco's forces.[113] December saw the beginning of a number of military reverses for the Huertistas: on 12 December Rómulo Figueroa recaptured Huitzuco, and six days later he took Buenavista de Cuéllar.[114] By February 1914 Julián Blanco was threatening the state capital, and on 13 February Rómulo Figueroa, in conjunction with the Zapatistas Julio Gómez and Chon Díaz, entered Chilapa. Four days later Figueroa captured Tixtla, and, after an abortive combined attack on Chilpancingo, he and Blanco took Ayutla on 3 March.[115]

The stage was now set for the final assault on the state capital, an event which was to signal a decisive shift in the relative strengths of the contending factions in Guerrero. The prime mover in the attack was Emiliano Zapata, who needed a victory of such importance to establish his position as the principal revolutionary leader of the south, with authority, not only in Morelos, but also in Guerrero and Puebla. The Morelos chieftain had acquired a number of local allies, notably Jesús H. Salgado, Chon Díaz, and Heliodoro Castillo, who were joined in November 1913 by Julián Blanco.[116]

The preparations for the capture of the state capital moved apace. By 9 March all the Guerrero chiefs had gathered their forces for the assault on Chilpancingo. Zapata himself supplied nearly 2,000 troops, although Salgado was designated as the commander of the rebel forces. The attack was scheduled for 26 March, but Chon Díaz, impatient for action, led a vigorous charge three days early which broke the federals' lines, and the city fell the next day.[117] This triumph was the most decisive action of the campaign against the Huertista government in Guerrero. Consul Edwards reported from Acapulco that "Federal officers who escaped to this city admit that the state is irretrievably lost to the government."[118] Edwards proved to be correct in his assessment of the situation, since on 7 April Iguala fell to the besieging forces of Jesús H. Salgado, and Julián Blanco moved against Acapulco, although the port remained in federal hands until 7 July, when the garrison evacuated the city, allowing Blanco to occupy it without firing a shot.[119]

Huerta himself remained in power in Mexico City until 15 July, but to all intents and purposes his regime in Guerrero collapsed on 24 March with the fall of Chilpancingo. The Huerta interlude was not just a mere hiccup in the revolutionary process, for it led to a realignment of the rebel factions and pointed up quite clearly the division of the revolutionary forces of the state into four broad geographical groups. In the north the Figueroa family still predominated, and Rómulo's forces were able to strike as far south as Chilapa and, in conjunction with Julián Blanco and others, also operated from Chilpancingo to the Costa Chica. In the center and on the Costa Chica Julián Blanco had emerged as the main revolutionary leader. Although he still operated with Figueroa on occasion, the relationship was now one of equally independent chieftains, rather than of a superior and his subordinate. Moreover, Blanco's recognition of the Plan of Ayala, albeit it for pragmatic reasons, drove a clear ideological wedge between him and the Figueroas. On the Costa Grande the power of Silvestre G. Mariscal was undisputed, while the Tierra Caliente was controlled by Jesús H. Salgado, who was beginning to extend his influence toward Iguala and Chilpancingo, and even, on occasion, raided into Michoacán and the state of Mexico.

Thus the balance of power in the state had shifted decisively away from the ranchero Liberals of northern Guerrero who had dominated the scene in 1911. The crucial victories of 1914 were won by Zapata and his local allies, while the power of the Figueroas had declined considerably, but despite the preeminence of the Morelos chieftain, Rómulo refused to recognize the Plan of Ayala and to submit himself to Zapata's authority. He had withdrawn briefly to Michoacán to avoid clashes with the Zapatistas, and in early June he once again went to join the forces of Gertrudis G. Sánchez in the neighboring state. The Figueroa Brigade, as his troops became known, fought for a time in Michoacán and later joined the Constitutionalist forces in the offensive against Villa in the north. Rómulo Figueroa would not return to Guerrero until 1917,[120] and in the meantime the Zapatistas briefly called the tune.

After the fall of Chilpancingo, an assembly of the main Guerrero chiefs who had signed the Plan of Ayala elected Jesús H. Salgado as director of the provisional government of Guerrero,[121] a procedure laid down in article 13 of the plan. The power of Zapata in the state was unquestioned, for he had just won the most important victory of the campaign against Huerta in the south, although the local rebels had, in fact, done most of the fighting, while Zapata occupied himself with the wider strategic design. Zapata's ability to dictate events in Guerrero was evident when, after the fall of Chilpancingo, he ordered Julián Blanco to hand over to him all the arms and ammunition taken in the capture of the city. Blanco promptly complied.[122] Nevertheless, although Zapata temporarily dominated Guerrero, his control of the state would soon fall victim to fragmentation and factionalism in the revolutionary ranks. Indeed, it is clear that the Guerrero Zapatistas never formed a cohesive part of the Ayala movement. Most of them adhered to Zapatismo "out of convenience," in the words of one Constitutionalist veteran.[123]

The history of Zapatismo in Guerrero cannot be separated from the name of Jesús H. Salgado, an owner of lands and mines from the Teloloapan area. Despite the fact that he was the principal Zapatista chief in the state, the history of Salgado's movement is rather obscure. He initially rebelled in conjunction with Ambrosio Figueroa's subordinate, Leovigildo Alvarez, but soon declared his independence of the Figueroa group, rebelling repeatedly in 1911 and 1912, although he did not formally adhere to the Zapatista movement until 1913.[124] Like the Morelos uprising, Salgadismo espoused the cause of *agrarismo*, although its program for distribution of land was by no means as clear and specific as the Plan of Ayala. Salgado issued a statement of the objectives of his rebellion in November 1911 (the same month the Plan of Ayala was published). After railing against the attempts of Ambrosio Figueroa to establish himself as the cacique of Guerrero, Salgado's proclamation asserted that "those who had been despoiled of their lands have not got them back again, despite the fact that the Plan of San Luis Potosí offered to do so." Every soldier who joined Salgado's forces was promised a parcel of land as well as a daily wage.[125]

The appeal of Salgado's program was clearly to the popular masses, and contemporary reports show quite clearly that he drew

his support from a social stratum very different from that of the rancheros who formed the nucleus of the Huitzuco rebels led by the Figueroas. Governor Lugo, for instance, told Madero that "Salgado's
people are all criminals whom he has taken out of the prisons and
who have seized other people's lands, for this is the bait which
[Salgado] has used in the ungrateful task he has taken upon himself."
Lugo added that Salgado had caused considerable agitation among
the ignorant masses and that there was a serious danger that he
might joint forces with Zapata.[126] Another observer described Salgado's followers in similar terms: "Salgado has gathered many people in . . . the Tierra Caliente . . . offering the Indians a distribution
of land when the rebellion triumphs; he has also used all sorts of
criminal types."[127] While the accusations that many of Salgado's followers were criminals may perhaps be discounted as the prejudice of
his enemies, it seems clear from the evidence available that the Salgadistas were landless peasants, often of indigenous ethnic origin.
Such people had more in common with the Zapatistas than with the
rancheros of northern Guerrero, and the danger of Salgado joining
forces with Zapata was realized long before it actually occurred.

Nevertheless, despite certain broad ideological affinities, complete harmony never existed between the Guerrero Zapatistas and
the Morelos chieftains. Shortly after Salgado's appointment as director of the provisional government of Guerrero, the Guerrero
Zapatistas conferred on their relationship with Zapata. While they
agreed to support the Plan of Ayala and join Zapata in the fight
against Carranza, they did so only on condition that they be independent of the command in Morelos. Moreover, as an incentive to
Zapata to respect their demands, they offered him a monthly payment of $50,000 from the mines of Guerrero if he stayed out of the
state.[128]

In the north of the state, where Zapatista bands from Morelos
and the state of Mexico frequently crossed into Guerrero, relations
with the local Zapatistas were tense. As early as November 1914
Colonel Victorino Bárcenas complained from Huitzuco that General
Genovevo de la O and other Zapatista chieftains had for some time
been stealing the cattle of ranchers and merchants in the area. If this
continued, Bárcenas asserted, the local revolutionaries would not be
able to sustain themselves.[129] As early as 1913 the Morelos Zapatistas had begun to plunder the possessions of Constitutionalist supporters in the north of Guerrero,[130] but indiscriminate pillage of their
own allies was quite another matter. The pressure on the towns of
northern Guerrero increased in the following years. In 1916 the citizens of Cacahuamilpa were obliged to abandon their village, and

Tetipac was temporarily evacuated in 1917.[131] Friction between the Morelos Zapatistas and their allies in northern Guerrero climaxed with the rebellion on 30 April 1917 of the people of Buenavista de Cuéllar, a town of smallholders and cattle ranchers, against the excessive exactions of General Pedro Saavedra and other Zapatista chiefs. This revolt led to the defection of the Zapatista general Victorino Bárcenas, himself a small landowner and cattle rancher near Huitzuco.[132] The tension between the Morelos rebels and their allies in Guerrero also manifested itself in the execution of a number of Guerrero Zapatistas on the orders of the Morelos command. Those killed included Chon Díaz, Julio Gómez, and Fidel Fuentes (formerly a close friend of the Figueroas).[133]

Given the narrowly regional mentality of the Morelos peasantry, it is not surprising that tensions should have developed between the Morelos movement and its allies in Guerrero. This is easily explained in the case of the northern portion of the state, which provided a number of nominally Zapatista chiefs, since the agrarian structure here was radically different from that of Morelos. The first Zapatista in Guerrero, Pablo Barrera, directed his attention to the abuse of the rental system, rather than to the despoilment of the lands of the pueblos. If differences existed between the tenants of northern Guerrero and the villagers of Morelos, the gulf was even wider when it came to the rancheros of the districts of Alarcón and Hidalgo. Thus the smallholder Victorino Bárcenas turned against Zapata when his fellow cattle ranchers in Buenavista de Cuéllar could no longer tolerate the exactions of the Morelos revolutionaries. Nor did the communal villages of the Taxco region provide a natural constituency for Zapatismo, since they shared none of the agrarian grievances of the Morelos pueblos. In any case it was no surprise that from 1916 onward the towns and villages of Guerrero began to turn against the Zapatistas and their allies in the state.[134]

Nevertheless, despite underlying tensions between the Morelos and Guerrero revolutionaries, the fall of Chilpancingo opened the brief period of Zapatista dominance in Guerrero. Initially the Zapatistas' power rested on the alliance between Blanco and Salgado which had been forged in negotiations between Blanco and representatives of Zapata. The negotiations bore fruit in July 1914, when both of the Guerrero chieftains signed the ratification of the Plan of Ayala.[135] Their alliance prospered only briefly, however, for already, beyond the mountainous confines of Guerrero, events on the national scene were moving fast, and Blanco's alliance with the Zapatistas never amounted to anything more than the ink with which he signed. Huerta had already resigned, and on 15 August the

Constitutionalist forces of Alvaro Obregón entered Mexico City, followed five days later by the First Chief of the Constitutionalists, Venustiano Carranza. Changes on the national scene inevitably led to much jockeying for position at the local level. Blanco did not immediately break with Salgado, but concentrated on his campaign against the forces of his rival Silvestre G. Mariscal on the Costa Grande. However, at the same time Blanco attempted to bolster his local position by negotiating an accommodation with Carranza, a course which sooner or later was bound to lead to conflict with the local Zapatistas. Meanwhile, Mariscal was likewise busy negotiating the incorporation of his forces into the Constitutionalist ranks, and for a time managed to outflank Blanco by cutting off his communications with Mexico City.[136]

It was perhaps the lack of communication with Guerrero which led Carranza to take a rather extraordinary step in the last days of September. Evidently unaware of Salgado's Zapatista affiliation, the First Chief appointed him Constitutionalist governor of Guerrero. About the same time Carranza accepted Mariscal into the Constitutionalist ranks, and ordered Blanco, now also affiliated with Carrancismo, to suspend his offensive against his rival's forces. However, Carranza's efforts to enjoy the best of both worlds took no account of the balance of forces on the ground. No sooner was he appointed Constitutionalist governor than Salgado publicly rebelled in favor of Zapata.[137]

Meanwhile, Blanco and Mariscal, unwilling brothers in Constitutionalist arms, were at loggerheads. In July 1915 Vice Consul Edwards returned from a temporary absence from Acapulco to find that the military position had resolved itself as follows: the Carrancistas, represented by Blanco and Mariscal, controlled most of both coasts, while the rest of the state was under Zapatista control. However, although Blanco and Mariscal were both nominally Constitutionalists, the two men had until recently been enemies, and the two sets of troops were divided by considerable bitterness. Edwards, who conferred with both leaders, "was led to infer that while General Mariscal is nominally for Carranza, as he has been to my personal knowledge for Madero and for Huerta, he is primarily for any successful faction which may succeed in establishing a government in Mexico City. In the meantime it is his intention and ambition to dominate the situation in this state and to be a factor in the final settlement of the affairs in the country. . . . the people have confidence in his ability to maintain order which is all they want." While evidently impressed with the abilities of the former schoolmaster, his political inconstancy notwithstanding, Edwards found Blanco, a man of humble origins, "a very ordinary person and one would judge him to be a man of mediocre ability. His secretary frequently took the conversation from him and made replies to my questions." There was a considerable potential for conflict in the Carrancista camp, for, while Blanco's status as governor was unquestioned, both men claimed the military command of Guerrero. The conflicting status of the two generals, Simón Díaz, commander of the Acapulco garrison, explained, was due to the fact that Carranza's government was not yet strong enough to control the local chiefs but was trying to keep them happy until the Carrancistas were able to establish a greater degree of control over local affairs.[138]

Edwards's fears of a clash between the forces of Mariscal and Blanco soon proved correct. Indeed, it was inevitable that the ambitions of the two chiefs to call the tune in the Constitutionalist camp in Guerrero should lead to an armed conflict. On 3 or 4 August troops commanded by one of Blanco's subordinates, Andrés Carreto, fought with troops of Martín Vicario (now a member of Mariscal's general staff) in Tierra Colorada. Then on 5 August Blanco came under fire from Mariscal's troops while out riding in Acapulco. Blanco immediately gathered his troops together, and he and his son Bonifacio led an attack on Mariscal's forces, but after a brief battle they were forced to take refuge in the Castle of San Diego. On the following day Blanco surrendered, and shortly afterward he and his son were shot dead. Blanco's assassination was followed by the execution of a number of his troops and his principal officers.

Mariscal and his supporters alleged that Blanco was planning to rebel against Carranza and join the Zapatistas. In addition, they claimed, Blanco had launched an unprovoked attack on the forces of Vicario and Mariscal. Blanco's supporters denied that he had planned to betray Carranza, and similarly alleged that Mariscal had launched an unprovoked attack on Blanco and had subsequently murdered him.[139] Whatever the truth, the latent hostility of the two groups had come to the surface, and Mariscal had eliminated his main rival in the Constitutionalist camp. Of the four main groups which emerged in 1911 and 1912, only those of Mariscal and Salgado had stood the pace in Guerrero.

Having eliminated his rival, Mariscal moved to formalize his dominance in the Carrancista camp. On 8 August an assembly of his officers and of prominent civilians met to discuss the selection of a new governor. The first name proposed was that of the veteran of the 1900–1901 campaigns against Mercenario and Mora, Rafael del Castillo Calderón, now a colonel in Mariscal's forces. Castillo Calderón modestly declined the offer, however, whereupon Mariscal nominated Lieutenant Colonel Simón Díaz, who was duly elected.[140]

With the question of the choice of governor settled, Mariscal, whose position as military commander of Guerrero was now undisputed, was free to devote himself to the campaign against the Zapatistas, and in late September he launched an offensive with some 1,200 men. Chilpancingo, Chilapa, and other towns in central Guerrero fell rapidly, allowing Mariscal to advance swiftly on Iguala. His *costeños* were able to penetrate as far as the border of Morelos, but there met a large force of Zapatistas led by Jesús H. Salgado. The fighting lasted nineteen days, at the end of which Mariscal was forced to retreat through the Tierra Caliente, suffering heavy losses, but despite this setback, Mariscal was able to reinforce and retain Chilpancingo, thus giving the Constitutionalists control over a roughly triangular area, with both coasts as its base and the state capital at its apex.[141] By January 1916, however, many of these gains had been lost, and the Zapatistas threatened Chilpancingo, Tixtla, and Tlapa in the center and operated in large numbers on the Costa Grande. In fact on the coast the Constitutionalists exercised little control outside Acapulco.[142]

An already adverse military outlook was aggravated by divisions in the Carrancista ranks. On 1 May 1916 General Pablo Vargas launched a surprise attack on Rafael del Castillo Calderón, commander of the garrison in Chilapa, who fled to the mountains with his entire command of 500 troops.[143] With the local Constitutionalists divided by internal bickering, the Zapatista hold on Guerrero was loosened not by Mariscal's forces but by Carrancista generals moving into the state from Michoacán. In April Héctor F. López and Joaquín Amaro launched an offensive through Salgado's home base in Tierra Caliente, and on 11 May captured Apipilulco and Cocula, entering Iguala on the following day. They still held on to these towns, and also Tepecoacuilco, in September, although their grip was rather precarious.[144] Zapatismo would continue to be a problem until 1918, but the back of the resistance had been broken.

Mariscal, freed from the heaviest of his military responsibilities, was now able to assume direct command of the state's political affairs, taking office as governor of Guerrero on 9 November.[145] With all the reins of power in the state now firmly in his hands, Mariscal had clearly emerged as "the boss and cacique of Guerrero," especially since Héctor F. López and Joaquín Amaro, his only possible rivals in the local military, were ordered to leave Guerrero by Carranza.[146] This was a watershed in the Mexican revolution in Guerrero, since, after more than five years of struggle between contending factions, a single group had emerged as the controlling force in the state. If the revolution in Guerrero had taken the form of a contest for the inheritance of the Alvarez *cacicazgo*, it was perhaps fitting that the winner should be a native of Atoyac, the birthplace of Juan Alvarez.

Guerrero thus entered a brief period of relative quiet, almost of normality, but the state had entered the Constitutionalist fold quite late. Two years previously, in April 1915, Alvaro Obregón had inflicted two heavy defeats on Villa, Carranza's principal rival, at Celaya and had subsequently driven him back to his mountain hideouts in Chihuahua. Zapata likewise had been pushed back to the confines of Morelos, and the victorious Constitutionalists had already held a constitutional convention and promulgated a new constitution in January 1917. Gradually, Carranza'a northern generals were restoring the federal government's control over the nation, and Guerrero was no exception to this process of normalization, but before the Carrancistas could exercise a degree of power in the state, they would have to confront the entrenched local interests of the Mariscalistas.

Mariscal was busily consolidating his political position. In July 1917 he took a step in this direction with his election as constitutional governor, and further strengthened his military hold on Guerrero by forming *defensas sociales* in the north to ward off the Zapatista threat.[147] He took little trouble to conceal his political ambitions, pressing Carranza to give him control of military operations in Morelos as well as in Guerrero. However, Mariscal's unbridled ambition for local political power was soon to lead to open confrontation with the First Chief, who, firmly entrenched in the presidency since April, was quite obviously unwilling to permit Mariscal to stake out Guerrero, and still less Morelos, as his private domain. By the end of the year the decision had been taken to oust Mariscal from control of the "South," and the occasion was Mariscal's visit to Mexico City to confer with Carranza in mid December. He met with the First Chief on a number of occasions, but suddenly, on 25 January, he was arrested for allegedly attempting to prevent his escort of *guerrerense* troops from being dispatched to Manzanillo, a clear breach of military discipline.[148]

The effects of Mariscal's arrest in Guerrero were electrifying. On 17 February his escort in Mexico City attempted to return to Guerrero, but was attacked by federal forces before it could leave

the city. Meanwhile, Major Gatica, the commander of the Mariscalista garrison in Iguala, was threatening that if Mariscal "was not
promptly released there would be disorders in the state." Gatica,
General Pablo Vargas, a senior Mariscalista officer, Interim Governor Julio Adams, and the state Congress all withdrew to Acapulco to
give themselves time to consider their best course of action.[149] In all
likelihood, they would have accepted a *fait accompli* which they
could do little to change, but Carranza was clearly anxious to press
home the advantage gained by the arrest of Mariscal by using the
ensuing disquiet as an excuse to dispatch troops to Guerrero to dis-
mantle Mariscal's military organization. Mariscal's remaining supporters clearly had little choice but to resist when General Fortunato
Maycotte arrived in Acapulco on 10 March with federal troops, pos-
ing a direct threat to Mariscal's forces in particular and to local autonomy in general. The U.S. vice consul neatly summed up the mood
among the Mariscalistas:

> Before the arrival of Government troops there appeared to be a
> desire on the part of the local soldiers to return to their homes
> and let matters quiet down, hoping that . . . General Mariscal
> would be dealt with justly. . . . The arrival of the troops has
> enabled the leaders to incite the soldiers to open rebellion with
> the cry of "Mariscal" and "The State of Guerrero." An aggra-
> vated condition seems to have been brought about in the Cen-
> tral Government's attempt to eliminate the Mariscal power.
> With tact Mariscal could have been held in line with other
> Central Government supporters. . . . The action determined
> upon bids fair to throw local troops and many of the people of
> the state in opposition to the Central Government.[150]

Mariscal's supporters prepared to resist the federal intrusion. In
March Interim Governor Adams and General Vargas travelled to
Chilpancingo and Chilapa to raise funds for revolutionary activities,[151] and in April the state legislature and the governor formally
protested Mariscal's arrest and demanded his release. However,
while eager to retain their hegemony in Guerrero, Mariscal's followers were, at the same time, reluctant to incur the wrath of Carranza, whose Constitutionalist faction had emerged triumphant
from the struggle with Villa and Zapata. Thus, while protesting the
dispatch of federal forces to the state and Mariscal's arrest, Governor
Adams left the door open to reconciliation, claiming that the hostile
attitude of General Maycotte had forced the local troops to take de-

fensive action, but that, nevertheless, they remained loyal to the Constitutionalists.[152] However, although the Mariscalistas seemed willing to negotiate, and despite reverses suffered by Maycotte on the Costa Grande, the government was clearly determined to crush all local opposition.

Since the outsider Maycotte had met with little success, Carranza turned to one of the state's native sons for help: Rómulo Figueroa, who had established his military and Carrancista credentials in Francisco Murguía's campaigns against Villa in the north, and who had, in 1914, for a time been governor and military commander of Zacatecas. The services of other members of the family to the Constitutionalist cause increased Carranza's confidence in Rómulo still further. Andrés, a young cousin who had first joined the revolutionary ranks in February 1914, had risen to command Murguía's Second Division, and Rómulo's brother Francisco had rendered service on the political front as a staunchly Carrancista delegate to the Convention of Aguascalientes, and later as a delegate to the constitutional convention of 1916–1917.[153] Of Guerrero's native revolutionaries, Rómulo was, then, an appropriate choice for the campaign against the Mariscalistas, and on 25 March he landed with his troops in Acapulco, immediately launching an energetic offensive on the Costa Grande.[154] By late July a number of Mariscalistas had capitulated, and on 11 August Interim Governor Adams surrendered to the forces of Maycotte.[155] However, the Mariscalista revolt did not finally come to an end until the last days of October, when the principal rebel leader, Silvestre Castro, an *agrarista* leader from Mariscal's native Atoyac, surrendered.[156]

The military phase of the revolution in Guerrero had now effectively come to an end. Only in the extreme north of the state and in Tierra Caliente did Zapatista bands still operate, but they were small groups of little military significance. Carranza was now able to appoint a new governor, and once again he looked to the Figueroas to protect his interests by appointing Francisco as provisional governor.[157] The revolution in Guerrero had thus come full circle. It had opened in 1911 with the rise to prominence of the group of Liberal rancheros led by the Figueroa brothers. Control of the state had, however, soon fragmented along more or less well defined regional lines: the Figueroas in the north around Iguala, Salgado in Tierra Caliente, Blanco in the center and on the Costa Chica, and Mariscal on the Costa Grande. From 1913 to 1918 the revolution in Guerrero bore a distinct resemblance to the nineteenth-century struggles between the local caciques for control of the "South." By 1919 all of these groups had torn themselves apart in the struggle, except for the Figueroas, who had absented themselves from the regional conflict in 1914, and thus were able to return to Guerrero in 1919 in a position of relative strength.[158]

However, the Figueroas did not return to Guerrero to enjoy the same apparently unassailable predominance which they had held, albeit fleetingly, in 1911; while in 1911 they had operated as powerful independent local chieftains, in 1919 they returned to the state with a command of federal troops as the agents of Carranza in his effort to establish a degree of control over the local political scene. After all, he had not put down the pretensions of Mariscal to dominate the state only to install a new set of regional caciques in the form of Rómulo and Francisco Figueroa, although, as time would show, Rómulo, at least, harbored ambitions to restore the family's grip on the reins of power in Guerrero.

While the political climate on the national level made the establishment of a regional *cacicazgo* ever more difficult, changes in the makeup of the revolutionary elite in Guerrero itself made the realization of Figueroa's ambitions still more problematical. With most of the main leaders of the revolution in Guerrero dead or in disgrace, a number of younger minor revolutionary figures would come to power from 1921 to 1941. These were, by and large, men whose careers had been mostly civilian in character, a fact which of itself set them clearly apart from the military chieftains of 1911 to 1919. A fairly typical example of these civilian revolutionaries was Eduardo Neri, nephew of General Canuto A. Neri, who led the 1893 revolt against Governor Arce, and one of a generation of young intellectuals who would play a significant role in the state's politics (among them, Miguel F. Ortega and Ezequiel Padilla). Closely associated with this group were Rodolfo Neri, Eduardo's uncle and a slightly older man, and Héctor F. López, unlike the others a man whose revolutionary career was made in the armed forces. López had been a close associate of Gertrudis G. Sánchez and had resigned from the army when his ambitions for the governorship had been frustrated in 1919 by the appointment of Mariscal to that post. Yet another state governor of the postrevolutionary period made his army career on the general staff of Sánchez: Alberto F. Berber, like López a military man, but one whose achievements on the battle field were fairly modest. Another military man was Gabriel Guevara, who was linked with the civilians by education, since he had been a contemporary in the Escuela Preparatoria y Normal in Chilpancingo of Eduardo Neri, Miguel Ortega, and Ezequiel Padilla.[159] The outsider in this list of postrevolutionary figures was Adrián Castrejón, a minor Zapatista general, who rose to prominence by supporting Obregón against the de la Huerta revolt in 1923. The story of the rise of these minor revolutionaries to power in Guerrero, and the elimination from the scene of the last of the revolutionary caciques, Rómulo Figueroa, was the next stage in the story of the revolution in the state.

6. The Eclipse of the Figueroas and the Emergence of the New Revolutionary State: 1920–1941

On the national level, the revolution came to an end with the promulgation of the new constitution on 31 January 1917. Although fighting continued, and both Zapata and Villa remained at large, the writing was on the wall for the opponents of the Constitutionalists. The new regime depended for its survival on the revolutionary army, which, led by Obregón, had saved the First Chief, Venustiano Carranza, from the Conventionist forces of Villa and Zapata. "But it was not a national army. It was a collection of chieftains . . . or robber barons. . . . Certainly it had no relation to that modern institution the state."[1] In short, as Raymond Buve has noted, during the armed struggle the country had reverted to the classic *caudillaje* of pre-Porfirian days.[2] It was Carranza's attempt to go over the heads of the military caudillos by imposing the candidacy of the civilian Ignacio Bonillas in the 1920 presidential elections which caused his downfall and finally his death on 20 May 1920.

The Agua Prieta revolt brought to power a group of Sonoran generals, chief among whom were Alvaro Obregón, Plutarco Elías Calles, and Adolfo de la Huerta. These men took up and refined a new style of government which sought "to manipulate (even to create) political institutions of a modern 'associational' character,"[3] which had been provided for in the constitution of 1917, but which Carranza had shown some hesitation to use to the full.[4] The basic implements of this new associational style of politics were the social reforms which the new constitution introduced, and which "were, before all and above all, political weapons in the hands of the rulers of the state. . . . In practice, the social reforms were employed as instruments of power."[5] The new regime, which "pitched a national appeal, in terms of concrete, articulate policies, to broad collectivities within Mexican society," stood in marked contrast to the more traditional currents of the revolution, whose "political objectives were usually couched in retrospective, even nostalgic terms," and who were "locked into local society" and proved unable to transcend localism.[6]

While this contrast had been evident on a national level in the rivalry between the Constitutionalists and the Villista-Zapatista alliance, it was equally obvious on the state level in the 1920s. The more traditional revolutionary leadership came from people of rural, often middle-class origin ("rancheros, petty traders . . . artisans" and the like), whose "objectives, whether social, political or economic, were both local, and, inasmuch as they derived from an opposition to change, conservative. They lacked any sense of overall strategy for national development."[7] While a few of these men, like Saturnino Cedillo, might survive into the 1930s, by the early 1920s they already represented the wave of the past.

In contrast, in Jalisco, Veracruz, Tamaulipas, Tabasco, Yucatán, and elsewhere, a new breed of modernist political leader emerged in the 1920s. These men

> had an urban rather than a rural background. They had usually enjoyed secondary or even higher education, and . . . they had a clear idea of national economic and political developments. They . . . did not command loyalty through charisma or a record of military success . . . and . . . mobilised support through their control of the machinery of government. They helped the labor unions that backed them and created unions where none existed. Similarly they set up peasant organizations through which they gave *ejidal* grants in return for votes. Working from the centers of state [bureaucracy] they extended their influence into the rural sector. Their objectives were to obtain high office within the national [bureaucracy], from where they could create a power base similar in nature but larger in scale to the one they enjoyed in their home states.[8]

Its modern, bureaucratic, and associational character notwithstanding, this new political style could skillfully use and adapt more traditional political methods such as *caudillismo*, personalism, and *caciquismo*.[9] The 1920s were "the laboratory of the Revolution"[10] from which the contemporary political system emerged during the 1930s.

The new revolutionary regime rested on three pillars: the army, the labor unions (especially the CROM), and the *agraristas*. When 20% of the officers and 40% of the enlisted men of the army rebelled in 1923, Obregón's government was saved by the *agraristas* and the CROM, both of which gave invaluable services to the regime. The power of the army declined steadily throughout the 1920s, as the abortive rebellions of 1927 and 1929 bear witness, while the importance of the *agraristas*—and of the CROM, whose leader, Luis N. Morones, became the right-hand man of Calles—grew steadily.[11] The assassination of President-elect Obregón in 1928 led to the formation of the Partido Nacional Revolucionario (PNR). The PNR brought together and channeled the aspirations of the various groups on which the government's power rested, providing Calles and his allies, Saturnino Cedillo, Lázaro Cárdenas, Juan Andrew Alamazán, and Joaquín Amaro, with a potent instrument of political control.[12]

The regime of Lázaro Cárdenas (1934–1940) was the watershed of the Mexican revolution. Rather than breaking radically, as some historians have suggested, with the preceding revolutionary regimes, Cárdenas took up many of the policies followed more or less haphazardly by Obregón and Calles and pushed them to their logical conclusion.[13] Agrarian reform and labor organization were speeded up, the railways and the electrical and petroleum industries were nationalized, and the structure of the PNR was reformed, considerably reducing the influence of the military in the new Partido de la Revolución Mexicana.[14] Cárdenas "created a relationship of direct dependency on the machinery of government among the major interest groups in national life—the *ejidatarios*, the small farmers, urban labor, and the industrialists."[15] The Cárdenas regime laid the foundations of the contemporary Mexican political system and of the Mexican economic "miracle." In the long run, the central achievement of the Mexican revolution was to establish the absolute primacy of the national state.[16]

For Guerrero, the years of Obregón, Calles, and Cárdenas were a painful and chaotic experience. Rival groups jockeyed for power and influence in the state while the federal government struggled to reassert its control in Guerrero. Indeed, if any sense may be made of the political history of Guerrero in this period, it is in terms of a haphazard but relentless process of the reestablishment of central political control over the state. The revolutionary struggle itself had facilitated this task, since some of the most powerful revolutionary leaders in Guerrero had been eliminated by 1919. Ambrosio Figueroa had died in 1913, and Julián Blanco in 1915, while Jesús H. Salgado had been reduced to a negligible force in military terms. The removal of Silvestre G. Mariscal from the state governorship had been another step toward the reestablishment of central political control. However, one major revolutionary cacique, Rómulo Figueroa, still exercised a powerful influence on the course of events in the state, and the federal executive by no means had the last word in the affairs of Guerrero.

The military pacification of the state had still not been completed when Francisco Figueroa took office as governor in January 1919. Jesús H. Salgado was still at large in Tierra Caliente. Although he was killed in battle in June, in March elements of the forces of Cipriano Jaimes had rebelled against Carranza's government in Tierra Caliente, and on the Costa Grande Jesús Cíntora, an old Salgadista, roamed the countryside.[17] Nevertheless, the revolution now entered a phase of reconstruction, however slow. In the first months of 1919 the Comisión Local Agraria was established in Guerrero, and Governor Figueroa looked forward to the creation of small property, "which can be the basis of our agricultural development, as it has been in France and other cultured countries."[18] Plans were undertaken to establish an agricultural school in Iguala and a university in Chilpancingo, and a few small public works projects were put in motion.[19]

Politically the Figueroas were dominant in Guerrero. They occupied the civil government, and Rómulo was charged with an important role in the military pacification of the state. The two brothers further enhanced their standing in the state by supporting Alvaro Obregón in the successful Agua Prieta revolt of 1920. On 13 April of that year Obregón escaped the surveillance of Carranza's secret police and, disguised as a railway worker, made his way to Iguala. Obregón had already prepared the ground in Guerrero by obtaining the support of a number of important local figures. The federal *diputados* for Guerrero—Custodio Valverde, Miguel F. Ortega, Ignacio Pérez Vargas, José Castilleja—and Senator José Inocente Lugo, the former Maderista governor, had publicly declared their support for him.[20] Moreover, the day before Obregón's escape, Héctor F. López had set out for Guerrero to confer with Rómulo and Francisco Figueroa, and with the military commander of the state, General Fortunato Maycotte, in an attempt to enlist the support of the local military and civil administrations. Unable to contact Rómulo in Iguala, López arranged with Colonel Joaquín F. Romero, Profesor Urbano Lavín, and Lic. Trinidad Mastache to receive and protect Obregón on his arrival. Wasting no time, on 14 April López conferred with Maycotte, who agreed to join the rebellion, and on the following day with Governor Figueroa, who, however, was reluctant to commit himself before he was sure of adequate military support.[21] Pledges of support for Obregón came from other local luminaries, including Eduardo and Rodolfo Neri and Cipriano Jaimes.[22]

Upon his arrival in Iguala, Obregón met with Rómulo Figueroa, who had returned posthaste from his military duties in Tierra Caliente and who offered his unconditional support. On 17 April Obregón arrived in Chilpancingo with General Maycotte and his civilian allies,[23] and two days later Governor Francisco Figueroa publicly denounced Carranza, accusing him of attempting to impose Ignacio Bonillas in the presidency and a slate of Carrancista *diputados* in the federal Congress. Figueroa called on the state legislature to support the rebellion launched in Sonora by Adolfo de la Huerta and Plutarco Elías Calles,[24] which it duly did on the following day.[25] Events moved fast, and on 12 May Rómulo Figueroa led a column composed of regular troops and of volunteers from the *defensas sociales* in a drive toward Toluca, which he occupied unopposed a few days later.[26] Rómulo and Francisco's active support of Obregón's call to revolt contrasted sharply with the response of their cousin Andrés Figueroa (promoted to the rank of brigadier general by Carranza on 14 April), who mounted a fierce resistance to the rebel forces in Chihuahua.[27] Despite such pockets of resistance, however, Carranza's regime collapsed with remarkable speed, and on 20 May he was killed while fleeing toward Veracruz.

In the short term, the Figueroas' support of Obregón in 1920 did much to consolidate their position in Guerrero. No sooner had Carranza been deposed than Rómulo was named *jefe de las operaciones militares* in Guerrero on 5 June 1920,[28] thus giving the brothers control of both the civil government and the military command of the state. As in 1911, however, their grip on the reins of power in Guerrero was not as firm as it seemed, for, while Obregón had to reward the support and protection given by the Figueroas in 1920, he was not willing to allow them absolute control in Guerrero.

Local political conditions favored an attempt to clip the Figueroas' wings, for a younger generation of revolutionaries was coming to prominence in Guerrero which might be willing to exchange political support for the central government for patronage to advance their own careers. Rómulo and Francisco Figueroa were members of a generation of revolutionaries born between 1857 and 1870, a generation which also embraced Ambrosio Figueroa, Julián Blanco, and Silvestre G. Mariscal (and probably also Jesús H. Salgado). In 1920, however, Obregón received support from a number of younger men whose role in the revolution had been relatively minor. Of this group only General Héctor F. López had played any significant part in the military phase of the revolution, particularly in 1916 when he and Joaquín Amaro conducted an offensive which broke the back of Zapatista resistance in northern Guerrero. He was well connected politically, having been the secretary of the revolutionary chieftain

Gertrudis G. Sánchez in Michoacán, and was a close friend of José Inocente Lugo. In 1916 he had been the candidate for the governorship of the Club Liberal Constitucionalista Guerrerense, but the appointment of Silvestre G. Mariscal as governor of Guerrero had frustrated this ambition, and in the following year López resigned from the army. The fall of Carranza saw a revival of López's political fortunes, however, when he was elected senator for Guerrero, defeating the Figueroas' candidate, Donaciano López.[29] Other supporters of Obregón included Lic. Miguel F. Ortega, who was elected to the federal Congress in August 1920, and two years later to the Senate, and Lic. Eduardo Neri, an opposition *diputado* in 1913 under Huerta, who found his reward for his support of Obregón with his appointment as *procurador de justicia*, a post he held until August 1922.[30]

López, Ortega, Neri, and others were members of the younger generation of revolutionaries. Still more crucially, their power base, and the very structure of their revolutionary careers, was different from that of the older revolutionaries. Lacking an independent power base of political or military support in the state, these younger revolutionary politicians were dependent on Obregón and the federal government for support and for access to elective or appointed office. Furthermore, their careers were to be of a civilian bureaucratic hue, in contrast to the Figueroas, who had carved out their careers in the military struggles of 1911 to 1917. Ultimately, the future lay with these new civilian *políticos*, rather than with the established military caciques, a significant shift in the state's body politic which would become apparent in 1923, but whose beginnings could already be glimpsed in 1920.

By 1921, when elections for state governor were scheduled, the writing was already on the wall for the Figueroas. Their opponent was Lic. Rodolfo Neri, uncle of Eduardo, and son of General Canuto A. Neri, who had led the 1893 rebellion against Francisco O. Arce. Backed by his nephew, who had considerable influence in Mexico City, and "at the suggestion of General Obregón," a group of local citizens launched Neri's candidacy for the governorship of Guerrero.[31] Neri was opposed in the elections by Donaciano López, a close friend of Rómulo Figueroa, who had been one of his aides when Figueroa was military governor of Zacatecas in 1915, and who had been secretary of government in Francisco Figueroa's outgoing administration.[32] Neri's victory in the elections was overwhelming and was the origin of the conflict, which soon became evident, between Governor Neri and Rómulo Figueroa, who retained his command of the federal forces in Guerrero.[33] Thus the Figueroas' predominance in the state was short-lived. The political life of Guerrero from 1921 to the spring of 1924 was dominated by the struggle of the last of the revolutionary caciques to assert his ambitions for control of the state. In this he was opposed by the new generation of young revolutionaries of which Governor Neri was the figurehead, and which allied itself with Obregón, and, lacking military power in Guerrero, was dependent on his support. When the struggle between Obregón and the army broke out in 1923, the president backed this dependent civilian group rather than the independent military, represented by Rómulo Figueroa. Figueroa's local ambitions, combined with the bitter enmity of Rodolfo Neri, were key factors in the complex gestation of the de la Huerta revolt in Guerrero.

Figueroa and Neri drew their support from quite different power bases. Figueroa's influence was based on his control of the federal military and of the local volunteer forces, which he supplied with arms in the teeth of vigorous objections from Governor Neri. Neri, in contrast, was an active backer of *agrarista* and labor groups, which constituted his major source of support. Clashes between Figueroa's troops and the *agrarista* and labor supporters of the governor were especially frequent on the coast, where Juan R. Escudero, a radical politician based in Acapulco, was Neri's organizer, but Figueroa also actively opposed agrarian activity in the district of Mina in Tierra Caliente and in his own home base around Huitzuco.[34] In January 1923 Figueroa wrote to Obregón that *agrarista* politicians were undermining "the peace and security of the state, sowing a principle of anarchism [so] that Russia will be left far behind the directors of the said policies,"[35] and a few months later he told the *agraristas* of Iguala that "if we want lands we should buy them."[36]

Figueroa's distaste for *agrarismo* was an expression not only of his political differences with Governor Neri, but also of the ranchero's respect for private property. Thus, while he was unwilling to provide protection for the *agraristas* of San José Poliutla, he provided troops to protect landowners' interests.[37] Indeed, Figueroa's own Rancho de Tequicuilco was threatened by the *agraristas* of Cuacán and Tequicuilco. In May 1922 he had the agrarians disarmed, and in the following month a number of them were arrested by General Amador Acevedo on Figueroa's orders.[38] Elsewhere, in May 1923, the *vecinos* of Cocula, Atlixtac, Apipilulco, Apango, and Xonacatla, unable to obtain land to work, since the landowners refused to rent it to them, seized by force the land they needed, but federal troops were promptly sent and the offenders arrested.[39] In the following month, Figueroa's troops arrested the committee of the ejido of Río Balsas.[40]

The alignment of forces in Guerrero, with Neri and the *agra-*

ristas ranged against Figueroa and the federal troops, was reflected in the figures for land distribution. While in 1920 only 1,620 hectares had been distributed by resolutions of the state governor, in 1921 (Neri's first year in office) 25,843 hectares were given to ejidos. Neri continued to accelerate the rate of distribution to his *agrarista* clients, granting 35,813 hectares in 1922, and 37,692 in 1923. However, the political intent of Neri's reform efforts was dramatically underlined in 1924, when, as soon as the de la Huertistas had been defeated and Figueroa's power in Guerrero had been crushed, the rate of reform plummeted to a mere 4,084 hectares. The amount of land distributed by resolutions of the federal executive reflected similar political concerns, although Obregón reacted somewhat more slowly to local events than Neri. Thus in 1922, when the prospect of rebellion seemed less immediate, a mere 4,422 hectares were allocated to ejidos in Guerrero by the federal government. In 1923, however, as the local and national political crisis deepened, Obregón granted 37,022 hectares in Guerrero, over half of them in the district of Hidalgo, where Figueroa's headquarters and the vital rail link with Mexico City were situated.[41] Reflecting the concentration of the government's agrarian reform efforts in the north of the state, agrarian agitation and organization were particularly intense in the Iguala area. A *congreso de campesinos* was held in the city in January 1923, and Obregón showed himself sensitive to *agrarista* demands in the area.[42]

Thus, by 1923 the state and federal governments were lined up side by side with the *agraristas* against the local military. However, there was still one further element to the political crisis of 1922–1923: the state Congress, where a bloc of *diputados* hostile to Neri had formed. As early as July 1922, Saturnino Martínez, a congressman loyal to Neri, wrote to Héctor F. López that "the politics against the governor had taken on alarming characteristics to the point that the traitor *diputados* had pacted to reelect themselves." This was dangerous, since the next Congress (to be elected in November 1922) would oversee the election of Neri's successor in the governorship. It was, therefore, essential "that the legislature be formed by LOYAL men who would know how to live up to their duty," that is, to elect Neri's chosen successor, Héctor F. López.[43]

In early 1923 this local dispute became caught up in the national political struggle which was beginning to develop over the election of Obregón's successor in the presidency. In the 1922 elections for the federal Congress, the Partido Cooperatista Nacional (PCN), led by Jorge Prieto Laurens, had succeeded in wresting control of the legislature from the Partido Liberal Constitucionalista (PLC), of which Eduardo Neri, Governor Neri's nephew, was president. This was an important victory for the PCN, since the party which dominated the federal Congress would, in the last resort, decide who would be chosen as Obregón's successor. However, in order to exercise still greater control over the choice of the next president, the PCN strove to influence the state governments and launched a number of assaults on the administrations of states which were not sympathetic to its aims. Attempts were made to unseat the governors of Jalisco and Nuevo León, without success, but the strategy bore dividends in Puebla, in March 1922, when the PCN seized control of the state executive.[44]

Guerrero, with its governor linked by family ties to the rival PLC, and with a ready-made opposition, was an obvious target for the PCN's maneuvers. In September 1922, four of the dissident *diputados* went to Mexico City to confer with the leaders of the PCN, who offered them their support. The federal congressmen for Guerrero, Ezequiel Padilla, Arturo Martínez Adame, Moisés Herrera, and Ignacio Pérez Vargas (all PCN members), together with other PCN luminaries, traveled to Guerrero to support the dissidents in the November elections. On 29 November the dissident congressmen, led by Alberto R. Guevara (formerly *oficial mayor* in the administration of Francisco Figueroa), abandoned the local Congress, thus breaking the quorum and preventing any business from being carried out.[45] On 28 December the dissidents moved from Chilpancingo to Iguala to establish a rival Congress, claiming that they were being harassed by Neri.[46] Meanwhile, in concert with the PCN, they launched a public attack on Neri in Mexico City, denouncing him to President Obregón and the federal Congress, and Obregón responded to the pressure by promising the dissidents the protection of Rómulo Figueroa's federal troops.[47]

On 1 February 1923 the dissident *diputados* returned to Chilpancingo with a federal escort and established themselves as a rival legislature, electing Moisés G. Herrera, a PCN federal congressman, provisional governor. U.S. Vice Consul Harry K. Pangburn judged that "the defeat of Rodolfo Neri seems complete,"[48] and the *comisión permanente* of the federal Congress, controlled by the PCN, tacitly recognized Herrera as provisional governor,[49] thus apparently sealing Neri's fate. However, the final element in the political equation was President Obregón, and he was not prepared to let the PCN dictate events in Guerrero. On 9 February he conferred with Rodolfo Neri and declared that he recognized him as the only legitimate executive authority in Guerrero. The federal escort given to the dissident congressmen was withdrawn, and the federal authorities were instructed to give Neri "the guarantees and facilities necessary for the exercise of his functions."[50] Faced with Obregón's determination to maintain Neri in office at all costs, the PCN was forced to accept defeat, as it was seven months later in San Luis Potosí when Obregón frustrated the party's attempt to take over that state.[51] In April Saturnino Martínez, who a year earlier had feared that the governor might lose control of the state Congress, and thus of the gubernatorial election, could now report that all but one of the local deputies were ready to support Neri's designated successor, Héctor F. López.[52]

With the "undivided support of the central government," Neri now felt himself able to make "determined efforts to oust Gen. Rómulo Figueroa."[53] Figueroa became the subject of a hostile press campaign orchestrated by Governor Neri and his supporters, principal among whom was Saturnino Martínez, the Tepecoacuilco politician and nephew of the *hacendado* Miguel Montúfar.[54] In March the tensions between the supporters of Figueroa and Neri's *agrarista* followers on the coast led to a minor rebellion in the Tecpan area, when Valente de la Cruz, an agrarian supporter of Neri, led an attack on the federal garrison of San Luis, which successfully repulsed the attackers.[55] Violence continued to erupt between the two factions: for example, in October when a gun battle took place in Teloloapan between supporters of Neri and federal troops commanded by Colonel Francisco López. A number of Neristas were killed in the fighting, and each side accused the other of unprovoked aggression.[56]

By the autumn Rómulo Figueroa was committed to rebellion. During the summer he had interviewed President Obregón in an effort to stave off Neri's attacks on him, but Obregón apparently refused to take any action, and Figueroa consequently began to establish contacts with supporters of Adolfo de la Huerta, notably with Carlos Carranco Cardoso of Tepecoacuilco. In the last week of November Figueroa held a meeting of the senior officers under his command in Iguala, in which it was agreed to support any armed movement in favor of de la Huerta.[57] Obregón, however, clearly had wind of Figueroa's intentions, and decided to force his hand by ordering his transfer to the state of Hidalgo.[58] Figueroa was faced with a clear dilemma: either he accepted his transfer and abandoned his ambitions in Guerrero, or he risked a premature rebellion. He opted for rebellion, but, in order to buy time, telegraphed the secretary of war, stressing the local causes of the revolt and making no mention of de la Huerta, since the national rebellion was still not ready. Figueroa stated that the "pueblos of the state, tired of suffering ill-treatment by the local government and in view [of] having become aware [of the] removal [of] forces [under] my command . . . resolved to rise up in arms against [the] local government. . . . Faced with this attitude, which I consider justified . . . I find myself obliged to assume the leadership of the movement to guarantee order." In response, Obregón gave Figueroa until 6 A.M. on 1 December to reconsider his attitude,[59] but the deadline expired without any reply from the rebel camp.

At first, things did not go at all well for Figueroa. The premature nature of the rebellion scared off his allies, who were unwilling to commit themselves to such a risky enterprise. Carlos Carranco Cardoso failed to supply the hundred men he had promised in Tepecoacuilco, and General Epifanio Rodríguez, commander of the *defensas sociales* of the Cocula area, did not produce the militia forces he had pledged. Similarly, Figueroa's military subordinates in Chilpancingo, Tlapa, and Acapulco refused to join the revolt, leaving him with only the troops directly under his orders and 200 men of the *defensa social* of Teloloapan.[60]

On 1 December the government mobilized troops under generals Tomás Toscano Arenal, Fabricio Urbalejo, and Lucas González to suppress the rebellion in Guerrero, and on 3 December Urbalejo entered Iguala.[61] Obregón, however, was still willing to negotiate and had already sent General Fortunato Maycotte, Francisco Figueroa, and Ezequiel Padilla to contact Figueroa, but they were unable to do so. Now, in order to buy time, Rómulo offered to negotiate his surrender, but when news of the rebellion of General Guadalupe Sánchez in Veracruz reached him, he broke off negotiations.[62] He was now irrevocably committed to the de la Huerta cause, and the waverers, evidently confident of a de la Huerta victory, now joined him in revolt. The federal garrisons of Chilpancingo and Acapulco and the attacking forces of General Toscano Arenal all defected to Figueroa's cause.[63]

Guerrero thus fell into Figueroa's hands with scarcely a shot having been fired. Now assured of military superiority in the state, he demanded the resignation of Rodolfo Neri, offering him his safety in return, but Neri refused to submit, and, accompanied by his closest associates and a small escort, fled to the mountains, managing to reach the coast, where he received the protection of his *agrarista* allies. Escorted by the agrarian forces of Silvestre Castro, the governor escaped to Zacualpan, in the state of Mexico.[64]

Temporarily in the ascendant, the rebels proceeded to consolidate their hold on Guerrero. By the end of the third week of December a provisional governor had been appointed, Profesor Urbano Lavín, who in 1920 had received Obregón on his arrival in Iguala.[65] On 22 December Rómulo Figueroa's forces entered Puente de Ixtla, just over the state line in Morelos. In late December and throughout January, Figueroa undertook a number of attacks in Morelos and the state of Mexico with a view to advancing on Cuernavaca and Mexico City itself. However, de la Huerta refused to authorize such a bold attack, and by late January the reverses suffered by the de la Huertistas in Puebla, Veracruz, and Michoacán made the planned offensive impossible.[66]

Within Guerrero itself, the only opposition to the cause of de la Huerta came from the *agraristas*. In the north, *agraristas* from a number of towns left Guerrero and joined the forces of the former Zapatistas Abacuc Román, Genovevo de la O, and Adrián Castrejón in Morelos.[67] It was on the coast, however, that the agrarians, led by the Escudero brothers, Baldomero and Amadeo Vidales, Valente de la Cruz, and Alberto Téllez, posed the most serious threat to Figueroa's forces. On the outbreak of the de la Huerta rebellion, Obregón had authorized Rodolfo Neri's chief allies on the Costa Grande, Juan, Felipe, and Francisco Escudero, to arm the *agraristas* of the coast. However, before they could complete the organization of the Obregonista militias, the brothers were arrested by the federal forces of Colonel Crispín Sámano and, at the instigation of the Spanish merchants of whom the Escuderos were bitter enemies, the brothers were executed by the rebel forces of Rosalío Radilla on 20 December 1923.[68] The overall command of the *agraristas* of the Costa Grande then passed to the Vidales brothers, Baldomero and Amadeo. By late December numerous armed bands of agrarians were threatening the ungarrisoned towns of the coast,[69] and by the end of January 1924 Consul Bucklin was reporting from Acapulco that "the agrarians show increasing strength and now hold several towns."[70] The strength of the *agraristas* continued to grow, and in early February they decisively defeated the de la Huertistas at Petatlán, obliging Rómulo Figueroa himself to rush to Acapulco to drive them back from the city.[71] However, although Figueroa succeeded in driving the agrarians back temporarily, the Vidales brothers had established themselves as a force to be reckoned with and were to control the Costa Grande for the next five years. Thus Governor Neri's reliance on *agrarista* support to counter the military power of Figueroa injected an important new element into Guerrero's political geography.

Despite *agrarista* harassment on the coast, Figueroa's control of Guerrero remained firm. However, the collapse of the de la Huerta rebellion in other states rendered the Guerrero rebels' position untenable, and reports of the surrender of Figueroa's allies began to appear in the Mexico City press on 10 March.[72] On the previous day Figueroa had informed de la Huerta of his determination to negotiate his own surrender, and within little more than a week all the major rebel chiefs of Guerrero had capitulated. Rómulo, his brother Francisco, and his senior officers were imprisoned in Santiago Tlatelolco a few days later.[73]

The political fortunes of the Figueroa family in Guerrero had reached their lowest point. Of the entire family, only Andrés, who again took a course exactly opposite to that of his cousins, backed the winning side. Stationed in Coahuila at the outbreak of the revolt, he fought for the Obregonista cause on several fronts and at the end of the uprising received an appointment in the Ministry of War.[74] In Guerrero, however, Rómulo Figueroa's ambitions for regional domination had been dealt a decisive blow. The alignment of local political forces from 1921 to 1923 was an important factor in the development and outcome of the de la Huerta rebellion, but the key factor in the state's political crisis was the federal executive. Neri could not have survived the opposition of the local military and of dissident elements in the state legislature without the support of Obregón, who was not willing to countenance the establishment of a quasi-autonomous military *cacicazgo* in Guerrero, nor to permit the state government to fall into the hands of the PCN, which clearly had ambitions to determine the presidential succession, against Obregón's wishes if need be. The defeat of the de la Huertistas reasserted the presidential power to exercise ultimate control over local politics. Moreover, the last of the major revolutionary caciques had been eliminated from the local scene. The Figueroas had lost the battle for local political power, and the younger generation of revolutionaries, of whom Neri was the figurehead, retained power in Guerrero with the election of one of their number, Héctor F. López, as governor in 1925. The Figueroas would not begin their comeback until the election of Gabriel R. Guevara to the governorship in 1933.

The defeat of Rómulo Figueroa and the de la Huertistas left Neri's hand greatly strengthened in the elections for state governor for the period 1925 to 1929, although a number of his enemies deftly switched to the Obregonista camp at the last moment. Such was the case of Ezequiel Padilla, for example. The coming gubernatorial elections had been one of the undercurrents of the enmity between Rómulo Figueroa and Neri. The Neristas accused Rómulo of seeking to impose his brother Francisco in the governorship, an accusation which was hotly denied by Figueroa's supporters. The Figueroa faction replied that Neri himself was bent on imposing Héctor F. López as his successor, a charge which was almost certainly true.[75] The defeat of the de la Huertistas destroyed any possibility of a Figueroista candidacy, and the mechanics of López's election were, therefore, greatly simplified.

López had backing from the Partido Liberal Constitucionalista, of which Eduardo Neri was president, and of the Partido Agrarista, although at the same time he drew support from a group of landowners in Tierra Caliente.[76] Rodolfo Neri's erstwhile opponents, meanwhile, had thrown their support behind Profesor Adolfo Cienfuegos y Camus.[77] While the official results of the elections held on 8 November 1924 gave López a victory of 38,429 votes over 24,596 for Cienfuegos y Camus, some reports indicated that the real victor was Cienfuegos,[78] but, despite the agitation of the defeated Cienfueguistas, López took office as governor on 1 April 1925.[79]

López's election signaled a marked shift away from support of *agrarismo* by the state government. Although López had received the backing of the Partido Agrarista, and despite the fact that his predecessor Rodolfo Neri had relied heavily on *agrarista* support, the new governor did not clearly define his attitude to *agrarismo* during his electoral campaign,[80] and it was doubtless his equivocal position which cost him the support of some *agrarista* leaders, among them Silvestre Castro of Atoyac.[81] López's attitude toward the agrarian reform was of some importance, since the *agraristas*, who had flexed their muscles against the de la Huerta rebels, had become an important factor in local politics. After the de la Huerta revolt was over, less than half of the *agraristas* on the coast obeyed the orders of the federal commander, General Rafael Sánchez, to lay down their arms or join the regular army. Since the federals garrisoned only Acapulco, the entire Costa Grande was left in the hands of the *agraristas*, who drove out the landowners, cattle ranchers, and merchants of the region. However, the *agraristas'* bitterest hatred was reserved for the Spanish merchant houses of Acapulco.[82]

López waited until June 1925 to give his views on the agrarian reform. He told the secretary of agriculture and development that he considered it essential to respect the small property, to do justice to both landowners and *agraristas*, and to exclude any political influence in the reform process.[83] In his first report to the state Congress, López again stressed the need for equal treatment of both landowners and agrarians, "that is to say, that the quality of the lands with which grants are made should be the same as those which are left to the landowners, since to establish a privilege of one or the other would be to violate one of the fundamental principles of the revolution."[84] López ordered that ejidos should preferably be granted uncultivated land, "because initiative and work should be respected," and in López's native Coahuayutla the *agrarista* movement was vigorously suppressed.[85] Nevertheless, despite his evident distaste for agrarian reform, in his first year in office López distributed 49,946 hectares. In 1926, however, the figure fell to 14,689 and in 1927 to 8,481 hectares.[86]

López's anti-agrarian policies were a direct challenge to an interest group which had become a major factor in Guerrero since 1923 and consequently provoked considerable hostility on the part of the local *agraristas*. Agrarian discontent was evident from the very month in which he took office. On the coast Valente de la Cruz, who had been one of Neri's supporters in 1923, attempted to start an uprising in Tecpan. In the same month the *agraristas* of Coyuca de Benítez and Pungarabato, in the district of Mina, where López had received support from landowning groups during the elections, deposed a number of *ayuntamientos* composed of "persons not very congenial to the *agraristas*."[87]

The most serious outbreak of agrarian discontent during López's administration, however, was the rebellion of the *agrarista* leaders of the Costa Grande, Amadeo and Baldomero Vidales. Owners of an Acapulco trading company, Hermanos Vidales, the two brothers engaged in selling seeds and vegetable products along the coast of Guerrero. They owned two ships, and their company had branches in ten coastal towns (including one in the state of Oaxaca). However, the coastal economy was dominated by the Spanish merchant houses of Acapulco, which owned considerable areas of land, controlled the fishing industry, and plied the shipping routes from Acapulco to Salina Cruz and Manzanillo.[88] The economic power of "the three houses" (as the merchant companies were known) was testified to by Vice Consul Pangburn, who had lived in Acapulco since before the revolution. The Spaniards, he noted, "have practically controled [sic] the commerce of this region and through their money and influence have exerted a dominating influence upon the local State government. They have controlled the sale and export of agricultural products of the coast district of Guerrero and, through combinations with corrupt local authorities, they have forced the farmers to sell to them only and at their own price." In addition, "they are large landowners and, probably through poli[ti]cal influence, they have avoided to date the partition of their land holdings as 'egidos' [sic] under the communal land law, even when American owned lands of this region had been so sacrificed."[89]

The competition between the Vidales brothers and the Spaniards was bitter,[90] and, when a political and labor movement directed against the Spaniards was organized in Acapulco, Amadeo and Baldomero became active members. The organizer of this movement was Juan R. Escudero, an associate of Ricardo Flores Magón, whom he had met in California during his student days, and like the Vidales a scion of a quite well heeled Acapulco trading family. Founder of the Liga de Trabajadores a Bordo de los Barcos y Tierra (the League of Ship and Shore Workers), Escudero formed the Partido Obrero de Acapulco (the Acapulco Workers' Party) for the 1920 elections.[91] As well as supporting the candidacy of Obregón, the party won control of the municipal government of Acapulco[92] and implemented a reformist program, forming consumer and fishing cooperatives and establishing a municipal paper bag and basket factory. The party also planned to found an agricultural colony by purchasing a local hacienda and pressed for the construction of a road linking Acapulco to Mexico City.[93] As an active supporter of Rodolfo Neri and *agrarismo*, and a bitter enemy of the Spaniards, Escudero was an obvious target for assassination when the de la Huerta revolt broke out, and on 20 December 1923 he and his two brothers were executed by rebel troops.[94] With the death of Escudero, the Vidales brothers emerged as the natural heirs to his movement.

While Escudero's Liga had begun as an urban labor union, the Vidales movement was entirely rural and, like many "revolutionary" rural movements in Mexico, looked to the past rather than to the future. In the nineteenth century land was often used by caciques to win support among the peasantry, and, in particular, to recruit soldiers. Similarly, some revolutionary chieftains—for example, Pancho Villa in Chihuahua and Saturnino Cedillo in San Luis Potosí[95]—founded military colonies as a reward to their troops. The Vidales brothers followed this same pattern of reward and recruitment, in 1925 forming a military agricultural colony known as the Unión de Ambas Costas on the land of two haciendas near Acapulco. Amadeo and Baldomero themselves contributed $20,979 to the project, while thirty-seven former members of their cavalry regiment chipped in with a total of $26,832.[96] However, the Vidales movement is most strikingly cast in a nineteenth-century mold by its Plan del Veladero, dated 6 May 1926, which denounced 300 years of "odious Spanish tyranny" and asserted that the Plan of Iguala, which had declared Mexico's independence, had protected the Spaniards' interests and enabled them to maintain their "monopoly," which had been left untouched by the Reforma, and had been actively protected by Porfirio Díaz. Thus the plan repeated the cry of "death to the *gachupines*" first heard in 1810 during the revolt of Hidalgo. However, now that the revolution had ushered in "National Socialism," the plan declared, all Spaniards should be expelled from Mexico, and all their property confiscated and turned over to the free municipalities.[97] The plan, therefore, blended the Vidales' own commercial interests with popular aspirations—the expulsion of the Spaniards and the strengthening of the municipalities.

Despite a split in the ranks of the Partido Obrero de Acapulco in 1925 which led the Vidales brothers to break away from the party first founded by Escudero, they easily mustered support for a revolt which they launched on 18 April 1926 with an attack on the cotton mill at Aguas Blancas, owned by one of the Spanish merchant houses.[98] American Vice Consul Pangburn believed that the revolt was sponsored by Mexico City politicians (perhaps by Alvaro Obregón himself), a belief fueled by the support Amadeo and Baldomero had received from both Obregón and Calles in founding the Unión de Ambas Costas.[99] In any case, the rebellion dragged on for almost three years, finally coming to an end in February 1929 with the surrender of Amadeo Vidales (Baldomero had been killed in battle) and his principal followers.[100]

The *agraristas* of Costa Grande were by no means Governor López's principal problem. Indeed, by a strange quirk of fate, he supported the rebellious Vidales faction in the 1926 congressional elections because of his own political difficulties with the Partido Obrero de Acapulco.[101] López faced further popular unrest in December 1926 when the Cristeros rebelled in Buenavista de Cuéllar and Tlapa, followed by uprisings in a number of towns throughout the state in May and June of the following year. In addition, the Cristeros soon established links with the Vidalista rebels.[102] On top of these troubles the governor was also facing a severe financial crisis,[103] but the real threat to his administration came, not from popular unrest or fiscal problems, but from the federal military command, which had been taken over by General Claudio Fox, sent to Guerrero to put down the Cristero and Vidalista rebellions.

López soon found himself at odds with Fox, who, according to Vice Consul Pangburn, "assumed arbitrary and despotic control over the political authorities of this state. He has, through his henchmen and the military authorities under his command, interfered directly in the installation of the 'Ayuntamientos' . . . at the cities heading the various districts of Guerrero as well as in the state and national congressional elections. No one has successfully opposed his wishes."[104] A showdown between the governor and the military was finally provoked by the question of the election of López's successor. The governor favored his secretary, Lic. Guillermo Miller, son of a landowner in Ometepec, while the military supported one of their number, the former Zapatista General Adrián Castrejón.[105] Unlike his predecessor Rodolfo Neri, López could not call on the *agraristas* for support against the military since he had alienated them by his hostility to agrarian reform. Therefore, unable to resist the military's maneuvers, López retired to Mexico City, leaving in his stead a local Congressman, Jesús B. Gutiérrez, and after an absence of several months finally resigned.[106]

Having squeezed López out of office, the military now moved to influence the choice of his successor. Although on the evening of 31 January López's supporters in Congress chose Jesús B. Gutiérrez as substitute governor, on the following day a session of Congress was called by López's opponents in the legislature, with the backing of the local military command. An anti-López majority was promptly manufactured by the handy expedient of forcing López's four closest followers in the legislature to resign, a fifth, who refused to resign, being promptly placed under arrest. The alternates of the *diputados* who resigned were summoned to constitute a quorum, and Colonel Enrique Martínez, a former state congressman and a native of Iguala, was appointed substitute governor.[107] Victory was not immediately assured, however, since López's supporters formed a rival legislature and continued to sustain the election of Gutiérrez as interim executive. Both groups began to lobby the federal Congress and President Calles, who on 14 February recognized Martínez as the legitimate governor of Guerrero, leaving Gutiérrez and his supporters little choice but to accept the verdict.[108]

Although there was probably more to López's resignation than meets the eye, his difficulties with General Fox were clearly a key factor in his ouster, as was his opposition to the election of Castrejón as his successor. Whatever other undercurrents there may have been, it was clear that, as in 1923, the deciding element in the local political conflict was the federal executive, which increasingly exercised ultimate control over state politics. At any rate, the removal of López was the prelude to a revival of agrarian radicalism in Guerrero which exemplified the associational style of government envisaged by Obregón and Calles.

Four months before Adrián Castrejón took office as governor of Guerrero an important event had taken place in Mexico City which was to form the basis of the contemporary Mexican political system. In July 1928 Alvaro Obregón had been assassinated shortly after being reelected as president, the constitution having been amended to permit him a second term. On 1 December, in an effort to heal the divisions caused in the revolutionary ranks by Obregón's death, Calles formed the Partido Nacional Revolucionario (the National Revolutionary Party, PNR) to provide an orderly institutional channel for resolving factional disputes. Although a response to an immediate political problem, the formation of the PNR proved to be a stroke of genius which was to shape the Mexican political system for decades.

Shortly after taking office, following the example of the new politics inaugurated in Mexico City, Castrejón founded two new political organizations to hold the state for Pascual Ortiz Rubio, the PNR candidate for the presidential elections of November 1929. These new organizations were the Partido Socialista de Guerrero (the Socialist Party of Guerrero, PSG) and the Liga de Comunidades y Sindicatos Campesinos del Estado de Guerrero (the League of Peasant Communities and Unions of the State of Guerrero).[109] The new organizations evidently carried out their task well: 40,855 votes were recorded for Ortiz Rubio in Guerrero against 216 for his two opponents.[110] The PSG and the Liga were, however, designed to do more than just win the elections for Ortiz Rubio. By means of the PSG it was hoped to affiliate the peasants and workers, "the immovable bulwark of our institutions and the magnificent support of Castrejón's government," to the new PNR.[111] The PSG was thus designed as a means by which to channel the support of the peasants and workers toward the new national party. As an extension of this role the PSG was also given the task of encouraging peasants to request land under the agrarian reform,[112] and, with the Liga, also represented peasants who had requested ejidos in their dealings with the agrarian and judicial authorities.[113] However, although these new political structures had potentially profound implications for the political organization of the state, they never approached the power achieved by similar parties and leagues in, for example, Veracruz and Tabasco. Indeed, the Liga and the PSG did not live long after Castrejón left the governorship, although the PSG did play its part in the elections for the governor's successor.[114]

In accord with the renewed emphasis on peasant support for the state government, Castrejón's first year in office was marked by a rapid increase in land distribution. In 1929 some 129,261 hectares were granted in resolutions signed by the governor, while presidential resolutions confirmed grants totaling 122,957, although actual distribution lagged behind somewhat (98,581 hectares were distributed in provisional possession, and 95,238 in definitive possession).[115] This sudden spurt in the rate of land distribution was repeated throughout the country and was principally a response to the growing threat of the Cristero rebellion.[116] In the following year, when the military crisis had passed, the rate of reform slumped by almost two-thirds and continued to fall during the rest of Castre-

jón's period in office. Indeed, in December 1930 Vice Consul Pangburn reported from Acapulco that Castrejón had "declared in my
presence that agrarian activities in this state were to shortly cease,
that new dotations of lands for ejidos were not to be made, but that
the dotations already under consideration were to be carried out."[117]
Certainly, Castrejón appeared to envisage a prompt end to the agrarian reform, since in September of the following year he declared his
determination to resolve the 393 *expedientes* still pending and reported that the PSG was urging all those entitled to request land to
do so.[118]

As the statistics indicate, Castrejón's agrarianism was quite
clearly as much a means of political manipulation, which could be
turned off and on at the government's convenience, as an instrument of social reform. Nevertheless, he was the clearest exponent in
Guerrero of the new associational style of government introduced
by Obregón and Calles. American Vice Consul Pangburn, a perceptive, although scarcely impartial, observer, painted a quite convincing picture of the governor. Castrejón, Pangburn wrote,

> has proved to be a good party man and undoubtedly has strong
> support from high officers in the national government.
> The July 1930 election for deputies and senators for the Mex-
> ican National Congress was carried by the governor to the con-
> trol of the National Revolutionist Party (P.N.R.) whose
> candidates (including at least two who were born outside of
> Guerrero) were accredited as winners by the State authorities.
> General Castrejon since his accession to power in the state
> of Guerrero has made every effort to hold the control of the
> lower classes, agrarians, etc., and has systematically opposed
> the property owners, merchants and industrialists by raising
> the state taxes from 25% to 33⅓% on rural and urban proper-
> ties, the establishment of the "business tax" (derecho de pa-
> tente) and the forced collection of the unjust so-called
> "catastral tax," the proceeds of which he has destined to form
> an alleged agricultural bank at the State Capital.[119]

Certainly, none of Castrejón's predecessors had so explicitly
sought the support of the peasantry and the workers as the basis of
the administration. Castrejón's populism had little in common, for
example, with the old-fashioned Liberalism of Héctor F. López, who
proclaimed the need to respect the rights of both *agraristas* and landowners and to draw support from all classes of society. The accelera-
tion of the agrarian reform during the administration of Castrejón

considerably expanded the government's clientele in Guerrero. More-over, land distribution was complemented by a reglamentary law of the federal law of idle lands (*tierras ociosas*) and a law creating the *fundo legal*. A state education law was drafted whose aim was to en-courage "social aspirations, feelings, and ideas which tend toward the improvement of the individual, of the home, and of the commu-nity in general, *improving the relations between society and the state*."[120] Castrejón's social reforms were designed to strengthen the dependency of the masses on the state apparatus, which, in turn, was to some degree dependent on popular support for its political survival.

Castrejón's period of office did not by any means transpire in an atmosphere of complete political calm. His administration was be-set by financial problems, and rumors that the governor was under heavy political fire and might lose his office circulated in 1929 and 1931. On the latter occasion, the arming of *agraristas* on the coast, led by the old rebel Amadeo Vidales, gave the rumors some cred-ence.[121] Nevertheless, compared to the turbulent years of Rodolfo Neri and Héctor F. López, Castrejón's term was remarkably quiet until the time came to elect his successor on 13 November 1932.

Castrejón, who had previously been compliant toward the wishes of the administration in Mexico City, threw his support be-hind the candidacy of Ezequiel Padilla, a prominent *guerrerense* pol-itician, and rallied the *agraristas* of Guerrero against the candidate of the PNR, General Gabriel R. Guevara, an *hacendado* with the rep-utation of being hostile to the *agraristas*, Castrejón's power base. Guevara had served in Guerrero for a time with Rómulo and Lino Figueroa, and his brother Alberto had been a close associate of both Rómulo and Francisco Figueroa.[122] His election marked the begin-ning of the comeback of the Figueroa family in Guerrero in the form of Ing. Rubén Figueroa, who in July 1934 was elected alternate *diputado* on the ticket of Alberto Guevara.[123] Once again, in the 1932 electoral campaign powerful local interests pitted themselves against the wishes of the central government and the national politi-cal machine. It was an uneven contest, and Guevara and the PNR won comfortably.[124]

Guevara's triumph in the elections, however, led to a bloody conflict between Guevaristas and Castrejonistas, partly because of the frustration of the latter, but also because the Castrejonistas won control of the *ayuntamientos* in the municipal elections in Decem-ber,[125] turning the tables on Guevara and the PNR. Why Guevara should have failed to control the *ayuntamientos*, while comfortably winning the state government, is not quite clear, but nevertheless this posed a serious threat to his ability to govern, since control of the municipal administrations was a vital element of the political base of the state government. The struggle between Guevaristas and Castrejonistas had already led to violence on 29 November when a PSG politician was murdered by Guevaristas in Mochitlán,[126] and in December a plot to murder Guevara was uncovered.[127]

The conflict took a turn for the worse when the solidly Guevarista state Congress took office on 1 March 1933. Castrejón refused to give a report of his administration as the constitution required, and the president of the legislature denounced the action of the governor, noting that "very soon the state will see its efforts crowned by the success of a new government which will know how to respect it."[128] The increasing tension between the two factions resulted in a bloody gun battle which took place in Chilpancingo on 22 March 1933, ten days before Guevara was due to take office. A group of Castrejón's supporters, stationed on the roof of his house, just off the main square of Chilpancingo, exchanged fire with a number of Guevarista state congressmen, leaving one *diputado* wounded and two other Guevara supporters dead. An official investigation found the Castrejonistas guilty of firing the first shots,[129] and, as a result, on 28 March Castrejón was removed from office by a vote of the Guevarista legislature, which appointed Deputy Ladislao Alarcón substitute governor, charged with handing the office over to Gabriel Guevara.[130]

With the election of Guevara, the PNR had won a famous victory over the political organization of an incumbent governor and had crushed Castrejón's attempt to assert a degree of independence from the national party. Nevertheless, on taking office, Guevara faced the task of securing a firm base of support for his administration, and as a first step purged the Castrejonista *ayuntamientos* in April 1933, charging that they "had joined together . . . to carry out a task of open opposition" to the new administration.[131]

Another important basis of support for Guevara's government was the control of the *comisariados ejidales*, the committees which administered the lands of each ejido. A report of the *departamento agrario* stated that

> in all the region of Iguala . . . only the *comisariados* of the *ejidos* of Acayahualco, Tepaxtitlán, and Rincón de la Cocina were not imposed by the . . . *jefe de la zona* José Luis Domínguez, for the rest in their totality were [imposed] . . . in the following manner: he called those who were in charge of the political campaign in favor of the candidacy of . . . General

Guevara, present governor of the state, and asked them for a
list of the individuals who in their respective towns had helped
them, with which elements he formed the boards of manage-
ment of the *comisariados*, in spite of the complete opposition
of the majorities [*sic*] of the *ejidatarios*.[132]

The representatives of one ejido complained that as early as August
1932 they were pressured by the agrarian authorities and officials of
Guevara's election campaign to support Guevara's candidacy.[133] In
other campaigns the *ejidatarios* were similarly used as electoral
cannon fodder, as the case of Maxela shows. In June 1934 the
ejidatarios of Maxela were "invited" to cast their votes in favor of
the candidacy for the federal Congress of Alberto R. Guevara, the
governor's brother. Their failure to heed the "invitation" subjected
them to harassment, and even physical assault.[134] Such cases are in-
dicative of the degree to which the ejidos and the agrarian bureaucracy had become instruments of political manipulation.

While this exploitation of the ejidos for political ends was
nothing new, Guevara's administration developed a distinctly *anti-
agrarista* tinge, despite his declarations to the contrary. He was alleged to have tolerated the existence of *guardias blancas* which
were responsible for the death of 200 peasants, and ejidos were said
to have been despoiled of land by members of Guevara's administration, although there is no evidence that the governor himself participated in such activities.[135] In any case, the rate of land distribution
certainly slumped during Guevara's years in office. In 1933 only
20,944 hectares were granted by the governor, and in 1934 he signed
resolutions for a mere 19,986 (against 105,584 granted that year by
President Lázaro Cárdenas). The year 1935 saw no change in this
pattern, Guevara granting only 5,695 hectares, while Cárdenas allocated 69,600.[136] Guevara, who was by reputation a Callista, was
clearly out of step with the new administration in agrarian matters,
and when the struggle for national political power between President Cárdenas and Plutarco Elías Calles came to a head, it was not
surprising that Guevara should fall from grace.

In 1935, as Cárdenas struggled for power with the "Jefe Máximo,"
seven Callista state governors were deposed, among them Gabriel
Guevara of Guerrero, and an eighth Callista state executive fell
the next year.[137] The excuse for Guevara's removal from office was
provided by the bloody events which took place in Coyuca de Catalán on 19 September 1935. After a bullfight in the bullring of Coyuca,
a gun battle broke out between supporters of the federal *diputado*
and landowner, General Salvador González, and the followers of the

agrarista leader Ernesto Gómez, a Guevarista, who was backed up by the local federal garrison. It is curious, and an interesting comment on the complexity of politics at the local level, that the supporter of Guevara, a man with an anti-*agrarista* reputation, should have been the *agrarista* Gómez, while his opponent was the landowner González. Whatever the political complexities behind the fighting, seven people were killed and seventeen wounded, among them the *presidente municipal* of Coyuca, who was an associate of General González. While it appears that personal rivalries and municipal politics were the immediate causes of these events, Guevara's enemies were quick to seize the opportunity to implicate him.[138]

A Senate investigation of the events of 19 September and other abuses alleged to have been committed by Guevara found that he was involved in the Coyuca massacre. However, while it is clear that Gómez's group were supporters of Guevara, and may have been the prime movers in the affair, there is little evidence to link Guevara himself to the events of Coyuca. The Senate investigating committee based its case on the testimony of a woman who claimed to have overheard Donato Gómez (presumably a relative of Ernesto) say that the governor had supplied the Gómez group with arms for the attack in the bullring.[139] Whatever the truth of the matter, on 5 November the Senate removed Guevara from office and appointed José Inocente Lugo, the former Maderista governor, to occupy the governorship until a new executive could be elected for the period 1937 to 1941.[140]

The first task of the new governor, and of President Cárdenas, was to secure political control of Guerrero. There were two key factors: the municipal councils and the army. Just as Guevara had purged the Castrejonista *ayuntamientos* in 1933, Lugo immediately proceeded to depose the Guevarista municipal councils: thirty-seven municipal authorities were removed from office, while another three resigned voluntarily.[141] President Cárdenas, meanwhile, assiduously courted the local military, among whom sympathy for Calles was said to be rife.[142] The ease with which Guevara and his supporters in the municipalities were removed from power was symptomatic of the central government's growing control over local political affairs. By the end of the presidential period of Lázaro Cárdenas, this control was virtually complete, as the case of Alberto Berber would show quite clearly.

General Alberto F. Berber took office as governor of Guerrero on 1 April 1937. A native of Chilapa, Berber was born in 1885. He had joined the Maderista forces of Tomás Gómez, and later fought under the orders of Rómulo Figueroa. He had been the private secretary of Héctor F. López, and during the administration of Gabriel R. Guevara he was a federal congressman and was rumored to be Guevara's choice for governor in 1937.[143] If these rumors were true, they may be an indication that the Guevaristas' defeat in 1935 had not been total, and that federal control of Guerrero was not yet complete, but the evidence to confirm any such speculation is lacking.

Berber was the fifth constitutionally elected governor to take office in Guerrero since the triumph of the Constitutionalist revolution. None of his predecessors had finished the term of office untroubled by serious political difficulties, and only one, Rodolfo Neri, had remained in office to hand over the governorship to his successor. If any trend may be discerned throughout the chronic instability of the years from 1919 to 1941, it is the steadily growing power of the federal executive and the national political machine to determine the broad lines of local political developments. One after another, the governors had learned this lesson the hard way, and Alberto Berber was soon to go the way of his predecessors.

Berber's difficulties with the national political machine (the PNR had now been reorganized as the PRM—Partido de la Revolución Mexicana) began in 1939. In January of that year

> the [PRM] Bloc of the Chamber of Deputies agreed to designate a commission to go to the state of Guerrero and investigate with full zeal the results of the municipal elections in [twenty-six municipalities]. . . . The report that the commission gives will be appended to the file which has been formed as a result of the accusations against the governor of the state of Guerrero for having violated the public vote, by recognizing the triumph of slates which had few votes and which were formed ex profeso by the local regime *to oppose those [slates] sustained by the Partido de la Revolución Mexicana.*

In addition, a number of *ayuntamientos* were seized by PRM supporters in the state.[144]

Berber's strained relations with the PRM came to a head in February 1941, over the question of the election of his successor. In the elections held in January 1941 there had been three candidates: the PRM candidate, Colonel Rafael Catalán Calvo; the federal *diputado* for Guerrero, Francisco S. Carreto; and General Cristóbal Rodríguez. On 12 January the state Congress ruled that Catalán Calvo was constitutionally ineligible for election, since he had not resigned his commission in the army six months before the date of the election as fraction 5 of article 58 of the state constitution required. Carreto was then declared elected as governor by an absolute majority.[145] The

PRM, ignoring the question of Catalán Calvo's constitutional eligibility, alleged that the popular vote had been violated and demanded that the executive powers of Guerrero be declared to have "disappeared."[146]

The pace of events accelerated on 19 February, when a statement from president Avila Camacho (Cárdenas's suc ːessor) was read to the Senate. The statement made no mention of tne January elections, but instead referred to crimes and abuses attributed to the "Public Powers" of Guerrero, and the violation of the popular vote in the municipal elections. The very heart of the matter was thus ignored. However, Senator Nabor Ojeda, an *agrarista* from Guerrero, hit the nail on the head: Berber had gone against the democratic will of the people and no less importantly, the resolutions of the PRM, both "constitutional precepts [*sic*: precedents?] which cause irreparable harm." Without further ado, the Senate declared that the powers of Guerrero had disappeared and appointed Carlos Carranco Cardoso, the former de la Huertista from Tepecoacuilco, as provisional governor.[147] New elections were held in May, and on 1 July Catalán Calvo took office as governor of Guerrero,[148] despite the fact that, according to the U.S. vice consul, the new executive, "although a native of the state, does not appear to be well-known locally. It is said that he was in Baja California until shortly before the election."[149]

The result of the elections was a resounding triumph for the PRM and the death blow to any prospect of a degree of genuine independence from the national political machine. In the twenty-two years since Francisco Figueroa had taken office as the Carrancista governor of Guerrero, the central government had steadily regained full political control of the state, crushing any ambitions for regional domination which the local revolutionary elite might still harbor. The PRM was able to impose its will with an ease which would have aroused the envy of Porfirio Díaz, who had bridled the ambitions of Jiménez, Neri, and Diego Alvarez, only to find himself faced with a growing middle-class revolt, of which the Castillo Calderón rebellion was a symptom, and the Mexican revolution the apotheosis.

Insofar as the Mexican revolution in Guerrero had been a reaction to the emergence of a strong national state under Porfirio Díaz, it may be defined as a traditionalist movement whose aim was to restore the nineteenth-century status quo, rather than to usher in a new political or social era. While this may appear rather paradoxical at first sight, it need cause no great surprise, for it is already clear that "revolutionary" uprisings in other areas of Mexico bore a distinct conservative or traditionalist stamp. Thus, the agrarian revolt of Morelos sought to restore a past which was perhaps as much imaginary as real, for one may doubt that the association of rural clans, of which the Zapatistas dreamed, had ever really existed. In Sonora the Yaquis fought for the land usurped by the whites and for the restoration of their tribal society.[150] In San Luis Potosí Saturnino Cedillo recalled the nineteenth-century tradition of the caudillos and their clientele, which supplied the leaders with soldiers in return for protection and land.[151] Francisco Villa displayed a similar concern to provide land for his soldiers, preferring to postpone efforts at agrarian reform until his soldiers' claims could be met,[152] for, "despite its impressive geographical extension, Villismo retained a localist, anti-national character, in keeping with its popular, 'traditional' essence."[153] Ultimately, of course, these traditionalist movements lost out to the modernizing Constitutionalist elements which swept down from Coahuila and Sonora, whose conception of Mexico's future was very different.

The traditionalist label covered a multitude of sins, and in Guerrero the revolutionary movement took a form quite distinct from the agrarian revolt in Morelos. Here the ranchero was the champion of the state's autonomy, for which Juan Alvarez had fought so tenaciously in the nineteenth century. Chief among them was a family from Quetzalapa, near Huitzuco. The Figueroas had launched the revolution in Guerrero, and various members of the family played an active role in the events of 1911 to 1919. In 1924, however, their political fortunes in the state had reached their nadir. Only one member of the family survived the debacle of the de la Huerta revolt with his revolutionary career intact. This was Andrés Figueroa, who had backed Obregón, while his cousins followed de la Huerta. In 1924 Andrés had been appointed *jefe del departamento de caballería* in the Ministry of War,[154] and for the next decade he carved out for himself a distinguished military career, which included a prominent role in the campaigns against the Cristero rebellion. Andrés forged his career outside Guerrero, avoiding the involvement in local politics which was the downfall of his cousin Rómulo, and in June 1935 he reached the peak of his career with his appointment as Cárdenas's secretary of war.[155]

In Guerrero itself the family did not begin its political comeback until 1934, when Ing. Rubén Figueroa was elected as an alternate congressman to the federal legislature. He followed a path to political prominence very different from that followed by his uncles Rómulo and Ambrosio, for Rubén developed his career within the official political system, serving in the bureaucracy, in elected office, and in the trade association of the trucking industry. In 1941 he played an active part in ousting from office Alberto F. Berber, and he was one of three men proposed by President Avila Camacho for the office of provisional governor.[156] Rubén's brother Rufo carved out a similarly classic career for himself, serving in important posts in the official party, labor unions, and government departments, as well as in elected office in the federal Congress and Senate, and as governor of Quintana Roo.[157] In Huitzuco itself, Jesús Figueroa, son of Don Rómulo, was elected *presidente municipal* in 1937, a post he was to occupy on three subsequent occasions. Moreover, despite the setbacks of 1923–1924, the Figueroas were still to be a force in state politics half a century later, and in 1975 Rubén Figueroa became the second member of the family to occupy the office of governor of the state of Guerrero. The Figueroas' comeback was possible because they had abandoned the role of autonomous local caciques and learned the rules of the political process of the new Mexico.[158]

7. Agrarian Reform in Northern Guerrero: 1919–1940

The three decades from 1910 to 1940 had seen many new faces on the political stage in Guerrero. Still more crucially, certain social groups had obtained a new access to political power in the state. Those who benefited most, as already noted, were the middle sectors (smallholders, petty traders, schoolteachers, small town lawyers, and the like) which had expanded considerably during the years of Porfirio Díaz and since the turn of the century had clamored for greater access to political office in their own state. However, from 1919 onward another group had also come to play an important role in the state's politics: the *agraristas*.[1] Guerrero's agrarians had been a vital source of support for Rodolfo Neri in his struggle with Rómulo Figueroa; for some eight years from 1921 to 1929, *agraristas* led by Amadeo and Baldomero Vidales had controlled the Costa Grande; and Governor Adrián Castrejón had taken a number of measures to enlist agrarian support for his administration. Thus, the agrarian reform which did much to change the pattern of rural society in Guerrero from 1919 to 1940 also had profound political implications. These political shockwaves were felt not only on the broader national and state scenes, but also on the more humble level of the municipality and the village. For the agrarian reform wrought profound changes in social relations at the local level and injected a completely new element into municipal and village politics. Before looking more closely at the reform process and the social and political changes it wrought, it is worth looking again at the rural society which it set out to change. My focus, by and large, will be on the village society affected by the reform, rather than on the larger-scale economies of the haciendas already examined in chapter 4, although the two were, of course, inextricably linked.

Small changes had taken place in the demographic structure of both districts during the years of revolutionary upheaval, but, fundamentally, northern Guerrero remained a rural and agricultural so-

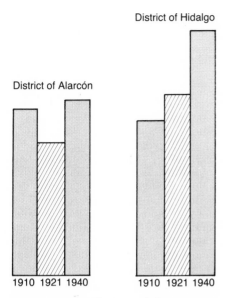

Figure 3. *Population of the Districts of Alarcón and Hidalgo, 1910, 1921, 1940*

ciety. In the district of Alarcón the population had declined somewhat between 1910 and 1921 from 38,739 to 30,942, but Hidalgo, in
contrast, had witnessed a growth in population almost equal to Alarcón's decline: from 35,542 to 41,668. After 1921 the population of
both districts followed an upward course, Hidalgo having 57,050 inhabitants by 1940, and Alarcón 40,676, less than 2,000 above its
1910 level.[2]

The distribution of population between urban and rural centers
had changed little since 1910, underlining the area's rural character.
In 1921 the district of Alarcón had an entirely rural population, although by 1940, 12% qualified as urban (Taxco had grown to 4,963,
crossing the threshold of 4,000 inhabitants needed to qualify as an
urban center). Hidalgo's population was 26% urban in 1921, but only
22% in 1940, the slight decline probably being caused by the stabi-
lization of the commercial boom in Iguala set off by the construction
of the Mexico City–Balsas railway around the turn of the century.[3]

The distribution of the economically active population by sector further underlined the agrarian nature of the region: by 1940,
75% of the economically active population of the district of Alarcón
worked in agriculture, and 80% did so in Hidalgo. Other sectors

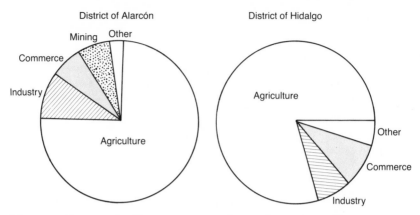

Figure 4. *Economically Active Population by Sector, 1940*

employed small numbers of workers: 10% in industry in Alarcón, a slight increase from 1910, while the percentage for Hildago remained virtually unchanged in the three decades from 1910 to 1940. Commerce had grown somewhat in both districts: from 3% to 7% in Hidalgo, reflecting the increasing importance of Iguala as a commercial center, and from 2% to 5% in Alarcón. In Alarcón mining occupied 7% of the workforce (against 3% in 1910).[4]

As one would expect, in such a predominantly rural society, access to the basic resources of the agricultural sector, land and livestock with which to work it, was quite crucial. Although the concentration of land in the hands of large landowners was not as pronounced as in other parts of Mexico, privately owned land was a rather scarce resource in a number of towns and villages in the area, as the data summarized in table 4 reveal. In almost half of the fifty-three towns and villages for which data were available, not one individual owned a plot of land, while in twenty-four of the remainder, 30% or fewer of the heads of family and adult males had their own land, and in only six cases did more than half have their own plots. Moreover, the amount of land owned was quite small, almost never exceeding fifty hectares (see table 5). These statistics are based on surveys carried out to determine the eligibility of individuals for *ejidal* grants who had an interest in reducing the amount of land ownership registered in their village and may, therefore, tend to underestimate the amount of land in private hands. Moreover, only villages which requested ejidos were surveyed, so that pueblos where smallholders were relatively numerous were underrepresented.

Table 4. Percentage of Heads of Family and Adult Males Who Owned Land in Fifty-three Towns and Villages of the Districts of Alarcón and Hidalgo (1919–1940)

None	Below 5%	5–10%	10–20%	20–30%	30–40%	40–50%	50–70%	70–90%	90–100%	Total
22	5	4	9	6	1	0	2	2	2	53

SOURCE: ASRA, Ramo Ejidal.

Table 5. Percentage of Heads of Family and Adult Males Owning Twenty Hectares or More in Six Towns and Villages of the Districts of Alarcón and Hidalgo (1919–1940)

Town/Village	20–50 hectares	50–100 hectares	Over 100 hectares
Apipilulco	0.34%	0.00%	0.00%
Huitzuco	0.41%	0.27%	0.41%
Tepecoacuilco	0.39%	0.13%	0.00%
Paintla	5.56%	4.17%	4.86%
Chontalcuatlán	10.43%	1.74%	4.35%
El Platanar	1.16%	0.00%	0.00%

SOURCE: ASRA, Ramo Ejidal.

Table 6. Percentage of Adult Males and Heads of Household Owning Livestock in Forty-five Towns and Villages in the Districts of Alarcón and Hidalgo (1919–1940)

None	0–10%	10–20%	20–30%	30–40%	40–50%	50–60%	60–70%	70–80%	80–90%	90–100%	Total
0	4	8	4	11	7	5	4	0	1	1	45

SOURCE: ASRA, Ramo Ejidal.

Table 7. Percentage of Adult Males and Heads of Household Owning Livestock in Forty-two Towns and Villages in the Districts of Alarcón and Hidalgo (1919–1940) by Types

Type	None	0–10%	10–20%	20–30%	30–40%	40–50%	50–60%	60–70%	70–80%	80–100%	Total
Mayor	0	5	8	12	11	2	1	1	1	1	42
Menor	23	16	2	1	0	0	0	0	0	0	42
Both	14	11	9	6	2	0	0	-	0	0	42

SOURCE: ASRA, Ramo Ejidal.

However, the figures are probably correct in suggesting that the supply of land was rather tight.

In contrast, livestock was a much less scarce resource than land. In a sample of forty-five towns and villages, at least some heads of family and adult males owned livestock in every case, and usually at least 30% owned some animals (table 6). Thus, even if they owned no land, a significant proportion of the rural population did own livestock. Moreover, the majority of livestock owners possessed *ganado mayor* (milk cows, slaughter cattle, beasts of burden, and work animals such as oxen, horses, and mules), which were essential as a source of animal protein and for tilling the fields (table 7). Fairly widespread ownership of livestock combined with a more limited supply of privately owned land suggests that access to communal land or to pasture rented from the haciendas must have been vitally important to the villages.

Lack of one or both of these vital resources, land and livestock, could have quite a considerable effect on living standards. For example, it was reported in 1931 that in San Nicolás "the social and economic conditions of the village are, moreover, precarious and distressing, since on account of the scarcity of cultivable lands and on account of the situation in which they have always been of obligatory tributaries of the Hacienda [de Tepozonalco], [the people of San Nicolás] have always been absolutely unable to achieve the least progress or economic relief."[5] In nearby Xonacatla the position was no better, and, indeed, for those unfortunates who lacked both land and oxen, perhaps still worse. The *vecinos* of Xonacatla cultivated maize "and this on a small scale, as they cannot extend and increase their sowings because of the excessive rents which the [land]owners demand[; the *vecinos*] are made to pay for each three hectares up to 1,400 kilograms of maize, and, if [the landowners] provide a pair of oxen, 900 kilos more, with the result that for each three hectares of land sowed they pay 2,300 kilograms of maize and with a total production of 5,500 kilos they are left only 3,200."[6] In Tetelilla, the rental of land and oxen accounted for well over half the tenants' crop. The rental of four hectares of land in 1928 cost $35, and the hire of a pair of oxen $30, while the value of the crop amounted to $108.80. Thus, even if the tenants owned oxen, almost one-third of the value of the crop had to be paid to the landowner. Indeed, where land and livestock had to be rented, the tenants could extract a surplus from the land only if they and their families provided the necessary labor, since the hire of a day laborer would cost $14, leaving the unfortunate tenants virtually no surplus.[7]

Since many campesinos did not possess land of their own, access to land through rental was important. The rents charged for land (nearly always paid in kind) varied considerably. Among the lowest were the two *cargas* (four hectoliters) per *yunta* (about two and a half hectares) charged in El Ejido, El Fraile, Hueymatla, and Santa Rosa, while about the highest was the eight to twelve *cargas* per hectare charged in Acayahualco. The proportion of the crop taken by the landowner likewise varied considerably from a low of 10% to a high of 60% (and if the crop failed, of course, the percentage could be higher). The norm seems to have been between about a quarter and a third of the crop, although the rent was fixed independently of the crop harvested.[8]

In pueblos which had communal lands, it is true, the landless peasant need not necessarily have recourse to renting land, but the quality of communal land was not always high, and not all villages had sufficient land for their needs. In Taxco el Viejo, for example, there were some 320 hectares of privately owned small properties. While those who did not own land had access to "a moderate area of communal lands, these are of bad quality, incapable of producing sufficient for all the *vecinos*."[9]

Those who neither owned nor rented land, or tenants who wished to supplement their income from rented land, were obliged to hire their labor out for a daily wage. This varied somewhat from place to place, but the usual wage throughout the period 1919 to 1935 was about $0.50. Occasionally, higher rates of $0.60 or $0.75 a day were paid, and in a few places the pay was as high as $1.00. Local availability of labor and seasonal demand were no doubt the determining factors. There seems to have been no perceptible increase in the agricultural wage between 1919 and 1935.[10]

Although agriculture was, no doubt, often a subsistence occupation, some did manage to produce a marketable surplus, and any such surplus was usually sold in local markets. The peasants of Coxcatlán, for example, sold any surplus maize they produced in Tlamacazapa, a mere stone's throw away, since prices there were higher than in Iguala. This was because Tlamacazapa made its living from the manufacture of matting and hats, and, maize production there sometimes being insufficient, demand tended to be high.[11] The peasants of El Platanar marketed their goods in the nearby towns of Pilcaya, Noxtepec, Tetipac, and Taxco,[12] while the village of Palmillas sold its produce slightly further afield, in Iguala, Buenavista de Cuéllar, and Puente de Ixtla (the latter just over the border in Morelos).[13] Apparently, the improvement in communications brought by the construction of the Mexico City–Balsas railway around the turn of the century had not stimulated the small producers to seek wider markets for their crops.

The standard of living which agriculture afforded those who depended on it for their livelihood was generally poor. One reason was the shortage of good arable land in the districts of Hidalgo and Alarcón. Many peasants were obliged to adopt the slash and burn *tlacolol* system, one which was "laborious and unproductive."[14] In Coxcatlán, for example, the value of the maize crop barely covered the costs of cultivation, although beans and squash were sown in between the maize furrows to increase the yield.[15] A further example of the hand-to-mouth existence of many peasants in northern Guerrero could be found in San Isidro, where "beans, which [the people] usually sow together with maize, constitute, along with [maize], almost their only nourishment. Tomatoes and chile form the complement of this rickety diet: but these products are usually sold to solve the problem of obtaining clothing, which is usually limited to white trousers of *manta* and a shirt of the same material, . . . [and] *huaraches.*"[16] Similarly, in Las Mesas it was estimated that in 1936 a family needed a yearly income of $550 to meet its needs, but the average family income was only $480,[17] while in El Sauz the yields of land rented from the Hacienda de Juchimilpa were low, and consequently the tenants were sometimes quite unable to pay their rent. In this case the landowner allowed a moratorium, but then demanded payment in cash instead of in kind, assessing the cash equivalent of the maize rent at inflated values.[18]

While detailed statistics are lacking on the income obtained from the land by those who depended on it for their livelihood, it is clear from numerous descriptive accounts that the peasants' standard of living was far from adequate. To the tenants the agrarian reform offered a higher income by freeing them from the obligation of paying out part of their crop as rent to the landowner. To the wage laborers the reform offered greater status and independence, and a chance to improve their standard of living. In either case, there was clearly a strong economic incentive to seek land under the reform program, although the actual benefits would sometimes prove to be more illusory than real.

From 1919 to 1940, 127 pueblos in the districts of Alarcón and Hidalgo presented 132 requests for land under the agrarian reform. Of these, 115 were requests for a direct grant (*dotación*), and a further 17 were for restitution of communal lands said to have been despoiled illegally from the pueblos (table 8). Although not one of the requests for restitution was successful, 7 villages which origi-

Table 8. *Requests for Ejidos in the Districts of Alarcón and*
Hidalgo (1919–1940)

Year	Dotación	Restitución	Ampliación
1919	21	1	0
1920	22	2	0
1921	15	4	0
1922	2	4	2
1923	4	1	5
1924	2	0	6
1925	4	0	0
1926	2	0	3
1927	0	0	1
1928	2	0	0
1929	8	0	0
1930	4	1	0
1931	5	0	1
1932	2	1	0
1933	1	0	1
1934	2	0	4
1935	3	1	13
1936	5	0	6
1937	2	0	4
1938	2	2	2
1939	3	0	5
1940	4	0	2
Total	115	17	55

SOURCE: ASRA, Ramo Ejidal.

nally requested restitution were granted an ejido by means of *dotación*. From 1919 to 1940, 85 ejidos were established in the districts
of Alarcón and Hidalgo, and by 1940, 84 of them had received definitive possession of their land; the remaining ejido had provisional
possession while it awaited final confirmation of its grant. Twelve
pueblos were refused the grant of an ejido.

Beginning in 1921, a number of ejidos began to request an extension (*ampliación*) of the land granted to them, and by 1940, 57 (67%)
of the area's ejidos had filed requests for additional land. However,
less than half were successful in seeking to expand their allotments:
by 1940, only 22 had received presidential approval of an extension,
and 2 had been refused outright for lack of affectable land. Two oth-

ers had been granted an extension by the state executive, but were still awaiting presidential confirmation of the additional land.

More than two-thirds (70%) of requests resolved by the state governor were processed within three years, while just under half (46%) received approval from the federal executive in the same period. In one case, however, seventeen years elapsed between the date of the request and the presidential resolution, and thirty pueblos were still awaiting presidential confirmation of their request for land in 1940. On balance, however, the processing of requests appears to have been fairly expeditious, in this area at least.

From 1919 to the end of 1940, the governors of Guerrero signed resolutions distributing a total of 751,843 hectares. The area of land granted in Guerrero by the federal executive was somewhat larger: 1,006,188 hectares. In the district of Alarcón the area of land granted was 15,418 and 16,085 hectares, respectively, while in the district of Hidalgo the figures were 90,444 and 112,765.[19]

The amounts of land distributed in Guerrero varied considerably from year to year, and it is clear that the fluctuations in the rate of reform were quite closely linked to political developments, both on the state and national levels. Thus, the first real leap forward in the rate of land reform came in the period 1921 to 1924 (see figures 5, 6, and 7), and corresponded to the buildup and denouement of the de la Huerta revolt. The rate of reform sagged under Governor Héctor F. López, who was known to be hostile to *agrarismo*, but picked up under the administration of the former Zapatista Adrián Castrejón, especially in 1929 when the Cristero rebellion was at its worst in Guerrero. The reform slowed again under Governor Gabriel Guevara, a Callista with an *anti-agrarista* reputation, in spite of the fact that from 1934 onward the federal government's policy was to speed up distribution of ejidos. Throughout the period of Cárdenas the amount of land distributed in presidential resolutions considerably exceeded that granted by the local executive. Although Governor Alberto F. Berber brought the state government's agrarian policy more closely into line with that of President Cárdenas, from 1934 to 1940 the main thrust of reform came from Mexico City and obeyed national policy objectives.[20]

The brunt of the land reform in northern Guerrero was borne, of course, by the hacienda, although in the district of Alarcón almost one-third (31%) of the land expropriated was taken from small landowners (table 9). If we discount 12,998 hectares of publicly owned land, a total of 97,436 hectares were expropriated from private landowners in the district of Hidalgo, of which 78,798 hectares (81%) were taken from only sixteen major landowners whose holdings ex-

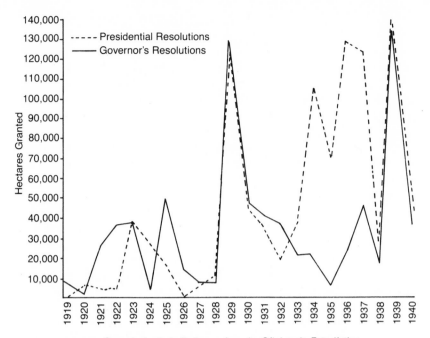

SOURCE: *Secretaría de la Reforma Agraria, Oficina de Estadística.*

Figure 5. *Area of Land Granted in Guerrero, 1919–1940*

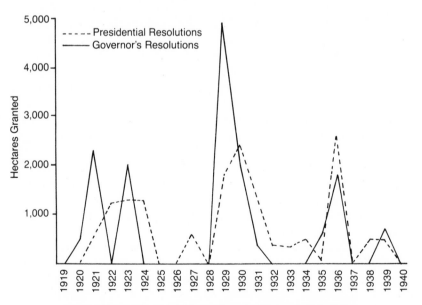

SOURCE: *Secretaría de la Reforma Agraria, Oficina de Estadística.*

Figure 6. *Area of Land Granted in the District of Alarcón, 1919–1940*

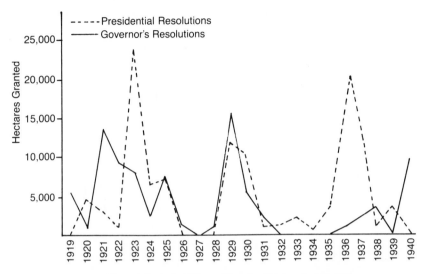

SOURCE: *Secretaría de la Reforma Agraria, Oficina de Estadística.*

Figure 7. *Area of Land Granted in the District of Hidalgo,*
1919–1940

ceeded 2,000 hectares. The remaining 18,638 hectares were expropriated from a number of ranchero smallholders. In the district of Alarcón, in contrast, large landowners contributed a smaller proportion of the land taken to form ejidos: 11,095 hectares (taken from four landowners of over 2,000 hectares), or 69% of the total amount of land expropriated. Consequently, in Alarcón the burden fell somewhat more heavily on smaller landowners. At least eleven of those affected in the district of Alarcón owned less than 1,000 hectares, and in one case the affected property was as small as seventy-six hectares. By 1940, in both districts, it was getting increasingly difficult to find legally affectable land to distribute to landless peasants.

Despite a growing shortage of land available for distribution, by the end of 1940 there were 10,525 *ejidatarios* in the districts of Alarcón and Hidalgo, although 1,418 of them (13%) could not be assigned their own parcel of cultivable land in their ejido, and had to settle for access to communal pasture and forest land. Of the eligible individuals who petitioned for land, 2,025 (16%) could not be granted any. The proportion of unsuccessful petitions was not spread evenly across the region, however. While in the municipalities where the hacienda was preponderant (Cocula, Iguala, and Tepecoacuilco)

**Table 9. Landowners Affected by the Agrarian Reform in the
Districts of Alarcón and Hidalgo (1919–1940)**

1. District of Alarcón

Landowner	Total area affected (hectares)	Area of land owned (hectares)	% of land affected
Isaac Mathewson	5,157	5,477	94%
Filomena Muñoz	2,249	3,592	63%
Jesús O. Martínez	2,160	2,898	75%
Luis Maldonado	1,589	1,654	96%
Mucio Romero	1,529	2,216	69%
Josefa Ramos	716	766	93%
Emanuel Amor	570	no data	
Vicente Gómez	545	952	57%
Manuel Meléndez	480	850	56%
Justiniano Jaimes	449	679	66%
José Ramos	153	203	75%
Bernardino Ramírez	88	288	31%
Juan Figueroa	82	732	11%
Francisco E. Camacho	71	313	23%
Luis Ordorica	67	no data	
Blanca Inclán Ordorica	67	no data	
Rómulo Figueroa	67	67	100%
Guadalupe Rocha	26	76	34%
Concepción Díaz Leal	20	220	9%
Total	16,085		

2. District of Hidalgo

Landowner	Total area affected (hectares)	Area of land owned (hectares)	% of land affected
Alberto Rivera	10,965	19,193	57%
Miguel Montúfar	10,902	22,346	49%
Febronia Gómez	10,774	13,832	78%
Emigdio Pastrana	10,339	14,160	73%
Felix Marbán and seven others	9,399	no data	
Atlixtac y Anexas S.A.	8,916	9,357	95%
National Lands	8,821	no data	
Manuela Mojica	6,414	6,825	94%
Julián and Ponciano Salgado	4,774	5,200	92%
Rafael del Castillo Calderón	4,251	11,799	36%
Ayuntamiento de Tepecoacuilco	3,778	3,778	100%

Table 9 *(continued)*

2. District of Hidalgo

Landowner	Total area affected (hectares)	Area of land owned (hectares)	% of land affected
Adela Cervantes Vda. de C.	2,838	3,310	86%
Francisco Fernández de la V.	2,303	2,334	99%
Manuel N. Mora	1,847	1,997	92%
Filomena Muñoz	1,343	3,592	37%
José Nava	1,288	2,130	60%
Manuel Roa	1,184	1,330	89%
Petra C. Vda. de Castro	1,139	3,800	30%
Lucía Patiño Vda. de C.	1,069	3,600	30%
Joaquina Martínez Vda. de P.	832	1,196	70%
José María Montes	754	2,655	28%
Luis Hernández	733	no data	
Diódoro Pastrana	729	2,072	35%
Emeterio Salgado	502	no data	
Enrique Pedrote	461	1,308	35%
Government of Guerrero	399	no data	
Pío Sandoval	386	no data	
Trinidad Mastache	385	705	55%
José María Velázquez	343	343	100%
Beatriz Fuentes Vda. de C.	314	no data	
José María Suárez	277	534	52%
Juan Chávez	246	947	26%
Clemente Jardón	222	no data	
Cutberto Villalva	218	557	39%
Jesús Villalva	213	1,216	18%
Señores Ayala Aponte	210	610	34%
Jesús Soto	197	1,359	14%
Joaquín Hernández	192	1,325	14%
Natalia Mastache	181	985	18%
Thomas K. Mathewson	110	800	14%
Heriberta C. Vda. de Suárez	56	no data	
Pantaleón Cerón	78	351	22%
Manuel Cerón	42	372	11%
Epifanio and Luis Peralta	10	1,650	1%
Total	110,434		

SOURCE: ASRA, Ramo Ejidal.
NOTE: Figures are taken from presidential resolutions, giving, in the case of the district of Hidalgo, a total slightly lower than the amount of land granted, since in some cases it was not possible to determine from which property land was taken.

only 11% of the applicants for grants were unsuccessful, in the municipality of Huitzuco 13% could not be given land, in Tetipac 16%, and in Taxco fully 65% of petitioners failed to receive land. Moreover, while in the hacienda zone very few *ejidatarios* (only 9%) failed to receive parcels of cultivable land, in Huitzuco over a third of petitioners could be granted only general rights to communal land (table 10).

Moreover, even when an applicant was successful, the chances were that the land granted would be of rather poor quality, as table 11 suggests. As one would expect, irrigated land constituted only a tiny portion of the total amount granted, since the supply of irrigated land in the area was small. In both the district of Alarcón and that of Hidalgo land cultivated by means of seasonal rainfall (*temporal*) represented just over 10% of *ejidal* lands, while more than half consisted of pasture and woodland, of which between 10% and 15% might be cultivable, if only by means of the slash and burn method (*tlacolol*). In addition, just over one-third of the land granted was of unspecified quality (*terrenos en general*), of which between 20% and 25% at most was cultivable. Thus, the actual or potential amount of crop land granted to the ejidos of the districts of Alarcón and Hidalgo came to between 30,326 and 36,033 hectares, or some 24% to 28% of the total amount of land granted. In sum, in terms of cultivable land, the resources allocated to the ejidos clearly left much to be desired.

No statistics exist to show the benefits which *ejidatarios* could expect from their pieces of land, but, from the numerous descriptive accounts available, it is possible to obtain a general impression of the extent to which the agrarian reform affected standards of living. We know that only a small proportion of *ejidal* land was arable, and it is further clear that cultivable land was by no means evenly distributed among the ejidos, largely due to the uneven geographical distribution of good crop land. This was especially true of irrigated land, which was concentrated in a few small pockets. Thus, for example, the ejidos of Apipilulco and Atlixtac accounted for 96% of the irrigated land granted in the district of Hidalgo, while Santiago received almost two-thirds of the irrigated land distributed in Alarcón.[21] *Temporal* was often no better distributed, as the case of some ejidos in the district of Hidalgo showed. While the proportion of arable land granted in the district was at most 27%, some ejidos received a much larger share than others. For example, the original grant to both Polocingo and Tonalapa del Norte was two-thirds cultivable, while fully 86% of the ejido of Sacacoyuca was crop land.[22]

Two examples will suffice to illustrate the poverty of the lands

Table 10. *Numbers of Eligible Individuals Granted and Refused Land in the Districts of Alarcón and Hidalgo (1919–1940)*

Municipality	Granted parcel	Granted rights to communal lands	Refused land	Totals
Taxco	702	152	1,597	2,451
percentage	29	6	65	100
Tetipac	750	0	145	895
percentage	84	0	16	100
Cocula	1,604	158	37	1,799
percentage	89	9	2	100
Huitzuco	671	527	186	1,384
percentage	48	38	13	100
Iguala	2,287	26	60	2,373
percentage	96	1	3	100
Tepecoacuilco	3,093	555	0	3,648
percentage	85	15	0	100

SOURCE: ASRA, Ramo Ejidal.

Table 11. *Type of Land Granted in Presidential Resolutions in the Districts of Alarcón and Hidalgo (1919–1940)*

Municipality	Irrigated (hectares)	Temporal (hectares)	Pasture, hill, and woodland (hectares)	Unspecified and urban Zone (hectares)	Totals
Taxco	101	638	3,408	5,502	9,649
Tetipac	350	1,059	4,232	795	6,436
Dt. Alarcón	451	1,697	7,640	6,297	16,085
percentage	3	11	47	39	100
Cocula	463	1,595	17,919	5,129	25,106
Huitzuco	0	452	21,758	6,303	28,513
Iguala	0	6,495	4,937	4,316	15,748
Tepecoacuilco	0	3,552	19,831	20,015	43,397
Dt. Hidalgo	463	12,094	64,445	35,763	112,764
percentage	0	11	57	32	100

SOURCE: ASRA, Ramo Ejidal.

for which many ejidos had to settle. In 1936 an engineer of the Mixed Agrarian Commisson described the ejido of El Fraile thus: "The zone inspected is a series of very high hills, steep slopes, and ravines where the inhabitants carry out cultivation by resorting to the *tlacolole* [*sic*] system, a system [which is] laborious, slow, and not very productive."[23] In the ejido of Santa Teresa the situation was no better, since most of the *temporal* land was of no use to the *ejidatarios* because crops planted on it were frequently lost, and consequently only part of the ejido was cultivated.[24]

Some ejidos, of course, constituted exceptions which did not, however, disprove the rule. For example, Ing. Ernesto Angeles wrote of the ejido of Acalman that "its people are very hard-working and industrious, having marked tendencies to improve themselves, since by their own efforts they have constructed a magnificent school[;] they are organizing their village in the proper way and have asked the respective authorities to commission an engineer and to provide the necessary tubing to bring water to the center of their village."[25] In some cases, furthermore, ejidos received more land than they could actually cultivate, and in such circumstances it was common to rent the excess land out to residents of other villages. Such was the case of the ejidos of Maxela, Palapa, and Ceja Blanca.[26] An interesting case was that of the ejido of Chontalcuatlán, which apparently rented quite large areas of its ejido, charging even higher rents than the private landowners. The enterprising *ejidatarios* of Chontalcuatlán sowed only the land close to their village and rented out the more distant parts while they devoted themselves to various cottage industries. One ejido complained that Chontalcuatlán even tried to take away its *ejidal* land in order to rent it out.[27] Needless to say, Chontalcuatlán's relations with its neighbors were none too cordial.

It is well known that the renting of *ejidal* land, an illegal but nevertheless common practice, is often linked to the fact that the *ejidatarios* lack sufficient capital to cultivate their land themselves.[28] Similarly, lack of capital or access to credit may often be responsible for under-utilization of *ejidal* land, rather than the granting of an excessive area of land, as the case of Las Mesas illustrates. In 1939 Ing. Ernesto Angeles reported that the lands of the ejido of Las Mesas, "although mountainous, have parts [which are] quite good for agriculture, [but it is] indispensable that the National Bank of Ejidal Credit finance [the *ejidatarios*], since, given their poverty, they almost [completely] lack even the most rudimentary implements for the exploitation of their lands."[29] If land was of poor quality, relatively large investments of capital might be necessary to obtain full benefit from the ejido. This capital was, needless to say, generally lacking, as was the case in Acayahualco, where the *ejidatarios* complained in 1923 that "as the cultivable land [of the ejido] is very little, in order to carry out intensive cultivation, it would be necessary to be capitalists to acquire fertilizer, but, as we say, we are poor."[30]

Thus, with some few notable exceptions, the ejido of the districts of Alarcón and Hidalgo was characterized by a shortage of good cultivable land, and, in some cases at least, a lack of capital to work this land efficiently. Moreover, in some ejidos these problems were aggravated by an uneven distribution of land among the *ejidatarios*. Consider the case of Pantla del Zapotal, which was provisionally granted 564 hectares for forty-seven *ejidatarios* in 1930, a grant confirmed in 1935. The cultivable land of this ejido was distributed among the *ejidatarios* in lots varying from one and a quarter hectares to five and a half hectares.[31] Similarly, in Palmillas, because of an inequitable distribution of cultivable land, only forty-six of the ninety-eight *ejidatarios* granted land in 1929 actually had a parcel of crop land.[32] Finally, in some cases, such as that of Hueymatla, it was impossible to distribute the parcels as the original grant specified because the arable land was scattered about the ejido in small lots of differing sizes.[33]

Thus, the physical conditions of the ejido were often not conducive to raising the standard of living of the peasantry. Moreover, an institutional factor further exacerbated the problems of the *ejidatario*, since the ejido, by virtue of its very nature, proved incapable of absorbing the rate of population growth in northern Guerrero. The definitive grant of an ejido was based on the eligible population at the time the presidential resolution was signed, but this meant that the grant made no allowance for population increase; and, although an extension of the grant could be applied for, this usually took much longer than the original *dotación*. Moreover, the scope for further grants to many existing ejidos was narrowing considerably, especially in the municipality of Taxco, as legally affectable land became more and more scarce. In Hueymatla, for example, Ing. Rodolfo Garduño reported in 1936 that "the present census shows that there are . . . fifty-seven individuals with a right to a parcel . . . a group for which subsistence constitutes a problem of fearful proportions, since, lacking land to sow, and since there are not . . . centers or means of permanent work, the state of these fifty-seven citizens borders on misery and represents a burden which those who have a parcel [try to] sustain without success."[34] There was no way out of this dilemma, for two months after this report was written, Hueymatla was refused an extension of its ejido since there were no legally affectable properties within the required distance of the village.[35] Furthermore, this case was by no means an exception; for example, in Las Mesas in 1940 there were twenty eligible individuals who had no land, and the village could be granted only twelve hectares by way of extension.[36] Similarly, in 1937 the *ejidatarios* of Real del Limón wrote that those who had a parcel of arable land had only two hectares each, and, moreover, twenty individuals had no land at all.[37]

However, the stress was not altogether on the debit side of the balance sheet. The major benefit which the *ejidatarios* derived from the agrarian reform in the districts of Alarcón and Hidalgo was that it freed them from the obligation to pay rent to the landowner. This represented a saving, on the average, of about one-quarter to one-third of the average yield of the land rented. Moreover, most large landowners were completely ruined by the agrarian reform, and some simply abandoned land which still had not been affected, leaving it to be worked rent-free by whoever wished to do so. This was the case of the properties La Mohonera, Joya de Pantla, and Tecuex-contitlán, which had been abandoned by their owner by the late 1930s.[38] Similarly, Manuela Mojica, the wife of the eminent politician Miguel F. Ortega, had abandoned the remainder of her haciendas Santa Teresa and Acayahualco by 1936,[39] and one owner gave up her land even before it had been touched by the reform.[40]

The balance of power had clearly shifted against the large landowner, and many of the large properties became economically unviable. For example, in 1921 the Banco Hipotecario Internacional began an attempt to recover the money owed it by the Hacienda de Atlixtac. Work was begun to recommence the production of sugar, but in 1935, most of the hacienda's land having been expropriated, the sugar-processing machinery was sold off.[41] Similarly, by 1936 the Hacienda de Santa Fe Tepetlapa had been embargoed by the state government for nonpayment of taxes.[42]

Thus, with few exceptions,[43] the former tenants had been largely freed from the yoke of the large landowners by 1940. However, to some extent the landowners had been replaced by the tax collectors. Whereas before the tenants had usually paid rent only on crop land, when they were granted land in an ejido they had to pay taxes, not only on their parcels of cultivable land, but also on their shares of the ejido's pasture and woodland, whether or not this was of much use to them. One engineer of the agrarian commission who visited Xonacatla in 1932 found the *ejidatarios* very hostile. They complained that the land of their provisional ejido was of poor quality and that they had to pay high taxes on it.[44] Similarly, the *ejidatarios* of

Santa Fe Tepetlapa, who received their ejido in 1924, flatly declared that the product of their land was insufficient to pay the taxes on it, and, indeed, they paid no taxes at all in 1925, 1926, or 1927.[45]

In short, while the *ejidatarios* no longer labored under the obligation to pay rent to the landowners, and while the power of the large landowners had been largely undermined (as the rather high incidence of land invasions in the 1920s and 1930s bears witness), the balance sheet was by no means all positive. Where the *ejidatarios* were unable to satisfy their needs from the land of the ejido, they might still find themselves partially dependent on private landowners to rent them extra land, or to hire them for wage labor.[46] The debits also included the generally poor quality of the ejido's land, a problem aggravated by the uneven distribution of resources, both between and within the ejidos, problems made no easier to bear by a shortage of capital and credit. Given these difficulties, it is not surprising that the *ejidal* parcel proved an inadequate unit for capital accumulation and the production of a marketable surplus.[47]

The effects of the agrarian reform were not only economic, however, and in the long run the economic impact was perhaps not as important as other factors, for the reform had profound effects on the relations between the various social groups of northern Guerrero. Indeed, one could argue that one of the most important consequences of the reform was to create a series of deep and bitter divisions in the rural society of northern Guerrero which led to frequent outbreaks of violence. Broadly speaking, one may distinguish five ways in which the reform divided the inhabitants of the area. First, of course, it set the *agraristas* at odds with the larger landowners who had most to lose. Second, the *agraristas* came up against the opposition of the small landowners, which took slightly different, and often more violent, forms from the resistance of the larger landowners. In addition, the reform split the landless peasantry itself, first into *agrarista* and *anti-agrarista* factions, for the landless peasants were by no means always keen to receive land in the fashion stipulated in the reform legislation, and then by driving still deeper the wedge of traditional hostility between landowning villages, which manifested itself in a more generalized form as villages vied for land. Finally, the ejidos were often plagued with very serious internal divisions.

The most predictable opposition to the *agraristas* came from the large landowners. Saturnino Martínez, the representative and nephew of the *hacendado* Miguel Montúfar, doubtless expressed the sentiments of many a landowner when he wrote that the *agraristas* who sought to take other people's land were individuals of "bad habits which after the revolution have become more deeply rooted in these men."[48] The weapon which the large landowners most frequently wielded against those who had requested their land was to refuse to rent it to the *agraristas* who had not yet received their ejido, a practice clearly common throughout the state. For example, in 1925 Julio Cuadros Caldas wrote that

> The latifundists of Guerrero have adopted a tactic of exquisite egoism which is sowing disorders and misery everywhere and [which] consists in obstinately refusing [to rent] lands to neighboring pueblos and bringing from distant villages blackleg peasants. Cases have arisen, like that of Acayahualco, in which the pueblo has collected in advance the value of the rent and deposited it with . . . the governor of the state who provided his good offices, to no avail to this day, so that one Licenciado [Miguel F.] Ortega, the representative of the farm, should rent lands to the residents [of Acayahualco]. There have been cases in which an *hacendado* prefers to leave the lands idle rather than give them to the people, with a spirit of base vengeance for [their] having asked for ejidos.[49]

As a result of these tactics, land seizures by the pueblos became frequent, since many municipal authorities were hostile to the *agraristas* and refused to use their legal powers to allocate them land under the Law of Idle Lands.[50]

The first mentions of the landowners of northern Guerrero refusing to rent land to *agraristas* date from March and April 1918,[51] and by 1923 the practice was causing serious disorders. For example, in November 1922 the *agraristas* of Cocula began to complain that the local landowners would rent them land only under onerous conditions, and in May 1923 the leaders of Cocula informed President Obregón that they had decided to seize the land they needed, "rather than see [their] families die [of] hunger and poverty." As a consequence of this illegal invasion, on 28 May the *agrarista* leaders of Cocula, Atlixtac, Apipilulco, and Xonacatla were arrested by federal troops.[52] Such events were so widespread that the state government had to issue a circular in July ordering *presidentes municipales* to allow the pueblos to occupy uncultivated lands so as to avoid disorders.[53]

At times, the tactics employed by the landowners and their allies in the municipal and, on occasion, state authorities succeeded in dividing the *agraristas*, setting one group against another. Thus, in 1935 the *presidente municipal* of Tepecoacuilco, who had close links with the landowner Miguel F. Ortega, refused to allow the *agraristas* of Rincón de la Cocina and Acayahualco to work Ortega's land as idle lands. Instead, the municipal authorities rented this land to the *agraristas* of Tierra Colorada.[54] In this case, the municipal authorities were applying the policy of Governor Gabriel R. Guevara, who had ordered that they refuse "all the requests for idle lands which in their judgment they thought it prudent to turn down."[55]

The support of the civil or military authorities was often crucial to the success of the landowners' tactics, and both elements were present in the case of Río Balsas, which had been in possession of its ejido since 1922. In 1925 the president of the Comisón Nacional Agraria wrote to President Calles that, although Río Balsas's possession of its ejido was perfectly legal, one of the affected landowners refused to let the *ejidatarios* work the land taken from her property, while another, Rafael del Castillo Calderón, continued to charge rent for the land taken from him. Consequently, "the *vecinos* of Río Balsas have not been able to enjoy . . . the lands which were given to them, since the aforementioned landowners, supported by the municipal authorities, and, on some occasions, by the federal forces, continue their lamentable attitude, flaunting the impunity which they enjoy."[56]

Other means of harassing the ejidos were open to the landowners. For example, in December 1920 the *ejidatarios* of Apipilulco complained that the administrator of the Hacienda de Atlixtac had diverted the course of the River Cocula, thus depriving them of irrigation water.[57] Then again, on occasion the large landowners found allies among the smallholders of the region. For example, in 1922 the Italian manager of the Hacienda de Santa Fe Tepetlapa, Antonio Valezzi, won the support of the militia of the smallholding town of Buenavista de Cuéllar, in order to collect rents from the *agraristas* of Santa Fe. Later, in 1925, when Santa Fe had been granted its ejido, Valezzi and the officer commanding the militia of Buenavista attempted to take over the day-to-day running of the ejido. Valezzi was further aided on this occasion by a group of prosperous *anti-agrarista* peasants in Santa Fe itself.[58]

If the opposition of the large landowners to the agrarian reform was constant and determined, still more so was the resistance of the smaller landowners. The ranchero's attitude to the reform was well expressed in a letter which 121 smallholders from Huitzuco wrote to President Cárdenas in 1938. Huitzuco, they said, did not need an ejido. Moreover, communal ownership of the land had been proved a failure, for it promoted laziness and criminal behavior, as well as reducing the volume of production. "Many of those who sign this memorandum," they told Cárdenas, "have been born and have grown

up on the small piece of land which we possess today and which . . .
we have managed to buy by dint of perseverance and sacrifices; we
are satisfied at having always fulfilled our duties and obligations as
citizens and taxpayers, even in the periods of armed agitation."[59]
These people, proud of their status as respected citizens who had
carved out their position in society by dint of self-help and hard
work, could hardly be expected to be sympathetic to the new doctrines of *agrarismo*. After all, the roots of ranchero society in northern Guerrero lay in the Reforma, which regarded private property as
inviolable, rather than in the doctrines of the social function of
property.

The resistance of the small landowners tended to be much more
violent than that of the larger owners. Perhaps the most violent
struggle between *agraristas* and rancheros was that of Tlaxmalac, a
town close to Huitzuco. In 1939 there were in Tlaxmalac 178 small
landowners, who owned farms ranging from less than a hectare to
180 hectares.[60] Division of the land was a continuing process in
Tlaxmalac, and by 1949 there were 270 owners of a total of 388 properties, only 26 of which exceeded 100 hectares, and only 2 individuals possessed more than 500 hectares.[61] When an *agrarista* group was
formed in Tlaxmalac, a fierce struggle broke out between the landowners and those who sought an ejido. In 1925 a group of thirty-
seven landowners murdered the leader of the *agraristas*, Sabino
Loza, and nine years later a member of the agrarian committee was
murdered by a hired assassin.[62] In 1948 the struggle continued una-
bated, according to Salvador Loza, son of the murdered *agrarista*,
who complained that since his father's death "an era of terror was
implanted, for the majority of the *agraristas* have had to emigrate,
seeking refuge in other parts of the republic."[63]

The struggle was especially bitter in the municipality of Huitzuco, where the ranchero element was numerous. For example, in
Quetzalapa, like Tlaxmalac a smallholding town, it was reported in
1940 that "there exists pressure on the part of some small landowners on the few peasants that there are in the village who lack
lands, since . . . [the landless peasants] are terrorized in different
ways, until . . . they abandon the place to go and settle in another
place. . . . the present residents of the village in the majority are
small landowners and are opposed to any agrarian question."[64] Likewise, in neighboring Chaucingo, "despite the fact that . . . they are
nearly all relatives, in this question of lands [the *vecinos*] are very
divided."[65]

As these last two cases suggest, the countryside was by no means
unanimously *agrarista*. Moreover, it was not only landowners who

opposed the agrarian reform, for the landless peasantry was by no means united, nor was it always in sympathy with the reform program. Jean Meyer has shown that a deep rift divided the *agrarista* and the *anti-agrarista* peasants,[66] and this rift could be quite clearly observed in the districts of Alarcón and Hidalgo. In Tonalapa del Sur, for example, of 153 eligible individuals only 35 wanted land, "the rest having said that they do not want lands which they have not bought."[67] Even more vigorous opposition to the reform was encountered by the *agraristas* of Santiago, who received definitive possession of seventy-two hectares in 1935, but were unable to use the land because the campesinos of Agualulco, Tlachichilpa, El Ranchito, and Noxtepec, who had always refused to petition for ejidos, threatened to kill any *ejidatario* from Santiago who attempted to work the land.[68] In El Platanar, more than half the eligible individuals wrote to the Agrarian Commission that they did not wish to be included in the petition for an ejido because the local landowner, Amado Figueroa, treated them well, providing them with work animals and credit.[69] Likewise, in Santiago Temixco the *anti-agrarista* faction, allied with the local owner of a 220-hectare sugar farm, outnumbered the agrarians by five to one.[70]

Still further lines of division pitted peasant against peasant in northern Guerrero in the 1920s and 1930s, for the *agraristas* were often deeply divided among themselves. Frequently one ejido was engaged in bitter enmity with another, or, indeed, with several others. We know already that something of a precedent existed for rivalry between ejidos in the form of the often violent quarrels which had divided the communal landowning villages of the area since colonial times. Indeed, one dispute over *ejidal* lands began even before the reform program was officially under way and continued on into the 1970s. In 1916 the local Zapatistas carried out a *reparto* of the lands around Cocula and Apipilulco, which gave rise to a dispute over some 100 hectares of land which Epifanio Rodríquez, a general from Apipilulco, claimed for his town, while two Cocula Zapatistas, Hesiquio Román and Pedro Suárez, asserted that Cocula was entitled to the land. The quarrel nearly came to a fight there and then, but tempers cooled and Cocula eventually won control of the disputed land. Shortly afterwards, however, Rodríguez had Suárez killed in revenge.[71] This did not end the matter, and the enmity between the two pueblos flared up again in 1920, when Apipilulco was granted an ejido which included 290 hectares of irrigated land. However, due to an improper classification of the land, and also because Cocula deprived Apipilulco of irrigation water, the latter never actually received the irrigated land to which it was entitled. The *agraristas* of

Apipilulco made good this oversight, however, by simply seizing a further portion of irrigated land, which, however, was allocated to Cocula in 1930 when it received its own ejido. The old conflict of 1916 was thus revived. Two unsuccessful attempts were made to solve the problem in 1932 and 1934, but after this the authorities appear to have neglected the question until, in 1970, the dispute led to a fracas in which two or three *ejidatarios* lost their lives.[72]

While not all disputes were quite so long-lived as that of Apipilulco and Cocula, numerous conflicts arose as villages vied for the best land, or for control of water rights. Thus, in 1935 the representatives of Acalman complained that "since we began to request *Dotación* of our Ejido we have suffered certain disagreements with the *Ejidatarios* of the *Cuadrilla* of Tlanipatlán of this Municipality who have interfered to prevent us from being given the piece of land which we already have mapped out." The reason for the opposition of Tlanipatlán was that the proposed grant to Acalman included a small stream which watered land cultivated by the *ejidatarios* of Tlanipatlán.[73]

Poor definition of the boundaries of the ejidos was often the cause of disputes. For example, in 1925 the *agraristas* of Palmillas complained that "in view of the fact that the *vecinos* of Coxcatlán have tried to charge rents to the *vecinos* of this *cuadrilla* who have planted fields even within the urban zone of [Palmillas], various difficulties having arisen through this cause, since [the *ejidatarios* of Coxcatlán] recognize even our houses as [part of their] *dotación*, we ask most attentively that [the Procuraduría de Pueblos] see fit to send an engineer to mark the boundaries of this *cuadrilla* until the procedure of *dotación* is completed."[74] This evidently was not done, however, since agreement between the two villages was not reached until 1929.[75]

If disputes between ejidos were harmful to the interests of the *ejidatarios*, still more damaging to the success of the reform were the frequent internal disputes and tensions to which the ejido lent itself. For, if agrarianism on the national and state level was a particularly effective instrument for mobilizing peasant support for the regime, at the municipal and village level the reform provided ample opportunities for factionalism, political intrigue, and manipulation. This was partly due to the fact that the ejido proved a uniquely suitable vehicle for furthering the ambitions of local *politicastros*, the ejido of Iguala being a case in point. The president of the Executive Committee which negotiated the grant of Iguala's ejido was one Jesús Nava, a man active in *agrarista* political circles and a committee member of the League of Agrarian Communities formed in

Iguala in 1923. Nava worked closely with Primitivo Torres, the local agent of the Partido Nacional Agrarista in Iguala. After the grant of Iguala's ejido in 1921, Nava and Torres exercised control over the functions of the ejido by means of the president of the Administrative Committee, Encarnación Bello, who worked hand in glove with the two politicians. Thus, Torres, and not the elected representatives of Iguala, carried out the distribution of the ejido's land, charging the *ejidatarios* from $1 to $5 apiece for the parcel to which they were entitled without charge. Nava and Torres also used their control of the ejido as a means to control the municipal elections of 1921 and 1922. However, in September of 1922 Bello broke with Torres and Nava, who held a meeting of a sizable group of citizens (fifty-nine of whom were not even *ejidatarios*) to expel Bello from office. Bello, however, refused to relinquish his post and carried out a new distribution of part of the ejido's lands. Nevertheless, Nava and Torres kept up their attacks on Bello, and in March 1923 officially sanctioned elections were held for a new Administrative Committee.[76] This was not the end of the story of political interference in the ejido, however, since a rift promptly developed between Nava and Torres, and the latter absented himself from Iguala for a time, only to return in 1924 as a member of the *ayuntamiento* of Iguala. Torres used his municipal office in an attempt to take over part of the ejido's land to form an agricultural colony, apparently without success.[77]

The potential for internal dissension in the ejido was to some degree due to its role as an instrument of political patronage. For example, in 1920 the commander of the militia in Polocingo, Germán Sánchez, offered the best land of the ejido to those who followed him in support of Obregón's revolution of Agua Prieta. Seventeen volunteers took up Sánchez's offer and participated in General Rómulo Figueroa's march on Mexico City, and in May 1922, when Sánchez's control of the ejido was challenged, he obtained from General Figueroa a certificate detailing his services in Obregón's cause and used this to petition the president for his support. However, Sánchez failed to retain control of the ejido, since a year later new elections for the administrative committee ousted him from office.[78]

The ejido was quite clearly regarded as a political, as well as an economic, institution, as the case of Tuxpan further illustrates. In 1934 Julio O. Hernández wrote to the federal congressman Ezequiel Padilla, a prominent Callista politician, explaining the internal difficulties afflicting the ejido of Tuxpan. The agrarian authorities, he explained, had ordered an equal distribution of the ejido among all of the 203 *ejidatarios* who had been granted land. Tuxpan, Hernández wrote, did not have enough land for all its *ejidatarios*, and anyway he believed that only the "true *agraristas*," who had supported the government during the Escobarista rebellion five years earlier, should be entitled to land. Those who had joined the rebel cause should be excluded from participation in the benefits of the agrarian reform.[79]

Such internal divisions along national political lines were not infrequent. In Cocula a conflict evolved after the de la Huerta revolt of 1923 between those *ejidatarios* who fought for the rebels and those who campaigned in the loyalist forces of Adrián Castrejón. The quarrel led to the death of at least one *ejidatario*. Moreover, the divisions in the ranks of the *ejidatarios* were exploited by local merchants and wealthy peasants for their own ends, notably by the owner of the sugar mill in Apipilulco where Cocula's cane crop was processed, and by two men who, despite the fact that they were not *ejidatarios*, were able to grow sugarcane on *ejidal* lands with the connivance of the *ejidal* authorities.[80]

The political role assigned to the ejido, a source of much internal factionalism, also made it an attractive instrument of political manipulation to outside interests. Gabriel R. Guevara was one politician who made particular use of the ejidos for electoral ends. Thus, in 1932 the president and secretary of the agrarian committee of Pantla del Zapotal complained that an agrarian reform official had visited their ejido with several propagandists of Guevara, who was "pre-candidate" of the PNR for the state governorship, and had ordered the committee to support the general's candidacy or face removal from office if they failed to do as ordered.[81] Similarly, in 1934 the *ejidatarios* of Maxela were "invited" to vote for Alberto Guevara, the governor's brother, in the elections for the federal Congress. When they refused to support Guevara, the governor ordered that they be punished for their insubordination.[82]

In the municipality of Tepecoacuilco, one Antonio Moyado B. was particularly active in interfering in the affairs of the ejidos during the latter part of the administration of Adrián Castrejón and the governorship of Gabriel Guevara. In June 1928 Moyado, a classic agrarian cacique, deposed the administrative committee of the ejido of Mayanalán and endeavored to repeat this success in nearby Polocingo. In Maxela he supported a family of small landowners named Martínez, who attempted to seize part of the ejido's land and, in return for Moyado's support, acted as his agents in the area.[83]

At once an instrument of social reform and of political manipulation, the agrarian reform's impact on the rural society of northern Guerrero was extremely complex. Not only did the traditional hostility between landholding villages become more generalized and acute, but a number of new rifts divided the populace. By 1940 the agrarian reform had left the peasantry divided and weakened and had created a large group (10,525 *ejidatarios*) which was dependent on the state for the land which it held in usufruct. Although one cannot assert with confidence that the creation of these divisions in Mexican rural society was the work of a consciously pursued policy, it no doubt greatly facilitated the establishment of a degree of political control over the peasantry, and the pacification of the country in general. It is certainly clear that the ejido was seen not only as a unit of production and a means to bring a greater degree of "social justice," but also as an instrument of political control and manipulation. David Ronfeldt's study of Atencingo, Puebla, shows quite clearly that despite the rhetoric of social reform, "in effect the government officially licensed monopoly capitalism and exploitation." The real beneficiaries of the creation of the ejido of Atencingo were not the *ejidatarios*, but the entrepreneur William Jenkins and the Mexican government.[84]

In Guerrero the reform had considerable political implications. On the state level it provided a readily available power base for the local politicians. Rodolfo Neri, for example, had proved that the *agraristas* could provide potent military and political support, even against the army and the volunteer forces armed by Rómulo Figueroa. This was a lesson which was not completely lost even on generally *anti-agrarista* politicians such as Héctor F. López and Gabriel Guevara, who, while generally opposed to agrarian reform, nevertheless allied themselves with *agrarista* groups in some parts of the state. At the municipal level, the ejido constituted, in fact if not in law, a parallel power base from which the *ayuntamiento* could often be controlled, as Jesús Nava and Primitivo Torres had learned in Iguala. Finally, at the village level the ejido could often be divided into squabbling factions, which could ally themselves with national factions: in Cocula with Obregón or de la Huerta, in Tuxpan with Calles or Escobar.

As a unit of production, the ejido (with some notable exceptions such as the collective farms of La Laguna and the sugar-growing ejidos of Morelos) could never produce sufficiently to provide anything more than bare subsistence for the average *ejidatario*. Few *ejidatarios* could hope to produce a sizable marketable surplus, and, indeed, many had to rely on wage labor and other means to supplement the production of the *ejidal* parcel. Nevertheless, the rural society of the districts of Alarcón and Hidalgo had undergone a profound transformation by 1940. Many large landowners had lost nearly all their land, while others had lost at least a considerable portion. While the enterprising ranchero—of which the Figueroa family was perhaps the most notable example—would continue to play a considerable part in the social and economic life of northern Guerrero, the large landowner who lived from renting land—of whom Miguel Montúfar and Alberto Rivera were the supreme examples—would no longer figure prominently. For not only had they lost much of their land, but the discipline on which rent collection depended had been largely destroyed by the years of revolutionary upheaval and the new doctrines of *agrarismo* and the social function of private property. The *ejidatarios* may well be said to have merely exchanged one form of domination for another, but they had, at least, gained a piece of land which, in some senses, was their own. As François Chevalier has pointed out, the *ejidatario* "is concerned above all with preserving results already achieved, even if these have now become more or less illusory from the economic point of view."[85] The role of the ejido in preserving political stability in Mexico has surely been one of its most significant contributions to the development of the contemporary Mexican state.

Epilogue

The Mexican revolution imposed on a reluctant peasant society a dynamic, modern nation-state dedicated to, indeed obsessed with, the development of a strong capitalist economy. The instrument of what Meyer has called this "capitalist project" (as opposed to the "peasant project" of the nation at large)[1] was the state. When all is said and done, all the complexities of the Mexican revolution can be reduced to this one dimension: the state. "Ironically enough," as Peter Smith has observed, "the PRI has not really institutionalized the Revolution, as its name proclaims. What it has done is to find a new formula for reinstitutionalizing the essence of the Porfiriato."[2] In the 1920s the energetic and ruthless leaders of the Sonoran dynasty built the foundations of this new state apparatus out of the ashes of a decade of revolutionary turmoil, and in the 1930s Lázaro Cárdenas polished and perfected the work of his predecessors. Obregón, Calles, and Cárdenas thus bestowed on their successors the basic levers of power with which they rule today.

In forging the new state, the revolution rode roughshod over a plethora of popular, nostalgic, and conservative movements. In Guerrero, the upshot was the death of efforts to restore the nineteenth-century *cacicazgo* of Juan Alvarez. Yet, curiously, the past lived on in revolutionary "dynasties" which have prospered for decades by following the new career paths mapped by the revolution. Thus the Figueroas, political pariahs in 1924, returned in the 1930s to the political stage of Guerrero. Theirs is not an isolated case, although it is perhaps the most striking and dramatic. On the Costa Chica the Guilléns, already prominent figures in the days of Porfirio Díaz, were revolutionaries in 1911 and were still making political careers for themselves in the 1940s. Still more long-lived were the dynasties of the Regueras and Añorves of Ometepec, where both families were prominent Royalists in the Wars of Independence, held local political office throughout the nineteenth century, joined the Maderista revolution, and were still holding political office decades later.[3] The Neris of Chilpancingo likewise bridged the Porfiriato and the revolution, and still other family names had a way of returning from the past to haunt the present.[4] Even the geographical patterns of conflict tended to repeat nineteenth-century motifs: in the previous century the interior (Bravo and Jiménez) had battled the coast (Juan and Diego Alvarez); during the revolution Julián Blanco from Dos Caminos, near Chilpancingo, disputed control of the state with Silvestre G. Mariscal of Atoyac, on the Costa Grande; and, similarly, in 1975 Rubén Figueroa (the interior) was locked in struggle with Israel Nogueda Otero (the coast).[5]

One might speculate that the revolution, whether as a matter of policy or merely through some accidental process, absorbed many of the established family dynasties in Guerrero and molded them into the new political system. In terms of its personnel at least, the new Mexico was, perhaps, not so very new after all.

Glossary

agrarismo   the ideology or political movement in favor of agrarian reform.
agraristas   supporters or beneficiaries of agrarian reform.
alcalde   alternative term for *presidente municipal.*
amparo   a legal term meaning "stay."
ampliación   the process of expanding the grant of an ejido.
ayuntamiento   a municipal government.
buscón   a freelance mine worker.
cacicazgo   the domain or region of influence of a cacique.
cacique   a local or regional boss.
campesino   literally, a person from the field; a peasant.
carga   a unit of measurement for grain equivalent to 200 liters.
casco de hacienda   the house, barns, storehouses (etc.) of an hacienda, usually the administrative core of the estate.
castas   people of mixed race; a term employed in colonial Mexico.
caudillaje   the phenomenon of caudillo politics.
caudillismo   an alternative term for *caudillaje.*
caudillo   a military-political strongman.
charro   a horseman, or one who wears the typical clothing of a Mexican rider.
colorados   troops of Ambrosio Figueroa, so called for their red shirts.
comandante de la división del sur   Commander of the Division of the South.
comisario   the principal public official in a town or village subject to the seat of municipal government.
comisión permanente   the Ways and Means Committee of the Mexican Congress.
costeño   a person from the coast.
cuadrilla   a village situated on land (private or communal) which it does not own.
cuartillo   a unit of measurement of grain approximately equivalent to ninety-six liters.
cuerpos rurales   corps of rural paramilitary police.
defensa social   a rural militia.
diputado   a congressman.

dotación   the process of granting an ejido.
ejidatario   a member of an ejido.
ejido   land held in usufruct from the government by a village or town.
fanega   a unit of measurement of grain approximately equivalent to one and a half bushels, and by extension an area of land capable of being sown with one fanega of seed.
gachupín   (derogatory) a Spaniard.
ganado mayor   beasts of burden or work animals.
gente de razón   literally "rational people," and by extension whites. A colonial term.
guardia blanca   private bodyguards or gang of thugs employed by a landowner.
guerrerense   a native of Guerrero.
hacendado   the owner of an hacienda.
hacienda de beneficio   an ore-processing plant.
huitzuquense   a native of Huitzuco.
jalisciense   a native of Jalisco.
jefe de las operaciones militares   a regional military commander.
juez municipal   municipal judge or magistrate.
juzgado de letras   a district court.
morelense   a resident of Morelos.
mostrenco   ownerless or unclaimed property.
oaxaqueño   a native of Oaxaca.
oficial mayor   chief administrative officer.
parcialidad   a form of communal land tenure.
parcionero   a member of a *parcialidad*.
partido   an administrative unit equivalent to the district.
pinto   a person of mixed Indian and black blood.
politicastro   (derogatory) a petty politician.
político   a politician.
prefecto político   an appointed official who administered a district, a unit of government comprising several municipalities.
presidente municipal   the chairman of a municipal council.
procurador de justicia   attorney general.
procurador general de la república   attorney general.
pronunciamiento   a *coup d'etat*.
pueblo   a village.
ranchería   a village formed by rancheros.
ranchero   a smallholder.
rancho   a smallholding.
secretaría de la reforma agraria   Ministry of Agrarian Reform.
secretario de gobernación   minister of the interior.
temporal   land cultivated using seasonal rainfall.
terreno baldío   vacant land.
tienda de raya   a company store on an hacienda or in an industrial concern.
tierras ociosas   lands deliberately left uncultivated.
tinterillo   (derogatory) a lawyer.

tlacolol the slash and burn method of cultivation, or land cultivated by that method.

vecino a resident of a town or village.

vicaría a parish.

yunta a unit of land measurement equivalent to about two and a half hectares.

Abbreviations: Archival Sources

AGGEG   Archivo General del Gobierno del Estado de Guerrero, Chilpancingo, Guerrero.

AGN   Archivo General de la Nación, Mexico, D.F.

AHDN   Archivo Histórico de la Defensa Nacional, annotated index of Luis Muro, Colegio de México, Mexico, D.F.

AM   Archivo de Madero, Biblioteca Nacional de México, Mexico, D.F.

AMT   Archivo Municipal de Taxco, Taxco, Guerrero.

AOM   Archivo del General Octavio Magaña, Universidad Nacional Autónoma de México, Mexico, D.F.

ARD   Archivo de Alfredo Robles Domínguez, Instituto de Estudios Históricos de la Revolución Mexicana, Mexico, D.F.

ASRA   Archivo de la Secretaría de la Reforma Agraria, Mexico, D.F.

AVC   Archivo de Venustiano Carranza, Instituto de Estudios Históricos de México, Condumex, S.A., Mexico, D.F.

MID   United States National Archives, Military Intelligence Division, Washington, D.C.

NA, RG 84   United States of America National Archives, Record Group 84, papers of the Acapulco consulate, Washington, D.C.

RDS   United States National Archives, Records of the Department of State Relating to Internal Affairs of Mexico, 1910–1929, Microfilm No. 274.

Notes

Introduction

1. Hans Gadow, *Through Southern Mexico: Being an Account of the Travels of a Naturalist* (London and New York, 1908), p. 364.
2. Jesús Figueroa Alcocer, *Crónica de la revolución en Guerrero* (Mexico, 1971), p. 16; Arturo Figueroa Uriza, *Ciudadanos en armas. Antecedencias y datos para la historia de la revolución mexicana* (2 vols.; Mexico, 1960), I, 40.
3. Figueroa Uriza, *Ciudadanos en armas*, I, 39–40.
4. Ibid., I, 45–47.
5. Frank Tannenbaum, *The Mexican Agrarian Revolution* (Washington, D.C., 1930).
6. David C. Bailey, "Revisionism and the Recent Historiography of the Mexican Revolution," *Hispanic American Historical Review*, 58 (1) (February 1978), 68–70.
7. Ibid., p. 63.
8. Ibid., pp. 73–74.
9. For example, Jean Meyer, *La cristiada* (3 vols., Mexico, 1973), has drawn on a wealth of local sources to reevaluate the Cristero rebellion in particular and the revolution in general.
10. Barry Carr, "Recent Regional Studies of the Mexican Revolution," *Latin American Research Review*, 15 (1) (1980), 4.
11. The bible of the microhistorian is Luis González, *Invitación a la microhistoria* (Mexico, 1973).
12. Ibid., pp. 4–5, 9–10.
13. For a stimulating example, see Alan Knight, "Peasant and Caudillo in Revolutionary Mexico 1910–17," in D. A. Brading (ed.), *Caudillo and Peasant in the Mexican Revolution* (Cambridge, 1980), pp. 17–58.
14. John Womack, Jr., *Zapata and the Mexican Revolution* (Harmondsworth, 1972).
15. Héctor Aguilar Camín, *La frontera nómada: Sonora y la revolución mexicana* (Mexico, 1977).
16. Ibid., pp. 19–124, especially pp. 39–49, 70–76, 88–94.
17. A phrase coined by David Brading—see Gilbert M. Joseph, "Caci-

quismo and the Revolution: Carrillo Puerto in Yucatán," in Brading (ed.), *Caudillo and Peasant,* p. 208.

18. Aguilar Camín, *Frontera nómada,* p. 132.
19. Héctor Aguilar Camín, "The Relevant Tradition: Sonoran Leaders in the Revolution," in Brading (ed.), *Caudillo and Peasant,* p. 117.
20. Ibid., pp. 92–123; Aguilar Camín, *Frontera nómada,* pp. 411–46.
21. Douglas W. Richmond, "Factional Strife in Coahuila, 1910–1920," *Hispanic American Historical Review,* 60 (1) (February 1980), 49–56, 64–68.
22. Friedrich Katz, "Pancho Villa," in George F. Wolskill and Douglas W. Richmond (eds.), *Essays on the Mexican Revolution* (Austin, Texas, 1979), pp. 28–31.
23. Mark Wasserman, "The Social Origins of the 1910 Revolution in Chihuahua," *Latin American Research Review,* 15 (1) (1980), 17–38; Mark Wasserman, "Oligarquía e intereses extranjeros en Chihuahua durante el Porfiriato," *Historia Mexicana,* 22 (3) (enero–marzo 1973), 279–93; Robert Sandels, "Antecendentes de la revolución en Chihuahua," *Historia Mexicana,* 24 (3) (enero–marzo 1975), 390–402.
24. Katz, "Pancho Villa," pp. 28, 35. For a comparison of Chihuahua and Morelos, see Friedrich Katz, "Peasants in the Mexican Revolution of 1910," in Joseph Spielberg and Scott Whiteford (eds.), *Forging Nations: A Comparative View of Rural Ferment and Revolt* (East Lansing, Michigan, 1976).
25. Aguilar Camín, *Frontera nómada,* pp. 289–94, 329–34.
26. Friedrich Katz, "Agrarian Changes in Northern Mexico in the Period of *Villista* Rule, 1913–1915," in James W. Wilkie, Michael C. Meyer, and Edna Monzón de Wilkie (eds.), *Contemporary Mexico: Papers of the IV International Congress of Mexican History* (Berkeley and Los Angeles, 1976), pp. 270–73; see also Katz, "Pancho Villa, Peasant Movements and Agrarian Reform in Northern Mexico," in Brading (ed.), *Caudillo and Peasant,* pp. 70–75.
27. Romana Falcón, "¿Los origenes populares de la revolución de 1910? El caso de San Luis Potosí," *Historia Mexicana,* 29 (2) (octubre–diciembre 1979), 197–240.
28. Dudley Ankerson, "Saturnino Cedillo, A Traditional Caudillo in San Luis Potosí 1890–1938," in Brading (ed.), *Caudillo and Peasant,* pp. 141–42; Victoria Lerner, "Los fundamentos socioeconómicos del *cacicazgo* en el México postrevolucionario. El caso de Saturnino Cedillo," *Historia Mexicana,* 29 (3) (enero–marzo 1979), 397.
29. Lerner, "Fundamentos socioeconómicos del *cacicazgo,*" p. 401.
30. Ibid., pp. 414–27; Ankerson, "Saturnino Cedillo," pp. 149–55.
31. Ankerson, "Saturnino Cedillo," p. 140.
32. Heather Fowler Salamini, *Agrarian Radicalism in Veracruz, 1920–1938* (Lincoln, Nebraska, 1978); Heather Fowler Salamini, "Revolutionary Caudillos in the 1920s: Francisco Múgica and Adalberto Tejeda," in Brading (ed.), *Caudillo and Peasant,* pp. 169–72, 182–92.
33. Fowler Salamini, "Revolutionary Caudillos," pp. 170, 172–81.

34. Gilbert M. Joseph, "Caciquismo and the Revolution," pp. 193–221.

35. Fowler Salamini, *Agrarian Radicalism*, pp. 73, 90–91, 163.

36. Paul Friedrich, *Agrarian Revolt in a Mexican Village* (Chicago, 1977).

37. Raymond Th. J. Buve, "Peasant Movements, Caudillos and Land Reform during the Revolution (1910–1917) in Tlaxcala, Mexico," *Boletín de Estudios Latinoamericanos y del Caribe*, 18 (June 1975), 121–49; "Protestas de obreros y campesinos durante el Porfiriato: Unas consideraciones sobre su desarollo e interrelaciones en el este de México central," *Boletín de Estudios Latinoamericanos*, 13 (diciembre 1972), 1–20.

38. Raymond Th. J. Buve, "State Governors and Peasant Mobilization in Tlaxcala," in Brading (ed.), *Caudillo and Peasant*, pp. 222–44.

39. Ronald Waterbury, "Non-revolutionary Peasants: Oaxaca Compared to Morelos in the Mexican Revolution," *Comparative Studies in Society and History*, 17 (1975), 410–42.

40. See, for example, David Ronfeldt, *Atencingo, Politics of Agrarian Struggle in a Mexican Ejido* (Stanford, California, 1973), as well as some of the local studies already cited.

41. As well as the studies already cited, see Barry Carr, "Las peculiaridades del norte mexicano, 1880–1927: Ensayo de interpretación," *Historia Mexicana*, 22 (3) (enero–marzo 1973), 324.

42. See, for example, Enrique Florescano and Isabel Gil Sánchez (eds.), *Descripciones económicas regionales de Nueva España* (2 vols.; Mexico, 1976), II, 75–76, 80–81, 97, 104, 140, *passim*.

43. For example, Carl Sartorius, *Mexico about 1850* (Stuttgart, 1961), pp. 84, 87, 93–94, 167, 179–81, 185–86; C. Harvey Gardiner (ed.), *Mexico 1824–1828: The Journal and Correspondence of Edward Thornton Tayloe* (Chapel Hill, North Carolina, 1959), pp. 45, 140, 143–44, 148, 184–86.

44. Wistano Luis Orozco, *Legislación y jurisprudencia sobre terrenos baldíos por el Licenciado Don Wistano Luis Orozco* (2 vols.; Mexico, 1895), II, 941–47; Andrés Molina Enríquez, *Los grandes problemas nacionales* (Mexico, 1909), pp. 81–104.

45. George M. McBride, *The Land Systems of Mexico* (New York, 1923), p. 101.

46. Paul S. Taylor, *A Spanish-Mexican Peasant Community: Arandas in Jalisco, Mexico*, Ibero Americana: 4 (Berkeley, 1933).

47. Luis González, *Pueblo en vilo. Microhistoria de San José de Gracia* (Mexico, 1968). All references here, however, are to the revised second edition (Mexico, 1972).

48. Ibid., pp. 29–43, 84–85.

49. See, for example, Tomás Martínez Saldaña and Leticia Gándara Mendoza, *Política y sociedad en México: El caso de Los Altos de Jalisco* (Mexico, 1976); Oriol Pi-Sunyer, *Zamora: Change and Continuity in a Mexican Town* (New York, 1973). An as yet unpublished study of a ranchero community in northern Jalisco is Robert Dennis Shadow, "Land, Labor and Cattle: The Agrarian Economy of a West Mexican

Municipio" (Ph.D. thesis, State University of New York, Stony Brook, 1978).
50. D. A. Brading, *Haciendas and Ranchos in the Mexican Bajío: León 1700–1860* (Cambridge, 1978).
51. Ibid., pp. 149–73, 208, 217.
52. Frans J. Schryer, *The Rancheros of Pisaflores: The History of a Peasant Bourgeoisie in Twentieth Century Mexico* (Toronto, 1980). See also Schryer's "A Ranchero Economy in Northwestern Hidalgo, 1880–1920," *Hispanic American Historical Review*, 59 (3) (August 1979), 418–43; and Schryer, "The Role of the Rancheros of Central Mexico in the Mexican Revolution (The Case of the Sierra Alta de Hidalgo)," *Canadian Journal of Latin American Studies*, 4 (7) (1979), 21–41.
53. Schryer, *Rancheros of Pisaflores*, pp. 71–76.

1. Political Opposition in Guerrero during the Rule of Porfirio Díaz

1. Daniel Cosío Villegas, "¿Dónde está el villano?" *Historia Mexicana*, 1 (3) (enero–marzo 1952), 434–35.
2. Raymond Th. J. Buve, "Patronaje en las zonas rurales de México," *Boletín de Estudios Latinoamericanos y del Caribe*, 16 (June 1974), 6–9; Buve, "Peasant Movements," pp. 118–20.
3. Daniel Cosío Villegas, *Historia moderna de México. El Porfiriato. La vida política interior* (2 vols.; Mexico, 1970–1972), II, 23.
4. Cosío Villegas, "¿Dónde está el villano?" p. 436.
5. Ibid., pp. 436–37.
6. Cosío Villegas, *Historia moderna de México. El Porfiriato. La vida política interior*, I, 295–98, 301, 309–10.
7. Ibid., I, 615–23, 627–46.
8. Ibid., II, 305.
9. Ibid., II, 110–22.
10. Ibid., II, 76–78.
11. Clyde Gilbert Bushnell, "The Military and Political Career of Juan Alvarez, 1790–1867" (Thesis, University of Texas, Austin, 1958), pp. 1–2.
12. Fernando Díaz Díaz, *Caudillos y caciques: Antonio López de Santa Anna y Juan Alvarez* (Mexico, 1972), pp. 103–4.
13. Ibid., pp. 105–6.
14. Ibid., p. 107.
15. Ibid., pp. 111–15.
16. Ibid., pp. 95–100.
17. Miguel Domínguez, *La erección del estado de Guerrero; Antecedentes historicos* (Mexico, 1949), pp. 24–25.
18. On the "Guerra de Castas" in Guerrero, see ibid., pp. 41–49; Bushnell, "Military and Political Career," pp. 136–43; Díaz Díaz, *Caudillos*, pp. 171–73.
19. Domínguez, *La erección del estado*, p. 45.
20. Ibid., p. 45.

21. Domínguez, *La erección del estado*, pp. 50–69; Bushnell, "Military and Political Career," pp. 220–21.

22. Bushnell, "Military and Political Career," p. 244.

23. For an outline biography of Jiménez, see General Héctor F. López [Mena], *Diccionario geográfico, histórico, biográfico y lingüístico del Estado de Guerrero* (Mexico, 1942), pp. 294–97.

24. Díaz Díaz, *Caudillos*, pp. 301, 304–5; Luis Guevara Ramírez, *Síntesis histórica del Estado de Guerrero* (Mexico, 1959), p. 94; Alberto María Carreño (ed.), *Archivo del General Porfirio Díaz* (29 vols.; Mexico, 1947–1960), IV, 168–70; V, 101–2, 336–37, 410; Laurens Ballard Perry, *Juárez and Díaz: Machine Politics in Mexico* (De Kalb, Illinois, 1978), pp. 90–96.

25. Carreño, *Archivo*, VII, 201; Moisés Ochoa Campos, *Breve historia del Estado de Guerrero* (Mexico, 1968), p. 221; Perry, *Juárez and Díaz*, pp. 95–96. Ochoa Campos states that Arce was a native of Zacatecas, which is clearly incorrect, as contemporary biographies show: *Periódico Oficial del Gobierno del Estado de Guerrero* (henceforth referred to as *Periódico Oficial*), 11 February 1891; Lázaro Pavia, *Los estados y sus gobernantes* (Mexico, 1890), p. 188.

26. Circular No. 28, 20 April 1869, in Guerrero, *Colección de decretos y circulares del gobierno del Estado de Guerrero* (Chilpancingo, Guerrero, 1869), I, 100–101.

27. "Manifiesto que el C. Gobernador Constitucional del Estado de Guerrero, general Francisco O. Arce, dirige a los pueblos del mismo," *Periódico Oficial*, 1, 12, 19, 26 October 1870. The Congress did not reach its verdict until 26 May 1870: Ochoa Campos, *Breve historia*, p. 221.

28. See Arce's "Manifiesto" of October 1870 for the judgment of the Supreme Court of Guerrero. See also Guerrero, *Memoria presentada ante la H. Legislatura del Estado de Guerrero por el C. Gobernador del mismo, General Francisco O. Arce, en cumplimiento de la fracción III del art. 57 de la Constitución* (Chilpancingo, Guerrero, 1872), pp. 6–7; Ochoa Campos, *Breve historia*, p. 221.

29. *Periódico Oficial*, 8, 19 October 1870; Arce's "Manifiesto," *Periódico Oficial*, 1, 12, 19, 26 October 1870; Ochoa Campos, *Breve historia*, pp. 221–22. On 21 November Neri attacked Chilpancingo itself: Guerrero, *Memoria* (1872), p. 21. On the national political contest, see Perry, *Juárez and Díaz*, pp. 144–46.

30. *Periódico Oficial*, 12 October 1870, which reproduces a speech to Congress given by Arce.

31. Ochoa Campos, *Breve historia*, p. 222.

32. Carreño, *Archivo*, IX, 176–77.

33. Ibid., IX, 167–68, 220–21, 240–42; Ochoa Campos, *Breve historia*, p. 223.

34. Guevara Ramírez, *Síntesis*, p. 100.

35. Cosío Villegas, *Historia moderna de México. El Porfiriato. La vida política interior*, I, 303; Moisés Ochoa Campos, *Historia del Estado de Guerrero* (Mexico, 1968), pp. 253–55. Cosío Villegas erroneously states

that Neri fought with Jiménez. The correspondence in Carreño, *Archivo*, concerning the events of 1876–1877 clearly shows that Neri sided with Alvarez.

36. Carreño, *Archivo*, XIV, 50–51, 62–63, 173–74, 223, 243–44.
37. Ibid., XVIII, 109–10, 286; XX, 30–31, 148–50.
38. Ibid., XX, 148–50; XXIV, 6–9; XXVI, 196–98.
39. Ibid., XIX, 25–28; XX, 260–61; XXI, 37–38, 41; XXII, 68–69.
40. Ibid., XIX, 25–28.
41. Ibid., XX, 100; XXI, 50–51.
42. Ibid., XXII, 129, 148–49; XXIII, 161–64.
43. Ibid., XXV, 213.
44. Ibid., XXIII, 21–22, 104–5, 204; XXV, 92; XXVI, 12.
45. Ibid., XXVI, 296–98.
46. Ibid., XXII, 275–76; XXIII, 182–84.
47. Ibid., XXIII, 193–94, 212, 258, 263–64, 290; XXIV, 119–20, 165–68, 206–7.
48. Ibid., XXIV, 183–86, 251–52; XXV, 112.
49. Ibid., XXIX, 14–17.
50. Ibid., XXIX, 112.
51. Ibid., XXIX, 202–4.
52. Ibid., XXIX, 200, 202–3. Neri had become vice-governor in October 1877: ibid., XXVII, 204.
53 Ibid., XXIII, 161–62.
54. Ibid., XXVII, 104, 122.
55. Ibid., XXV, 127; XXVI, 138–39, 143–44, 181–82.
56. Ibid., XXIX, 5–6, 14–17.
57. Cosío Villegas, *Historia moderna de México. El Porfiriato. La vida política interior*, I, 78.
58. On the crisis, see: *Periódico Oficial*, 2, 9, 16 February 1887; *El Diario del Hogar*, 19 January 1887.
59. *El Diario del Hogar*, 19 January 1887. Arce's apologists amitted the charge, but added that the requirement had never been observed in the past.
60. Ibid.
61. Ibid. Alvarez's influence in the legislature was evident: his son-in-law Cirilo Heredia held two seats, and his other sons-in-law, Lic. Rosendo Heredia and José G. Ney, also held seats, as did Félix P. Alvarez and Julio T. Alvarez. Relatives of Alvarez thus held six of the fourteen seats in Congress. See: Guerrero, *Memoria presentada al IX Congreso Constitucional del Estado por el Gobernador del mismo, General Francisco O. Arce, en cumplimiento de la fracción IV del artículo 4° de la Constitución* (Chilpancingo, Guerrero, 1886), p. 171.
62. Diego Alvarez to Ortiz de Montellano, 20 August 1886, *El Diario del Hogar*, 19 January 1887.
63. Arce to Alvarez, 20 October and 10 November 1886, and Alvarez to Arce, 3 November and 19 November 1886, in ibid. The emphasis is in the original.

64. Alvarez to *El Diario del Hogar*, 29 December 1886, in ibid.

65. In the correspondence published in *El Diario del Hogar* Ortiz de Montellano states that Arce "only came to help a friend, to keep his position for him." This would seem to imply that Arce was to be merely a caretaker, since Alvarez could not constitutionally be reelected without an intervening term. It may be doubted that this was ever the intention of Arce's protector, Porfirio Díaz, and perhaps this question was the true origin of the 1885 crisis.

66. *Periódico Oficial*, 18 May 1889.

67. Cosío Villegas, *Historia moderna de México. El Porfiriato. La vida política interior*, II, 79.

68. Article reprinted in *Periódico Oficial*, 14 December 1892.

69. Ibid., 17 December 1892.

70. *El Monitor Republicano*, 28 May 1893. For the election results, see: *Periódico Oficial*, 8 March 1893. For a biography of Ortiz de Montellano, see his obituary in *El Diario del Hogar*, 10 January 1901.

71. *La Federación*, 20 April 1893.

72. *El Monitor Republicano*, 9 April 1893.

73. *La Federación*, 20 July 1893.

74. *El Diario del Hogar*, 18 October 1893; *El Monitor Republicano*, 25 October 1893; *La Federación*, 19 October 1893.

75. Neri to Díaz, 18 October 1893, in *El Monitor Republicano*, 25 October 1893; *El Diario del Hogar*, 26 October 1893.

76. *El Diario del Hogar*, 2 November 1893.

77. *Periódico Oficial*, 20 and 27 December 1893, 10 January 1894; *El Diario del Hogar*, 8 December 1893.

78. *Periódico Oficial*, 18 October 1893; *La Federación*, 16 November 1893; *El Monitor Republicano*, 14 November 1893.

79. *El Diario del Hogar*, 5 November 1893; *El Monitor Republicano*, same date.

80. *Periódico Oficial*, 25 November 1893; *El Monitor Republicano*, 2 December 1893.

81. *Periódico Oficial*, 11 and 22 November 1893.

82. Decree No. 36, *Periódico Oficial*, 22 November 1893; *El Monitor Republicano*, 24 November 1893.

83. *La Federación*, 4 January 1894; *Periódico Oficial*, 12 January 1894.

84. *Periódico Oficial*, 7 March 1894; *El Diario del Hogar*, 24 January 1894. Mercenario was certainly not a native of Guerrero and was even rumored not to be a Mexican national. He had been administrator of the Acapulco customshouse, *prefecto político* of the districts of Tixtla and Hidalgo, a *diputado* in the state legislature, and at the time of Neri's revolt was *presidente municipal* of Huitzuco.

85. Both Neri and Diego Alvarez were presidents of clubs which endorsed both Mercenario and the reelection of Díaz: *El Imparcial*, 22 September and 17 November 1895.

86. Ochoa Campos, *Historia del Estado de Guerrero*, p. 264.

87. Alejandro Sánchez Castro, "La Revolución de Castillo Calderón," in

Fidel Franco, *Eusebio S. Almonte, Poeta mártir guerrerense* (Mexico, 1947), p. 29.

88. Castillo Calderón had been *secretario de gobierno,* and several times a *diputado* in the state Congress. In 1899 he had been an organizer of the "Gran Junta de Amigos del Senor General Díaz" in Guerrero, and a delegate to the Porfirista "Asamblea Constitucionalista de Mexico." See: *Periódico Oficial,* 6 May 1891, 15 March and 27 December 1899; *La Federación,* 8 June 1893.

89. See Decrees No. 47, 48, 15 January 1901, in Guerrero, *Memoria presentada al XVIII Congreso Constitucional, por el cuidadano Agustín Mora, Gobernador del Estado de Guerrero, en cumplimiento de la fracción IV del artículo 4° de la Constitución política local* (Chilpancingo, Guerrero, 1903), I, 184.

90. *El Diario del Hogar,* 6 April 1901.

91. Mora had virtually no connection with Guerrero: *El Diario del Hogar,* 20 April 1901. The appointment of a complete outsider no doubt aggravated the discontent of the people.

92. *El Diario del Hogar,* 16 April 1901; Sánchez Castro, "La Revolución," p. 30.

93. *El Diario del Hogar,* 17 April, 3 May 1901.

94. *El Diario del Hogar,* 17 April 1901. Ochoa Campos, *Historia del Estado de Guerrero,* p. 274, refers to a much more far-reaching plan, which rejected the Porfirian regime and called for effective suffrage, constitutional guarantees to meet the needs of workers and campesinos, and distribution of hacienda lands. Since he offers no proof of this plan, and cites no source, the existence of any such plan must be doubted. It is worth noting that both Castillo Calderón and Bello were *hacendados* in their own right.

95. *El Diario del Hogar,* 17 April 1901; *El País,* 12 April 1901; Franco, *Eusebio S. Almonte,* pp. 15–16.

96. *El Monitor Republicano,* 3 May 1901; Sánchez Castro, "La Revolución," p. 31.

97. Sánchez Castro, "La Revolución," pp. 31–33; Franco, *Eusebio S. Almonte,* pp. 16–17; *El Monitor Republicano,* 3 May 1901.

98. Circular of 29 October 1901, issued by the *presidente municipal* of Taxco: AMT, 1901.

99. On Blanco's participation, see: Custodio Valverde, *Julián Blanco y la revolución en el estado de Guerrero* (Mexico, 1916), p. 9.

100. Interview, Dr. Arturo Figueroa Uriza, Chilpancingo, 11 June 1975.

101. The following list (by no means comprehensive) gives some idea of the social status of the Figueroas: (1) Ambrosio: owner of Rancho de las Joyas; (2) Rómulo: owner of 67 hectares of irrigated land near Taxco, Rancho de Tequicuilco (2,400 hectares), a *nixtamal* mill, an ice plant, and a soap manufacturing business; (3) Francisco: from 1906 director of the school in Huitzuco; (4) Andrés: owner of a rancho; (5) Nicasio: owner of a rancho, shopkeeper; (6) Bernabé: owner of Rancho Nuevo.

Based on information in ASRA; Figueroa Uriza, *Ciudadanos en armas;* Figueroa Alcocer, *Crónica; El Diario del Hogar,* 20 December 1893.

102. Figueroa Uriza, *Cuidadanos en armas,* I, 47.

103. Figueroa Alcocer, *Crónica,* p. 13.

104. Guerrero, *Memoria* (1886), p. 172; Guerrero, *Memoria presentada al X Congreso Constitucional del Estado de Guerrero por el Gobernador del mismo, General Francisco O. Arce, en cumplimiento de la fracción IV del artículo 4° de la Constitución* (Chilpancingo, Guerrero, 1888), p. xxx; *Periódico Oficial,* 20 January 1892, 8 March 1893.

105. Juan Vicario, the principal Conservative chieftain, was a native of Huitzuco: Leopoldo Carranco Cardoso, *Acciones militares en el Estado de Guerrero* (Mexico, 1963), p. 22. Northern Guerrero generally was strongly Conservative: Daniel Muñoz y Pérez, *El General Don Juan Alvarez: Esbozo biográfico y selección de documentos de Daniel Muñoz y Pérez* (Mexico, 1959), pp. 452, 475–76.

106. Figueroa Alcocer, *Crónica,* p. 13; also Figueroa Uriza, *Cuidadanos en armas,* I, 28–30. Ambrosio and Francisco Figueroa were both students of Sáenz: José C. Gutiérrez Galindo, *Rubén Figueroa, permanencia de una revolución en Guerrero* (Mexico, 1975), pp. 27, 38.

107. *El Diario del Hogar,* 20 December 1893; Figueroa Uriza, *Ciudadanos en armas,* I, 33; Figueroa Alcocer, *Crónica,* p. 16; Gutiérrez Galindo, *Rubén Figueroa,* p. 83. The latter wrongly states that the shooting took place in 1910. The Christian name of the man killed varies in the accounts, but I assume that the contemporary account is accurate in this respect. Moronati's origins are obscure, but he had commercial and mining interests in Taxco from at least 1869: "Informe sobre la asignación hecha a D. Antonio Moronati por su capital como causante de la contribución de 1%," AMT, 1869.

108. *El Diario del Hogar,* 5 January 1894; Guerrero, *1894. Memoria presentada al XIV Congreso Constitucional por el Coronel Antonio Mercenario, Gobernador del Estado de Guerrero, en cumplimiento de la fracción IV del artículo 4° de la Constitución política local* (Chilpancingo, Guerrero, 1896), p. 40.

109. Figueroa Uriza, *Cuidadanos en armas,* I, 32; Figueroa Alcocer, *Crónica,* p. 15. For Moronati's group, see Figueroa Uriza, *Cuidadanos en armas.*

110. Guerrero, *Memoria* (1896), p. 40; Guerrero, *Memoria* (1903), p. 217; *Periódico Oficial,* 18 January 1896, 3 February 1897, 16 March 1898, 3 February 1900.

111. Figueroa Uriza, *Ciudadanos en armas,* I, 33–35; Figueroa Alcocer, *Crónica,* p. 15.

112. *Periódico Oficial,* 13 May 1905, 9 February 1910.

113. Sánchez Castro, "La Revolución," p. 32; Franco, *Eusebio S. Almonte,* p. 15; interview, Profesor Leopoldo Carranco Cardoso, Taxco, 14 June 1975; Leopoldo Carranco Cardoso, *Iniciación de la Guerra de Independencia en el Territorio del hoy Estado de Guerrero* (Iguala, Guerrero,

1967), p. 12. Silvestre G. Mariscal, a Maderista in 1911, may also have participated in the 1901 movement: Wilfrido Fierro Armenta, *Monografía de Atoyac* (Mexico, 1973), p. 167.

114. Cosío Villegas, *Historia moderna de México. El Porfiriato. La vida política interior*, II, 362–93.

115. Ibid., pp. 648–63.

116. Ibid., pp. 612–23; Jorge Fernando Iturribarría, "Limantour y la caída de Porfirio Díaz," *Historia Mexicana*, 10 (2) (octubre–diciembre 1960), 255.

117. On the Creelman interview, see: Charles Curtis Cumberland, *Mexican Revolution. Genesis under Madero* (Austin, Texas, 1952), pp. 47–48.

118. On Reyismo, see: ibid., pp. 81–85; Cosío Villegas, *Historia moderna de México. El Porfiriato. La vida política interior*, II, 807–16; Stanley R. Ross, *Francisco I. Madero, Apostle of Mexican Democracy* (New York, 1955), pp. 65–79.

119. On Anti-Reelectionism, see: Cumberland, *Mexican Revolution*, pp. 55–118; Ross, *Madero*, pp. 73–112.

120. A list of the social backgrounds of thirteen revolutionary figures is given in Vicente Fuentes Díaz, *La revolución de 1910 en el estado de Guerrero* (Mexico, 1960). The list includes six small landowners, three schoolteachers, one *hacendado*, two other landowners whose status is not specified, two mine owners, and one person from a well-off family. Some individuals fell into more than one category.

121. Héctor F. López Mena, "Pródromos," *El Nacional*, 6, 13 April 1953; and López's "Remembranzas maderistas," *Novedades*, 3 October 1938.

122. Cosío Villegas, *Historia moderna de México. El Porfiriato. La vida política interior*, II, 820–21.

123. Jesús Millán Nava, "Los iniciadores," *El Universal*, 18 August 1940.

124. Ibid.; Figueroa Uriza, *Cuidadanos en armas*, I, 51–54; Figueroa Alcocer, *Crónica*, pp. 10–11.

125. Figueroa Uriza, *Ciudadanos en armas*, I, 56; Figueroa Alcocer, *Crónica*, pp. 17–18.

126. Figueroa Uriza, *Ciudadanos en armas*, I, 57.

127. Ibid., I, 55.

128. Ibid., I, 56–57.

129. Ibid., I, 59–66, 73.

130. Carranco Cardoso, *Iniciación de la Guerra de Independencia*, p. 13; Ochoa Campos, *Historia del Estado de Guerrero*, pp. 284–85.

131. Millán Nava, "Los iniciadores," *El Universal*, 18 August 1940; Héctor F. López [Mena], "El maderisimo en Guerrero," *El Hombre Libre*, 1 September 1937.

132. Figueroa Alcocer, *Crónica*, pp. 19–24; Figueroa Uriza, *Ciudadanos en armas*, I, 77–85.

133. Figueroa Alcocer, *Crónica*, pp. 22–26; Figueroa Uriza, *Cuidadanos en armas*, I, 83–91; Millán Nava, "Los iniciadores," *El Universal*, 18 August 1940; Millán Nava, "La heróica defensa de Huitzuco," *Jueves de Excélsior*, 18 July 1957.

2. Economy and Society in Northern Guerrero: 1876–1911

1. Daniel Cosío Villegas, (ed.), *Historia moderna de México. El Porfiriato. La vida económica* (2 vols.; Mexico, 1965), I, 511, 625–28.
2. Ibid., pp. 488–634.
3. Fernando Rosenzweig Hernández, "Las exportaciones mexicanas de 1877 a 1911," *Historia Mexicana*, 9 (3) (enero–marzo 1960), 406.
4. On economic developments during the Porfiriato, see ibid.; Cosío Villegas, *Historia moderna de México. El Porfiriato. La vida económica*.
5. Daniel Cosío Villegas (ed.), *Historia moderna de México. El Porfiriato. La vida social* (2 vols.; Mexico, 1956–1957), I, 22–23.
6. John H. Coatsworth, "Railroads, Landholding and Agrarian Protest in the Early Porfiriato," *Hispanic American Historical Review*, 54 (1) (February 1974), 48–71.
7. Womack, *Zapata*, pp. 69–97, *passim*.
8. Evelyn Hu-Dehart, "Development and Rural Rebellion: Pacification of the Yaquis in the Late Porfiriato," *Hispanic American Historical Review*, 54 (1) (February 1974), 72.
9. Paul Friedrich, *Agrarian Revolt in a Mexican Village* (Chicago: University of Chicago Press, 1977), pp. 43–49.
10. Rosenzweig Hernández, "Exportaciones mexicanas," pp. 410–11.
11. Cosío Villegas, *Historia moderna de México. El Porfiriato. La vida económica, passim*.
12. For a comparison of an area of rapid modernization (Morelos) with one where the impact of Porfirian policy was minimal (Oaxaca), see Waterbury, "Non-revolutionary Peasants."
13. Moisés T. de la Peña, *Guerrero económico* (2 vols.; Chilpancingo, Guerrero, 1949), I, 10–15.
14. For maize production, see Dirección General de Estadística, *Anuario estadístico de la República Mexicana. Formado por la Dirección General de Estadística a cargo del Dr. Antonio Peñafiel* (15 vols.; Mexico, 1893–1912).
15. Ibid.
16. de la Peña, *Guerrero económico*, II, 290.
17. Ibid., p. 321.
18. *Anuario estadístico*, 1900, pp. 76–77.
19. See, for example, ibid., 1900, pp. 78–79; 1902, pp. 68–69; 1903, pp. 120–21; 1907, pp. 52–53.
20. de la Peña, *Guerrero económico*, I, 15.
21. Peter Gerhard, *A Guide to the Historical Geography of New Spain* (Cambridge, 1972), pp. 146, 252.
22. For administrative divisions, see: Secretaría de Fomento, Colonización, e Industria, *Censo general de la República Mexicana, verificada el 28 de octubre de 1900, conforme a las instrucciones de la Dirección General de Estadística a cargo del Dr. Antonio Peñafiel. Estado de Guerrero* (Mexico, 1905), pp. 16, 82, 148.
23. Gerhard, *Guide to Historical Geography*, pp. 146, 252.

24. AGN, Tierras, vol. 3601, expedientes 8 and 9.
25. *Censo 1900. Guerrero*, pp. 137–40.
26. Dirección General de Estadística, *Tercer censo de población de los Estados Unidos Mexicanos verificado el 27 de octubre de 1910* (3 vols.; Mexico, 1918–1920), I, 17.
27. Ibid., II, 35.
28. ASRA, 23/1223 (723.6) Toca No. 1, fols. 52–53.
29. *Censo 1910*, II, 544–47, 558–61.
30. All figures in this discussion of agricultural production are from *Anuario estadístico*.
31. "Voto de gracias al señor Don Manuel Guillén," *Periódico Oficial*, 19 August 1905.
32. Ibid., 16 April 1890.
33. Guerrero, *Informe leído por el C. Damián Flores, Gobernador del Estado, al abrirse el segundo perído de sesiones ordinarias del XX Congreso Constitucional el día 2 de septiembre de 1907 y contestación del C. Presidente de la propia cámara* (Chipancingo, Guerrero, 1907), p. 7.
34. Guerrero, *Memoria* (1888), p. xxx.
35. de la Peña *Guerrero económico*, I, 497.
36. Ibid., pp. 522–23; *El País*, 2 June 1909; *El Diario del Hogar*, 3 June 1909.
37. *Periódico Oficial*, 1 March 1899.
38. de la Peña, *Guerrero económico*, I, 162, 164–65; II, 505.
39. *Periódico Oficial*, 30 June 1900.
40. J. Villalva to Secretario General de Gobierno de Guerrero, 6 December 1911, AGGEG, Documentos Históricos 1911.
41. Celso Muñoz, "Apuntes estadísticos del Distrito de Tasco del Estado de Guerrero," *Boletín de la Sociedad Mexicana de Geografía y Estadística*, tomo 7, época 1a. (1859), 458.
42. *Periódico Oficial*, 13 November 1895.
43. de la Peña, *Guerrero económico*, II, 290.
44. Carlos Sellerier, "El mineral de Huitzuco," *Anales del Ministerio de Fomento*, II (1898), 69–71. Saulny died in 1886, leaving Romero Rubio as sole owner.
45. Ibid., p. 108.
46. Ibid., p. 109.
47. de la Peña, *Guerrero económico*, II, 445.
48. Ibid., II, 437–41.
49. AGN, Tierras, vol. 3601, expediente 9.
50. *Periódico Oficial*, 14 August 1889.
51. Richard E. Chism, "El distrito minero de Taxco," *Periódico Oficial*, 26 April 1890.
52. *Periódico Oficial*, 26 August 1893.
53. "Haciendas de beneficio o fundiciones, Distrito de Alarcón, 3 December 1899," AMT, 1923.
54. Dr. Antonio Peñafiel, *Ciudades coloniales y capitales de la república*

mexicana por el Dr. Antonio Peñafiel; se imprime por acuerdo del Señor general Porfirio Díaz, presidente de la república siendo secretario de fomento el Señor general Manuel González Cosío. Estado de Guerrero (Mexico, 1908), p. 14.

55. "Lista de las minas existentes en esta municipalidad y que durante el año de 1904 no estuvieron en producción," AMT, 1905.

56. de la Peña, *Guerrero económico,* I, 168, 174; II, 457.

57. Figueroa Uriza, *Ciudadanos en armas,* I, 187, 190–91, 311–12; RDS, 812.00/1136. Resentment of taxes on the production and processing of local agricultural produce was one cause of resentment which led to the outbreak of the revolution in Pisaflores, Hidalgo: Frans J. Schryer, "The Role of the Rancheros of Central Mexico in the Mexican Revolution (The Case of the Sierra Alta de Hidalgo)," *Canadian Journal of Latin American Studies,* 4 (7) (1979), 40, n. 41.

58. Schryer, *Rancheros of Pisaflores,* pp. 23–47; González, *Pueblo en vilo,* pp. 59–109.

3. Rancho and Community in Northern Guerrero in the Porfiriato

1. The standard account of the emergence of the hacienda is François Chevalier, *Land and Society in Colonial Mexico: The Great Hacienda* (Berkeley and Los Angeles, 1966).

2. Ibid., pp. 222–26.

3. González, *Pueblo en vilo,* pp. 39–43, 84–85; Schryer, *Rancheros of Pisaflores,* pp. 23–47; Schryer, "A Ranchero Economy in Northwestern Hidalgo," *Hispanic American Historical Review,* 59 (3) (August 1979), 418–43; Taylor, *Arandas,* pp. 27–29; Elinore M. Barrett, *La cuenca del Tepalcatepec* (2 vols.; Mexico, 1975), pp. 26–27.

4. Brading, *Haciendas and Ranchos,* pp. 17, 62–65, 149–73.

5. *Periódico Oficial,* 16 March 1912.

6. AVC, fondo XXI, carpeta 12, documento 13693.

7. Pedro Hendrichs Pérez, *Por tierras ignotas: Viajes y observaciones en la región del Río de las Balsas, por Pedro Hendrichs Pérez* (2 vols.; Mexico, 1945–1946), I, 29.

8. ARD, tomo 2, expediente 12, fols. 22, 29, 35; tomo 5, expediente 27, fols. 2–210. I am grateful to Alan Knight for bringing the case of Ometepec to my attention.

9. On the Valley of Mexico, see Charles Gibson, *The Aztecs under Spanish Rule: A History of the Indians of the Valley of Mexico* (Stanford, California, 1964). On the Valley of Oaxaca, see William B. Taylor, *Landlord and Peasant in Colonial Oaxaca* (Stanford, California, 1972).

10. José María Luis Mora, quoted in Charles A. Hale, *Mexican Liberalism in the Age of Mora, 1821–1853* (New Haven and London, 1968), p. 180.

11. Jesús Reyes Heroles, *El liberalismo mexicano* (3 vols.; Mexico, 1957–1961), III, 595.

12. *Diputado* Terán in the Federal Congress, 15 June 1822, in ibid., I, 135.

13. Guerrero, *Memoria* (1886), p. 4.

14. Jan Bazant, *Alienation of Church Wealth in Mexico: Social and Economic Aspects of the Liberal Revolution, 1856–1875* (Cambridge, 1971), p. 53.

15. Nathan L. Whetten, *Rural Mexico* (Chicago, 1948), pp. 85–86.

16. T. G. Powell, *El liberalismo y el campesinado en el centro de México (1850 a 1876)* (Mexico, 1974), p. 154.

17. Ibid., pp. 154–55.

18. Charles R. Berry, "The Fiction and Fact of the Reform: The Case of the Central District of Oaxaca, 1856–1867," *The Americas,* 26 (3) (January 1970), 281.

19. The Indians of Mayanalán, for instance, complained as early as 1740 that "the tenant rancheros called whites" had seized all but a very small part of their land: ASRA, 23/1309 (723.6) Toca, fol. 4.

20. Ian Edward Jacobs, "Aspects of the History of the Mexican Revolution in the State of Guerrero up to 1940" (Thesis, University of Cambridge, n.d.), pp. 293–94.

21. ASRA, 23/1392 (723.6) Restitución Local, fol. 84.

22. ASRA, 23/1392 (723.6) Restitución Local, fol. 80–81; Toca.

23. ASRA, 23/1392 (723.6) Restitución Local, fol. 326.

24. ASRA, 23/9749 (723.6) Toca No. 1, fol. 159.

25. Guerrero, *Memoria* (1886), p. 4.

26. Ibid.

27. Ibid., pp. 185–86.

28. Ibid., p. 237.

29. Files in ASRA show that disentailment had begun in at least twenty communities by 1886.

30. *Periódico Oficial,* 6 March 1903.

31. *Periódico Oficial,* 3 April 1909. Such delays in implementing the Reform Laws were not uncommon. Robert J. Knowlton chronicles a similar pattern of delay in Jalisco in "La individualización de la propiedad corporativa civil en el siglo XIX—notas sobre Jalisco," *Historia Méxicana,* 28 (1) (julio–septiembre 1978), 24–61.

32. Powell, *El liberalismo,* p. 75.

33. ASRA, 23/9749 (723.6) Toca No. 1, fol. 159.

34. See the *acuerdo* of the *prefecto* Francisco Olea, 13 October 1869, in AMT, 1869. There were similar cases in Oaxaca: Berry, "Fiction and Fact," p. 280.

35. ASRA, 23/1392 (723.6) Restitución Local No. 1, fol. 142.

36. ASRA, 23/1392 (723.6) Restitución Local No. 3, fols. 234, 254–59, 307–11, 325.

37. ASRA, 23/1392 (723.6) Documentación Complementaria, fol. 69.

38. ASRA, 23/1392 (723.6) Documentación Complementaria, fols. 72–74.

39. ASRA, 23/1459 (723.6) Local, fols. 5–14, 37–38, 182–84; Toca, fols. 13–14, 221–22, provides a detailed history of Chaucingo. Note that this was not a community of Indian origin, but rather a Spanish form of communal property known as *condueñazgo:* McBride, *The Land Systems of Mexico,* pp. 103–4. A similar *condueñazgo* founded on the Ha-

cienda de Tampochocho was the root of ranchero society in Pisaflores, Hidalgo: Schryer, *Rancheros of Pisaflores*, pp. 29–31.

40. ASRA, 23/1459 (723.6) Local, fols. 23–24, 37–38, 182–84; Toca, fols. 13–14; 23/11996 (723.6) Local, fol. 8.
41. ASRA, 276.1/539 (723.6) Local, fols. 149–50; also the report of Ing. Samuel Azuela in ibid.
42. Report of Ing. Pedro Alcántar, 19 September 1931, ASRA, 23/10225 (723.6) Local No. 1, fols. 185–87.
43. Elisa A. Vda. de Meléndez to Secretario de Agricultura y Fomento, 29 May 1918, ASRA, 23/9773 (723.6) Toca; Local fols. 2–3.
44. ASRA, 23/1244 (723.6) Local, fol. 38.
45. ASRA, 23/1413 (723.6) Restitución Local, fols. 15–17, 20–39, 81–84, 129–35; 276.1/1009 (723.6) Local, fols. 229–35, 239–43.
46. ASRA, 23/1413 (723.6) Restitución Local, fol. 54.
47. ASRA, 23/1384 (723.6) Restitución Local, fols. 240–41.
48. ASRA, 23/1384 (723.6) Restitución Local, fols. 242–57.
49. Report of Ing. Arnulfo Viveros, 6 March 1923, ASRA, 23/1384 (723.6) Restitución Local, fols. 25–33.
50. Presidente del Comité Ejecutivo Particular to Secretario de la Comisión Local Agraria, 16 January 1933, ASRA, 23/11133 (723.6) Local, fol. 45.
51. Report of Jesús de Anda Padilla, ASRA, 276.1/1025 (723.6), Trabajos Téchnicos.
52. On Ometepec, see note 8 above. On Tepoztlán, see Oscar Lewis, *Life in a Mexican Village: Tepoztlán Restudied* (Urbana, Illinois, 1972), pp. 51, 96–97, 115; on Pisaflores, see Schryer, *Rancheros of Pisaflores*, pp. 34–36.
53. Interview, Arturo Figueroa, Tetipac, Guerrero, 8 July 1975.
54. *Periódico Oficial*, 22 July 1893.
55. ASRA, 23/9860 (723.6) Toca, fols. 98–100.
56. ASRA, 23/1439 (723.6) Restitución, Anexo al Local, fols. 29–59.
57. ASRA, 23/1439 (723.6) Restitución, Anexo al Local, fols. 48–51.
58. Report of Ing. José Segundo Serrano, 7 June 1932, ASRA, 23/1439 (723.6) Restitución, Anexo al Local, fols. 101–3.
59. "Alegato presentado a la Suprema Corte de Justicia de la Nación por el Licenciado Faustino Estrada sosteniendo que debe ser confirmada la sentencia pronunciada por el Juzgado de Distrito de Guerrero amparando a los senores Eulalio, Gumaro y Narcisa Rosas," ASRA, 23/1439 (723.6) Restitución, Anexo al Local, fols. 148–56.
60. ASRA, 23/1439 (723.6) Restitución, Anexo al Local, fols. 8–9, 101, 106–7.
61. ASRA, 23/1439 (723.6) Restitución, Anexo al Local, fols. 146–47.
62. ASRA, 23/1218 (723.6) Ampliación Toca, fols. 39–40, 43–44b, 55.
63. ASRA, 23/1218 (723.6) Local, fols. 33–40.
64. ASRA, 23/1280 (723.6) Local, fols. 52–54; 23/21410 (723.6) Local, fols. 37–39.
65. ASRA, 23/21410 (723.6) Local, fols. 48–49.

66. For estimates of their holdings, see ASRA, 23/1280 (723.6) Local, fols. 15–17, 19–21, 103, 144–45.
67. ASRA, 23/1403 (723.6) Toca, fols. 29–31, 110, 112–13.
68. ASRA, 23/1403 (723.6) Local, fol. 120; Toca, fol. 454.
69. ASRA, 23/1403 (723.6) Local, fols. 38–39.
70. Jacobs, "Revolution in Guerrero," pp. 291–92; AOM, caja 2, expediente C-3, documento 386; El Diario del Hogar, 20 February 1912; "Informe sobre la actuación del Lic. y Coronel Trinidad Mastache," ASRA, 23/1280 (723.6) Toca No. 2, fol. 198.
71. Antonio Díaz Soto y Gama, "También en Guerrero se hizo labor agraria," El Universal, 15 December 1954.
72. See copies of the documentation in this dispute in ASRA, 276.1/1025 (723.6) Toca.
73. See the copy of the documentation in ASRA, 276.1/1009 (723.6) Toca.
74. Memoria (1886), pp. 3–4. See also Periódico Oficial, 22 May 1889.
75. See the amparo judgment of 13 February 1908 in AMT, 1919; Manuel Cornelio et al. to Governor of Guerrero, 24 October 1911, in AMT, 1911; ASRA, 276.1/539 (723.6) Local, fols. 41–42.
76. Periódico Oficial, 20 September 1933; de la Peña, Guerrero económico, I, 443. De la Peña incorrectly attributes the solution to Adrian Castrejón, Guevara's predecessor.
77. Periódico Oficial, 25 February 1891.
78. Circular No. 72, Periódico Oficial, 24 November 1897.
79. ASRA, 23/1309 (723.6) Local, fols. 16–17; Toca, fol. 3.
80. See table 1.
81. ASRA, 23/1413 (723.6) Restitución Local, fols. 174, 176–77.
82. ASRA, 23/1413 (723.6) Restitución Local, fol. 23; 276.1/1009 (723.6) Local, fols. 237–38.
83. ASRA, 23/1361 (723.6) Local, fols. 25–90, 362–63; Toca, fols. 48–63.
84. ASRA, 23/1361 (723.6) Local, fols. 151–57, 223–90; Toca, fols. 67–90; "Cuestión de terrenos entre los vecinos de Buena-vista y Coxcatlán," AMT, 1919.
85. Comisario 1° Jesús Velasco to Presidente Municipal de Taxco, 6 September 1911, AMT, 1911.
86. ASRA, 23/1361 (723.6) Toca, Deslindes Comunales, fols. 5–6.

4. The Hacienda in Northern Guerrero in the Porfiriato

1. Hendrichs Pérez, Por tierras ignotas, I, 36.
2. de la Peña, Guerrero económico, I, 449.
3. Ibid., p. 435. See also the protest of the residents of San Agustín Acayapitzalán Petaquillas against encroachment on their lands by Arce (owner of the Hacienda de Tepechicotlán) and Agustina Salinas (owner of the Hacienda de Mazatlán), El Diario del Hogar, 26 March 1893.
4. NA, RG 84—1921 (600), World Trade Report, 18 August 1921.
5. de la Peña, Guerrero económico, I, 434; G. Muñiz to H. H. Leonard, 12 January 1932, NA, RG 84—1932 (350).
6. RDS, 812.00/2178.

7. Carlos A. Miller to Marion Selcher (*sic*), 23 March 1910, NA, RG 84—1 January–30 June 1910 (Miscellaneous Letters Received); Clement S. Edwards to Secretary of State, 27 December 1912, NA, RG 84—1912 (310); Edwards to Secretary of State, 23 September 1912, NA, RG 84—1912 (320); "Inventario de las propiedades del señor Carlos A. Miller . . . 8 March 1912," NA, RG 84—1912 (Miscellaneous Letters); Germán Miller to John Gmon (*sic*), 1 July 1921, NA, RG 84—1921 (600).

8. Edwards to Secretary of State, 23 September 1912, NA, RG 84—1912 (320); "List of property owned by Stephens y Cia. Sucs. . . . 14 April 1912," NA, RG 84—1912 (Miscellaneous Letters); Edwards to Secretary of State, 27 December 1912, NA, RG 84—1912 (310); Stephens Hermanos to H. H. Leonard, 8 January 1932, NA, RG 84—1932 (350).

9. RDS, 812.00/2178; Henry Weiss to Marion Letcher, 17 June 1910, NA, RG 84—1 January–30 June 1910 (Miscellaneous Letters Received); Edwards to Secretary of State, 27 December 1912, NA, RG 84—1912 (310); Edwards to Secretary of State, 23 September 1912, NA, RG 84—1912 (320); H. H. Leonard to J. Ruben Clark, Jr., 11 November 1931, NA, RG 84—1931 (350); Frank Pettee to American Embassy, 18 March 1933, NA, RG 84—1933 (350).

10. Edwards to Secretary of State, 27 December 1912, NA, RG 84—1912 (310); Edwards to Secretary of State, 23 September 1912, NA, RG 84—1912 (320); W. M. Hudson to Dr. H. K. Pangburn, 17 August 1922, and Geo. B. Baker to Pangburn, 7 September 1922, NA, RG 84—1922 (350).

11. Edwards to Secretary of State, 23 September 1912, NA, RG 84—1912 (310); Mrs. J. D. R. McCabe to American Consul, 17 April 1925, NA, RG 84—1925 (350); Clarence A. Miller to American Ambassador, 26 June 1931, and Miller to Secretary of State, 30 June 1931, NA, RG 84—1931 (350).

12. Frank Pettee to C. E. Maleady, 11 June 1932, NA, RG 84—1932 (350).

13. Harry K. Pangburn to Alexander W. Weddell, 18 May 1926, NA, RG 84—1927 (800).

14. Díaz Díaz, *Caudillos y caciques*, pp. 98–99.

15. Eric R. Wolf and Sidney W. Mintz, "Haciendas and Plantations in Middle America and the Antilles," *Social and Economic Studies*, 6 (3) (September 1957), 380.

16. Taylor, *Landlord and Peasant*, pp. 121–22; Robert G. Keith, *Conquest and Agrarian Change: The Emergence of the Hacienda System on the Peruvian Coast* (Cambridge, Massachusetts, and London, 1976), p. 2.

17. Brading, *Haciendas and Ranchos*, pp. 1–12.

18. Compare table 2 to table 1 in chapter 3; according to the 1940 census the municipalities comprising the two districts totaled 459,325 hectares.

19. See Womack, *Zapata*, pp. 531–32, for a list of *hacendados* in Morelos.

20. ASRA, 23/11131 (723.6) Local, fols. 58–60; 23/1196 (723.6) Toca, fols. 22–23; 23/1197 (723.6) Toca, fols. 16–26; 23/1203 (723.6) Local, fols. 41–44; 23/1280 (723.6) Local, fols. 62–63.

21. Copies of the will are in ASRA, 23/1196 (723.6) Toca, fols. 54–55;

23/1197 (723.6) Toca, fols. 28–31; 23/1203 (723.6) Local, fols. 45–46.
22. See the partition of Juan Montúfar's estate in ASRA, 23/1351 (723.6) Toca, fol. 74; 23/9970 (723.6) Local. See also the will of Catalina Cuenca, ASRA, 23/1223 (723.6) Toca No. 2, fols. 10–22.
23. See Catalina Cuenca's will, ASRA, 23/1223 (723.6) Toca No. 2, fols. 10–22. See also the report of Profesora María Alday Adame on the history of Montúfar's holdings, ASRA, 23/1351 (723.6) Toca, fol. 74; 23/9970 (723.6) Local.
24. Will of Catalina Cuenca, ASRA, 23/1223 (723.6) Toca No. 2, fols. 10–22.
25. Ibid.
26. Report of Profesora María Alday Adame, ASRA, 23/21418 (723.6) Local, fols. 47–49; report of *juez registrador* de Iguala, ASRA, 23/1385 (723.6) Local, fol. 116.
27. Will of Catalina Cuenca, ASRA, 23/1223 (723.6) Toca No. 2, fols. 10–22; copy of the bill of sale of El Zoquital in ASRA, 23/1199 (723.6) Toca No. 2.
28. Will of Catalina Cuenca, ASRA, 23/1223 (723.6) Toca No. 2, fols. 10–22.
29. See the summary of Pastrana's titles in ASRA, 23/1232 (723.6) Toca.
30. ASRA, 23/1385 (723.6) Local, fol. 114.
31. See the will of Ponciano Salgado and other documents in ASRA, 23/1270 (723.6) Toca No. 1, fols. 191–97.
32. ASRA, 23/1235 (723.6) Local, fol. 2; Toca, fols. 37–38.
33. ASRA, 23/1194 (723.6) Local, fol. 5; 23/1223 (723.6) Toca No. 1, fols. 440–41.
34. ASRA, 23/1247 (723.6) Local, fols. 2–3; 23/1233 (723.6) Local, fols. 3–4.
35. Tannenbaum, *Mexican Agrarian Revolution*, pp. 9–11.
36. Friedrich Katz, "Labor Conditions on Haciendas in Porfirian Mexico: Some Trends and Tendencies," *Hispanic American Historical Review*, 54 (1) (February 1974), 4–6.
37. Report of 5 September 1919, ASRA, 23/1195 (723.6) Local, fols. 54–55. Reports of Guillermo Bazán, 21 and 23 July 1919, ASRA, 23/1196 (723.6) Local, fol. 35; 23/1197 (723.6) Local, fols. 26–28; report of José M. Núñez, 30 May 1922, ASRA, 23/1212 (723.6) Local, fols. 54, 57–59.
38. ASRA, 23/1195 (723.6) Local, fols. 30–46, 48; 23/1196 (723.6) Toca, fols. 4–22, 35. In rare cases the rent was paid in cash.
39. ASRA, 23/1196 (723.6) Toca, fols. 23–29.
40. ASRA, 23/1196 (723.6) Toca, fols. 54–55; 23/1197 (723.6) Toca, fols. 28–31; 23/1203 (723.6) Local, fols. 45–46.
41. Cuenca's will is in ASRA, 23/1223 (723.6) Toca No. 2, fols. 10–22.
42. Report of Ing. Guillermo Bazán, 6 October 1919, ASRA, 23/1194 (723.6) Local, fols. 90–91.
43. Report of 5 November 1919, ASRA 23/1198 (723.6) Local, fols. 65–66.
44. Saturnino Martínez to Comisión Local Agraria, 29 October 1921, ASRA, 23/1248 (723.6) Local, fol. 29. Mezcal was still being manufactured on Tecoacuilco in 1920, but by then the tenants were making it for their own profit: ASRA, 23/1248 (723.6) Restitución Local, fol. 26.
45. ASRA, 23/1234 (723.6) Restitución Toca, fol. 46.

46. ASRA, 23/1211 (723.6) Local, fols. 18–19.
47. ASRA, 23/1211 (723.6) Toca, fols. 19–20.
48. ASRA, 23/1199 (723.6) Local, fols. 64–67.
49. ASRA, 23/1199 (723.6) Local, fols. 68–69.
50. ASRA, 23/1241 (723.6) Local, fol. 15.
51. ASRA, 23/1235 (723.6) Local, fol. 2; Toca, fols. 37–38.
52. *Periódico Oficial*, 16 March, 20 April 1898.
53. Ramon Marrón to Secretario de Agricultura y Fomento, 21 June, 15 September 1920, ASRA, 23/1199 (723.6) Toca No. 1, fols. 63, 92.
54. ASRA, 23/1199 (723.6) Local, fols. 68–69; 23/1198 (723.6) Local, fols. 65–66.
55. ASRA, 23/1199 (723.6) Local, fols. 68–69; 23/1198 (723.6) Local, fols. 65–66; 23/1202 (723.6) Local, fols. 31–33; 23/1201 (723.6) Local, fols. 24–25.
56. ASRA, 23/1201 (723.6) Local, fols. 24–25; 23/1198 (723.6) Local, fols. 65–66.
57. ASRA, 23/1201 (723.6) Local, fols. 24–25.
58. Ramon Marrón to Secretario de Agricultura y Fomento, 21 June 1920, ASRA, 23/1199 (723.6) Toca No. 1, fol. 63.
59. In a letter of 26 February 1912 the owner referred to the presence of tenants on his land: RDS, 812.00/3478.
60. See the copy of the bill of sale of El Zoquital, ASRA, 23/1199 (723.6) Toca No. 2.
61. ASRA, 23/1384 (723.6) Restitución Local, fols. 44–49.
62. ASRA, 23/1204 (723.6) Local, fols. 52–57; 23/1208 (723.6) Local, fols. 54–56; Toca, fol. 85.
63. RDS, 812.00/3478.
64. In an interview in Chilpancingo, 26 May 1975, Ing. Manuel Mesa Andraca stated that Rivera and Montúfar always had a say in the selection of the *presidente municipal* of Iguala, and in property tax assessments.
65. Jacobs, *"Revolution in Guerrero,"* pp. 289–90.
66. Ibid.; ASRA, 23/1309 (723.6) Toca, fol. 3.
67. On Castillo Calderón's career, see *Periódico Oficial*, 6 May 1891; 15 March, 27 December 1899; *La Federación*, 8 June 1893.
68. See the reports on agricultural production in the municipality of Taxco in 1900 in AMT, 1901.
69. Interview, Carlos Albarrán Gómez, Cocula, Guerrero, 3 July 1975.
70. Comandante Odilón Figueroa to Gobernador J. I. Lugo, 20 December 1911, AGGEG, Pablo Barrera, Años 1911–12/39.
71. Oficial Mayor M. Rojas to Presidentes Municipales of Tepecoacuilco, Huitzuco, Apipilulco, 30 September 1917, AGGEG, Documentos Históricos 1917.
72. For the cases of Coxcatlán and Taxco el Viejo see Comisario 1° Jesús Velasco to Presidente Municipal de Taxco, 6 September 1911, in AMT, 1911, and ASRA, 23/10225 (723.6) Local No. 1, fols. 185–87.
73. On the case of Buenavista, see the following chapter.
74. On the Vidales brothers, see chapter 6.

5. Revolution in Guerrero: 1911–1919

1. Ankerson, "Saturnino Cedillo," p. 142.
2. Knight, "Peasant and Caudillo," pp. 26–35.
3. Ibid., p. 28.
4. Figueroa Uriza, *Ciudadanos en armas*, I, 28–30; Figueroa Alcocer, *Crónica*, pp. 14–15.
5. Figueroa Uriza, *Ciudadanos en armas*, I, 40–41; Gutiérrez Galindo, *Rubén Figueroa*, pp. 26, 38.
6. Figueroa Uriza, *Ciudadanos en armas*, I, 41; Gutiérrez Galindo, *Rubén Figueroa*, p. 39. Figueroa's biography of Juárez was published in *Periódico Oficial*, 4 April 1906.
7. Francisco Figueroa, "Causas que motivaron la revolución de 1910 en el Estado de Guerrero," *El País*, 22 August 1912.
8. Francisco Figueroa's *Informe* of 15 November 1911, quoted in Figueroa Uriza, *Ciudadanos en armas*, I, 312–13. The *Informe* was first published in *Periódico Oficial*, 18 November 1911.
9. *Informe*, 15 November 1911, Figueroa Uriza, *Ciudadanos en armas*, I, 306.
10. Francisco Figueroa to Francisco I. Madero, 11 November 1911, in Isidro Fabela (ed.), *Documentos históricos de la Revolución Mexicana* (27 vols.; Mexico, 1960–1973), Revolución y régimen maderista, II, 264–66. My emphasis.
11. See Figueroa's *Informe*, 15 November 1911, Figueroa Uriza, *Ciudadanos en armas*, I, 303–14. See also Francisco Figueroa, "Causas," and Figueroa's manifesto of July 1911, *El Diario del Hogar*, 10 July 1911.
12. *Periódico Oficial*, 13 September 1911.
13. The manifesto is quoted in full in Figueroa Uriza, *Ciudadanos en armas*, I, 232–34. Figueroa's remarks on the agrarian question are also quoted in Gildardo Magaña, *Emiliano Zapata y el agrarismo en México* (5 vols.; Mexico, 1951–1952), II, 19.
14. Figueroa Uriza, *Ciudadanos en armas*, I, 295–96.
15. *Periódico Oficial*, 1 March 1911.
16. Figueroa Uriza, *Ciudadanos en armas*, I, 92–95.
17. Ibid., I, 123–26.
18. Ibid., I, 105.
19. Ibid., I, 103.
20. Blanco's promotion to captain is recorded in AGGEG, Julián Blanco, 1899.
21. The foregoing discussion of revolutionary developments is based on the following sources: Figueroa Uriza, *Ciudadanos en armas*, I, 103–4, 125, 146–47; Fuentes Díaz, *La revolución de 1910*, pp. 96–97; Ochoa Campos, *Historia del Estado de Guerrero*, p. 286; Beatriz Hernández García, *Estado de Guerrero* (Mexico, 1968), p. 31; Millán Nava, "Los iniciadores", *El Universal*, 25 August 1940; Millán Nava, "La heróica defensa de Huitzuco," *Jueves de Excélsior*, 18 July 1957.
22. Figueroa Uriza, *Ciudadanos en armas*, I, 147; Millán Nava, "La Revo-

lución en Guerrero," *El Nacional*, 28 October 1934.

23. Harry K. Pangburn, U.S. Vice Consul in Acapulco, to Secretary of State, 19 March 1911, RDS, 812.00/1136.

24. Héctor F. López Mena, "El maderismo en Guerrero," *El Hombre Libre*, 6, 13 April 1953; López Mena, "Remembranzas maderistas," *Novedades*, 3 October 1938.

25. Fuentes Díaz, *La revolución de 1910*, p. 97.

26. RDS, 812.00/1564; "Alzuyeta y Cia. Sucs.: Relación de los daños sufridos por los que suscriben con motivo de la revolución desde el año de 1910," Acapulco, 8 August 1919, NA, RG 84—1919 (350).

27. Reports of Vice Consul Pangburn, 11, 18, 20, 21 April 1911, RDS, 812.00/1452, 1520, 1425, 1426, 1564.

28. Circular No. 45, 20 April 1911, *Periódico Oficial*, 22 April 1911.

29. Figueroa Uriza, *Ciudadanos en armas*, I, 191.

30. Millán Nava, "La Revolución en Guerrero," *El Nacional*, 4 November 1934.

31. Circular No. 54, 3 May 1911, *Periódico Oficial*, 6 May 1911.

32. Figueroa Uriza, *Ciudadanos en armas*, I, 113–14.

33. Ibid., pp. 110–11; Magaña, *Emiliano Zapata*, II, 15; Figueroa Alcocer, *Crónica*, pp. 31–32.

34. Figueroa Alcocer, *Crónica*, p. 32; Figueroa Uriza, *Ciudadanos en armas*, I, 110–11, 113–22; Magaña, *Emiliano Zapata*, I, 101; Millán Nava, "La Revolución en Guerrero," *El Nacional*, 28 October 1934; Millán Nava, "Los iniciadores," *El Universal*, 25 August 1940.

35. Figueroa Uriza, *Ciudadanos en armas*, I, 111–12, 125, 127–30; Womack, *Zapata*, pp. 124–25; Magaña, *Emiliano Zapata*, I, 110–12. While it is true that the Figueroas were personally close to a number of important Morelos *hacendados*, and while it appears that they did receive funding from landowners, it is by no means clear that this was tied to any commitment to dispose of Zapata, nor that any money had been received by the time of the advance of Jojutla. The payments to the Figueroas are referred to in Héctor F. López, "Datos para la historia. El maderismo en Guerrero," *El Hombre Libre*, 10 September 1937, but no mention is made of when the money was paid.

36. Figueroa Uriza, *Ciudadanos en armas*, I, 128–29; *El Diario del Hogar*, 11 December 1911; *El País*, 29 April 1911.

37. Figueroa Uriza, *Ciudadanos en armas*, I, 142–43.

38. Ibid., I, 135–36.

39. Francisco I. Madero to José Soto and Francisco Figueroa, 4 May 1911, AM, Telegramas 2 March–20 May 1911; Figueroa Uriza, *Ciudadanos en armas*, I, 137.

40. Figueroa Uriza, *Ciudadanos en armas*, I, 137–38.

41. Ibid., I, 139–41.

42. Ibid., I, 154–62; Figueroa Alcocer, *Crónica*, pp. 35–36; Fuentes Díaz, *La revolución de 1910*, pp. 108–9; Millán Nava, "La Revolución en Guerrero," *El Nacional*, 28 October 1934.

43. Figueroa Uriza, *Ciudadanos en armas*, I, 162–64; Fuentes Díaz, *La re-

volución de 1910, p. 109; Valverde, *Julián Blanco*, pp. 19–20; López, *Diccionario*, pp. 95–96.

44. RDS, 812.00/1947.
45. Figueroa Uriza, *Ciudadanos en armas*, I, 170–73; Fuentes Díaz, *La revolución de 1910*, p. 117.
46. Francisco I. Madero to Ambrosio Figueroa, 24 May 1911, AM, Telegramas 22–24 May 1911.
47. Figueroa Uriza, *Ciudadanos en armas*, I, 208–11, 217.
48. Ibid., I, 293–94.
49. Ibid., I, 309; *Periódico Oficial*, 4 September 1912.
50. Figueroa Uriza, *Ciudadanos en armas*, I, 222–24.
51. Ibid., I, 228.
52. Ibid., I, 231.
53. Ibid., I, 197–99; Womack, *Zapata*, pp. 133–34; Magaña, *Emiliano Zapata*, I, 136–37; Tomás Ruíz de Velasco to Ing. Alfredo Robles Domínguez, 26 May 1911, ARD, tomo 1, expediente 17, fol. 15.
54. Figueroa Uriza, *Ciudadanos en armas*, I, 173–75.
55. "Memorándum de la situación política del Estado de Morelos," ARD, tomo 7, expediente 37, fols. 5–11; Magaña, *Emiliano Zapata*, I, 134–35.
56. AOM, caja 1, expediente 3-R, documentos 480–81.
57. Ambrosio Figueroa to Francisco I. Madero, 28 May 1911, AM, Telegramas 27–28 May 1911.
58. Ibid., Figueroa to Madero, 29 May 1911, AM, Telegramas 29–30 May 1911.
59. Figueroa to Madero, 31 May 1911, AM, Telegramas 30–31 May 1911; Figueroa to Lic. Matías Chávez, 4 June 1911, AOM, caja 19, expediente 3, documento 90.
60. Epigmenio López Barroso, *Diccionario geográfico, histórico y estadístico del Distrito de Abasolo, del Estado de Guerrero* (Mexico, 1967), pp. 23–30; ARD, tomo 2, expediente 12; tomo 5, expediente 27.
61. Figueroa Uriza, *Ciudadanos en armas*, I, 318.
62. RDS, 812.00/2178.
63. Figueroa Uriza, *Ciudadanos en armas*, I, 319.
64. Gral. Julián Blanco and Coroneles Martín Vicario and Tomás Gómez to Francisco I. Madero, 9 July 1911, AM, Telegramas, 6–18 June 1911; RDS, 812.00/2242.
65. RDS, 812.00/2242.
66. Figueroa Uriza, *Ciudadanos en armas*, I, 319–29; Valverde, *Julián Blanco*, p. 25, Appendix pp. 5–11.
67. Fuentes Díaz, *La revolución de 1910*, p. 65.
68. Figueroa Uriza, *Ciudadanos en armas*, I, 329–32.
69. Lugo to Francisco León de la Barra, 23 October 1911, AOM, caja 12, expediente 2, documento 48.
70. RDS, 812.00/2346
71. *Periódico Oficial*, 2, 9 December 1911. On Ambrosio Figueroa's support for Vicario, see "Memorándum de la situación política del Estado

de Morelos," ARD, tomo 7, expediente 37, fols. 5–11; Figueroa Uriza, *Ciudadanos en armas*, I, 408.

72. Madero to Francisco Figueroa, 30 November 1911, in Fabela, *Documentos históricos*, Revolución y régimen maderista, II, 358–60.
73. Lugo to Madero, 10 December 1911, in ibid., II, 400–401.
74. Lugo to Madero, 8 December 1911, in ibid., II, 392–93.
75. Lugo to Madero, 24 December 1911, in ibid., II, 457–58.
76. Madero to Ambrosio Figueroa, 9 December 1911, in ibid., II, 395–96.
77. *Periódico Oficial*, 23 December 1911; Figueroa Uriza, *Ciudadanos en armas*, I, 335.
78. Figueroa Uriza, *Ciudadanos en armas*, I, 336, 440; *El País*, 16 January 1912; *El Diario del Hogar*, 16, 18, 23 January 1912. The reports in *El Diario del Hogar* must be treated with caution, since the paper was hostile to the Figueroas. Nevertheless, they do reflect the enmity between Salgado and the Figueroas.
79. On Barrera's activities, see AGGEG, Pablo Barrero, Años 1911–12/39; *El País*, 6 January 1912; Jesús Barrera to Lázaro Cárdenas, 4 January 1936, ASRA, 23/1229 (723.6) Toca, fol. 116.
80. Vicario to Governor José I. Lugo, 2 January 1912, and Ayuntamiento de Tepecoacuilco to Governor of Guerrero, 17 January 1912, AGGEG, Pablo Barrera, Años 1911–12/39.
81. Madero to Figueroa, 10 January 1912, in Fabela, *Documentos históricos*, Revolución y régimen maderista, III, 29–30.
82. Figueroa Uriza, *Ciudadanos en armas*, I, 277–90; Womack, *Zapata*, pp. 191–92.
83. Figueroa Uriza, *Ciudadanos en armas*, I, 342–43.
84. Circular of 12 February 1912, AMT 1912. On the law of suspension of guarantees, see Figueroa Uriza, *Ciudadanos en armas*, I, 359–61.
85. Tte Coronel Severo Carrasco Pérez to Secretario de Guerra y Marina, 21 July 1911, ARD, tomo 2, expediente 8, fols. 68–69; AOM, caja 2, expediente C-3, documentos 385–86; *El Diario del Hogar*, 17 February, 2 March 1912; Figueroa Uriza, *Ciudadanos en armas*, I, 126n, 349, 351–52; Franco, *Eusebio S. Almonte*, p. 15.
86. Figueroa Uriza, *Ciudadanos en armas*, I, 352–58.
87. Ibid., I, 347–49; *El Diario del Hogar*, 16, 17, 20, 25 February 1912; *El País*, 18, 19, 20 February 1912.
88. Madero to Ambrosio Figueroa, 24 February 1912, in Fabela, *Documentos históricos*, Revolución y régimen maderista, III, 14.
89. Figueroa to Madero, 17, 27 February 1912, in ibid., III, 107–8, 149–50. Madero repeated his order to Figueroa to leave Guerrero on 3 March, but Ambrosio again refused: Figueroa Uriza, *Ciudadanos en armas*, I, 370–72.
90. Figueroa Uriza, *Ciudadanos en armas*, I, 377–79; Figueroa Alcocer, *Crónica*, pp. 43–44.
91. For a summary of the military situation, see *Periódico Oficial*, 16, 27 March 1912.
92. Figueroa Uriza, *Ciudadanos en armas*, I, 391, 394–96; Figueroa Al-

cocer, *Crónica*, p. 44; *El País*, 26 July 1912.

93. Figueroa Uriza, *Ciudadanos en armas*, I, 395–400; Ambrosio Figueroa to Madero, 3 July 1912, in Fabela, *Documentos históricos*, Revolución y régimen maderista, IV, 13–14.

94. Figueroa Uriza, *Ciudadanos en armas*, I, 427–32.

95. On Radilla, see RDS, 812.00/5464, 5538, 5559, 5584, 5600, 5681, 5685.

96. RDS, 812.00/5835.

97. Figueroa Uriza, *Ciudadanos en armas*, I, 395; *El País*, 26 June 1912. In 1915 Francisco Figueroa objected to Blanco's appointment as governor of Guerrero on the grounds that he was a mere instrument of Lugo: AHDN, XI/481.5/129, fols. 15–16, caja 74.

98. George J. Rausch, Jr., "The Early Career of Victoriano Huerta," *The Americas*, 21 (2) (October 1964), 136–45.

99. Jesús Millán Nava, "Hacia el ocaso," *El Universal*, 29 September 1940; and Millán Nava, "José Inocente Lugo, el gobernador perseguido," *Jueves de Excélsior*, 7 November 1957.

100. *El País*, 3 March 1913.

101. *Periódico Oficial*, 13 March 1913. Lugo, however, was allowed to complete his term, which ran to 1 April: RDS, 812.00/6858; *El País*, 3 April 1913.

102. Figueroa Uriza, *Ciudadanos en armas*, I, 440; Valverde, *Julián Blanco*, p. 30.

103. Figueroa Uriza, *Ciudadanos en armas*, I, 440–41.

104. RDS, 812.00/6858, 7196.

105. Figueroa Uriza, *Ciudadanos en armas*, I, 451; Héctor F. López Mena, "Campaña contra el huertismo," *El Nacional*, 25 May 1953.

106. Figueroa Uriza, *Ciudadanos en armas*, I, 446–47; Valverde, *Julián Blanco*, p. 32.

107. Figueroa Uriza, *Ciudadanos en armas*, I, 449; José Andraca Ortega to Secretario General de Gobierno, 17 April 1913, AGGEG, Documentos Históricos, 1913.

108. Figueroa Uriza, *Ciudadanos en armas*, I, 452–56, 458–59, 467–68.

109. Ibid.

110. Ibid., I, 478–91.

111. Ibid., I, 461–67; II, 505–27.

112. Ibid., II, 504; RDS, 812.00/9999. Vice Consul Edwards noted that "Blanco is a strong man and can draw a great many recruits."

113. RDS, 812.00/9651, 9793, 10068, 10234.

114. Figueroa Uriza, *Ciudadanos en armas*, II, 558–61.

115. Ibid., II, 569–80; RDS, 812.00/11090.

116. Womack, *Zapata*, p. 252.

117. Ibid., pp. 252–55; Figueroa Uriza, *Ciudadanos en armas*, II, 583–86; Valverde, *Julián Blanco*, pp. 44–50; Jesús Millán Nava, "Encarnizada batalla para la toma de Chilpancingo," *Jueves de Excélsior*, 27 June 1957.

118. RDS, 812.00/11356.

119. Figueroa Uriza, *Ciudadanos en armas*, II, 586–87, 606–7.

120. On the deterioriating relations with Zapata which drove Figueroa out of Guerrero, see ibid., I, 454–56, 467–68; II, 588. Note that Figueroa's difficulties were mainly with the Morelos Zapatistas, not with Zapata's *guerrerense* allies, with some of whom he regularly operated.

121. Womack, *Zapata*, p. 255; Valverde, *Julián Blanco*, p. 51; Figueroa Uriza, *Ciudadanos en armas*, II, 587.

122. Womack, *Zapata*, p. 255; Valverde, *Julián Blanco*, pp. 49–50.

123. Interview, Jesús Figueroa Alcocer, Huitzuco, Guerrero, 1 July 1975.

124. Womack, *Zapata*, p. 241.

125. Figueroa Uriza, *Ciudadanos en armas*, I, 331–32.

126. Lugo to Madero, in Fabela, *Documentos históricos*, Revolución y régimen maderista, II, 388–89, 400–404.

127. José M. Ortiz, "Memorándum con relación al levantamiento de Jesús H. Salgado" (December 1911?), in ibid., II, 374–76.

128. Valverde, *Julián Blanco*, pp. 69–70.

129. Bárcenas to Emiliano Zapata, 9 November 1914, AOM, caja 30, expediente 8, documento 129.

130. Figueroa Uriza, *Ciudadanos en armas*, II, 566–67.

131. ASRA, 23/1439 (723.6) Restitución, Anexo al Local, fols. 101–3; interview, Arturo Figueroa, Tetipac, Guerrero, 8 July 1975.

132. Interview, Gabriel Velasco, Buenavista de Cuéllar, Guerrero, 9 July 1975; José Figueroa Ayala, "Buenavista de Cuéllar, Gro.: Epopeya" (unpublished ms.); Jean Meyer, *La révolution mexicaine: 1910–1940* (Paris, 1973), p. 76–77.

133. Figueroa Uriza, *Ciudadanos en armas*, II, 710; Figueroa Alcocer, *Crónica*, p. 170; Meyer, *La cristiada*, III, 121.

134. Interviews with the following Zapatista veterans: Carlos Albarrán Gómez, Cocula, Guerrero, 3 July 1975; Lucano Téllez Peralta, Iguala, Guerrero, 6 July 1975; Zeferino Bahena Bahena, Iguala, Guerrero, 1 July 1975; "Memorándum del Estado Mayor del C. Subsecretario de Guerra y Marina," 7 August 1918, AVC, carpeta 124, documento 13976; "Memorándum del Ayuntamiento de Chilpancingo," 20 March 1918, AVC, carpeta 121, documento 13693.

135. "Acta de Ratificación del Plan de Ayala," San Pablo Oxtotepec, 19 July 1914, RDS, 812.00/16115.

136. Valverde, *Julián Blanco*, pp. 56–66.

137. Ibid., pp. 67, 78; Figueroa Uriza, *Ciudadanos en armas*, II, 619–20, 648, 674; AVC, Telegramas 1914–1915, folders 5–6.

138. RDS, 812.00/15794. Edwards's assessment of Mariscal and Blanco was broadly confirmed by the captain of the U.S.S. *Yorktown* in October 1914: "Political and Social 'Whos-Who' in the State of Guerrero," RDS, 812.00/14239.

139. For the version of Blanco's supporters, see Valverde, *Julián Blanco*, pp. 98–110, 135–38, and the report of General Natalio Espinosa, in Fabela, *Documentos históricos*, Revolución y régimen constitucionalista, IV, 215–17. For Mariscal's version, see AVC, Telegramas 1915–1918, folder 4, and Valverde, *Julián Blanco*, pp. 131–34. For Martín Vicario's ver-

sion, which confirms that Blanco was fired upon while riding in Acapulco, see Figueroa Uriza, *Ciudadanos en armas*, II, 675–77.

140. Fabela, *Documentos históricos*, Revolución y régimen constitucionalista, IV, 200–202; Valverde, *Julián Blanco*, p. 104.

141. RDS, 812.00/16834.

142. RDS, 812.00/17256; Coronel Jefe M. (*sic*, Rafael?) del Castillo to Venustiano Carranza, 3 January 1916, AVC, Telegramas 1915–1918, folder 14.

143. RDS, 812.00/18134; Tte Coronel S. Díaz to Primer Jefe, 12 May 1916, AVC, Telegramas 1915–1918, folder 25.

144. Héctor F. López Mena, "Campaña contra villistas y zapatistas," *El Nacional*, 16, 23 November 1953.

145. Corl S. Díaz to Primer Jefe, 9 November 1916, AVC, Telegramas 1915–1918, folder 31.

146. Ochoa Campos, *Historia del Estado de Guerrero*, p. 298; López Mena, "Campaña contra villistas y zapatistas," *El Nacional*, 30 November 1953.

147. Figueroa Uriza, *Ciudadanos en armas*, II, 742–43.

148. Ibid., II, 743–45; *El Universal*, 17, 29, 31 December 1917; RDS, 812.00/21781.

149. RDS, 812.00/21781, 21943.

150. RDS., 812.00/21943.

151. "Memorándum del Ayuntamiento de Chilpancingo," 20 March 1918, AVC, carpeta 121, documento 13693.

152. AVC, carpeta 121, documentos 13708, 13714.

153. On the Figueroas' careers from 1914 to 1917, see Figueroa Uriza, *Ciudadanos en armas*, II, 563–722, *passim*.

154. For the Costa Grande campaign, see ibid., II, 705–65.

155. AVC, carpeta 124, documento 13980; Telegramas 1915–1918, folders 45–46.

156. Figueroa Uriza, *Ciudadanos en armas*, II, 764.

157. Ibid., II, 765.

158. The Figueroas' only remaining rival, Jesús H. Salgado, was killed by the forces of Maycotte on 8 June 1919: Figueroa Uriza, *Ciudadanos en armas*, II, 814–15.

159. *Memoria 1903*, I, 396, 413. Ortega, Padilla and Eduardo and Rodolfo Neri later studied together in Mexico City; *Periódico Oficial*, 13 January 1909.

6. The Eclipse of the Figueroas and the Emergence of the New Revolutionary State: 1920–1941

1. Ernest Gruening, *Mexico and Its Heritage* (London, 1928), p. 319. On the army during Carranza's regime, see: Edwin Lieuwen, *Mexican Militarism: The Political Rise and Fall of the Revolutionary Army, 1910–1940* (Albuquerque, 1968), pp. 29–55.

2. Buve, "Peasant Movements," pp. 114, 120.

3. Knight, "Peasant and Caudillo," p. 55.

4. Arnaldo Córdova, *La ideología de la Revolución Mexicana: Formación del nuevo régimen* (Mexico, 1973), pp. 205–17.

5. Arnaldo Córdova, *La formación del poder político en México* (Mexico, 1972), p. 21.

6. Knight, "Peasant and Caudillo" pp. 44, 51–52.

7. Ankerson, "Saturnino Cedillo," p. 140.

8. Ibid., pp. 140–41. One would not wish to push this rural-urban dichotomy too far, for, after all, the principal Constitutionalist caudillos were, in many cases, of rural origins. Nevertheless, the Tomás Garrido Canabals, the Emilio Portes Gils, or the Adalberto Tejedas of the 1920s did display a distinctly urban political instinct. For some case studies, see Fowler Salamini, *Agrarian Radicalism*; and Joseph, "Caciquismo and the Revolution," on Veracruz and Yucatán, respectively.

9. Buve's "Patronaje" is particularly suggestive in this regard. On *caciquismo* in revolutionary Mexico, see: Roger Bartra et al., *Caciquismo y poder político en el México rural* (Mexico, 1975).

10. The phrase was used by Cárdenas with reference to Tabasco: John W. F. Dulles, *Yesterday in Mexico: A Chronicle of the Revolution, 1919–1936* (Austin, Texas, 1967), p. 611.

11. On the political and military significance of the agrarian politics of Obregón and Calles, see Meyer, *La cristiada*, III, 60–64, 85–88. On the government's use of labor, see Jean Meyer, "Los obreros en la Revolución Mexicana: Los Batallones Rojos," *Historia Mexicana*, 21 (1) (julio–septiembre 1971), 1–37; Dulles, *Yesterday in Mexico*, pp. 271–79; Gruening, *Mexico and Its Heritage*, pp. 338–60.

12. Córdova, *La formación*, pp. 37–40; Lieuwen, *Mexican Militarism*, pp. 102–6; Dulles, *Yesterday in Mexico*, pp. 408–35.

13. Romana Falcón, "El surgimiento del agrarismo cardenista—Una revisión de las tesis populistas," *Historia Mexicana*, 27 (3) (enero–marzo, 1978), 338–86.

14. Lieuwen, *Mexican Militarism*, pp. 123–26.

15. William P. Glade, Jr., "Revolution and Economic Development," in William P. Glade, Jr., and Charles W. Anderson, *The Political Economy of Mexico: Two Studies by William P. Glade, Jr. and Charles W. Anderson* (Madison, Wisconsin, 1963), p. 27.

16. Knight, "Peasant and Caudillo," p. 3.

17. Figueroa Uriza, *Ciudadanos en armas*, II, 812–16.

18. Ibid., II, 776.

19. Ibid., II, 771–83.

20. *Excélsior*, 9 April 1920. See also Luis N. Ruvalcaba (ed.), *Campaña política del C. Alvaro Obregón, candidato a la presidencia de la República 1920–1924* (5 vols.; Mexico, 1923), III, 109–13. For Obregón's own account of his escape to Iguala, see Fabela, *Documentos históricos*, Revolución y régimen constitucionalista, VI, 435–39.

21. Héctor F. López Mena, "Campaña obregonista," *El Nacional*, 29 March 1954; Miguel Gil, "Por qué huyó de México el 12 de abril de 1920 el general Obregón," *La Prensa*, 13 April 1931.

22. López Mena, "Campaña obregonista," *El Nacional,* 29 March and 5 April 1954; Heriberto Barrón, "El tren dorado," *La Prensa,* 20 May 1934; Lic. Rodolfo Neri, *La rebelión delahuertista en el Estado de Guerrero* (Chilpancingo, Guerrero, 1968), p. 1; Ramírez to Gobernador del Estado, 2 (*sic*) April 1920, AGGEG, Documentos Históricos 1920.

23. Figueroa Uriza, *Ciudadanos en armas,* II, 824–27.

24. The speech is in "Actas taquigráficas de las sesiones de los días 19, 20 y 26 de abril de 1920," pp. 5–8, AGGEG, Documentos Históricos 1920. It is reproduced in Figueroa Uriza, *Ciudadanos en armas,* II, 827–32.

25. Decree No. 38, *Periódico Oficial,* 24 April 1920. The decree is re-produced in Figueroa Uriza, *Ciudadanos en armas,* II, 833–35.

26. Figueroa Alcocer, *Crónica,* pp. 206–8. Carranza's sole supporter in Guerrero was Silvestre G. Mariscal, who had been released from prison toward the end of 1919. He was captured and executed on 31 May 1920: Figueroa Uriza, *Ciudadanos en armas,* II, 859–61.

27. Figueroa Uriza, *Ciudadanos en armas,* II, 841–49.

28. Ibid., II, 888.

29. Héctor F. López Mena, "Campaña contra villistas y zapatistas," *El Nacional,* 9, 23, 30 November 1953; López Mena, "La campaña obregonista," *El Nacional,* 19 April 1954; Salvador Azuela, "Un luchador de la Revolución," *El Universal,* 4 May 1957; Jesús Romero Flores, "El Gral. Héctor F. López, un gran revolucionario," *El Nacional,* 21 February 1926.

30. López Mena, "Campaña obregonista," *El Nacional,* 8 March 1954; *Excélsior,* 12 August 1922; Amado González Dávila, *Geografía del Estado de Guerrero y síntesis histórica* (Mexico, 1959), p. 318; López, *Diccionario,* p. 457; RDS, 812.00/26209 and 812.002/154.

31. Neri, *La rebelión delahuertista,* p. 1; RDS, 812.00/26209.

32. Neri, *La rebelión delahuertista,* p. 1; Figueroa Alcocer, *Crónica,* p. 153; Figueroa Uriza, *Ciudadanos en armas,* II, 887.

33. Neri, *La rebelión delahuertista,* p. 1; Gruening, *Mexico and Its Heritage,* p. 431.

34. Gral. de Brigada Comiconado (*sic*) Samuel M. Santos to C. Presidente de la República, 7 July 1923, AGN, Presidentes Obregón/Calles, 106-1, 818-G-15; RDS, 812.00/26589, 26699; R. Neri and Teófilo Escudero to Presidente de la República, 30 May 1922, and Obregón to Gral. Rómulo Figueroa, 26 June 1922, AGN, Presidentes Obregón/Calles, 109, 818-S-78; Memorandum of Lic. D. Pastrana to Oficial Mayor de la Comisión Nacional Agraria, 14 April 1924, ASRA, 23/9749 (723.6) Toca No. 1, fol. 82. On the activities of Escudero, see Mario Gill, "Los Escudero de Acapulco," *Historia Mexicana,* 3 (2) (octubre–diciembre 1953), 291–308; Alejandro Martínez Carbajal, *Juan Escudero y Amadeo Vidales* (Mexico, 1961), pp. 35–82.

35. AGN, Presidentes Obregón/Calles, 106-1, 818-G-15.

36. Jesús Nava et al. to Obregón, 14 June 1923, AGN Presidentes Obregón/Calles, 106-1, 818-I-16.

37. R. Neri and Teófilo Escudero to Presidente de la República, 30 May

1922; Obregón to Gral. Rómulo Figueroa, 26 June 1922, AGN, Presidentes Obregón/Calles, 109, 818-S-78.

38. ASRA, 23/1453 (723.6) Toca, fols. 2, 11–16; 23/9794 (723.6) Toca.

39. For the correspondence in this case, see AGN, Presidentes Obregón/ Calles, 105, 818-C-82; 106-1, 818-C-15; ASRA, 23/1280 (723.6) Toca No. 1, fols. 29–30, 41, 73, 111–13, 117–19.

40. ASRA, 23/1270 (723.6) Toca No. 1, fols. 59–64. Rancheros were not always hostile to *agrarismo* when the political imperatives did not threaten their own property: Schryer, *Rancheros of Pisaflores*, pp. 85–100.

41. Jacobs, "Revolution in Guerrero," pp. 303–4, 307–8.

42. AGN, Presidentes Obregón/Calles, 106-1, 818-G-15.

43. Héctor F. López Mena, "Por qué y cómo fuí gobernador del Estado de Guerrero," *El Nacional*, 10 May 1954.

44. On the political background of the de la Huerta revolt, see Alonso Capetillo, *La rebelión sin cabeza. (Génesis y desarrollo del movimiento delahuertista)* (Mexico, 1925); Luis Monroy Durán, *El último caudillo: Apuntes para la historia de México, acerca del movimiento armado de 1923, en contra del gobierno constituído* (Mexico, 1924); Dulles, *Yesterday in Mexico*, pp. 126–35, 173–76, 181–96.

45. *Periódico Oficial*, 24 March 1923.

46. Ibid.; *El Universal*, 4, 5, 6 January 1923.

47. *El Universal*, 10, 25 January 1923.

48. RDS, 812.00/26209; *El Universal*, 3, 7 February 1923; *Periódico Oficial*, 24 March 1923.

49. *El Universal*, 8 February 1923.

50. Gobernador Constitucional Interino Teófile Escudero to Presidente Municipal de Taxco, 9, 10 February 1923, AMT, 1923; *El Universal*, 10 February 1923; *Periódico Oficial*, 24 March 1923.

51. On the San Luis affair, see Dulles, *Yesterday in Mexico*, pp. 181–87; Capetillo, *La rebelión sin cabeza*, pp. 59–68.

52. López Mena, "Por qué y cómo," *El Nacional*, 10 May 1954.

53. RDS, 812.00/26589.

54. Figueroa Uriza, *Ciudadanos en armas*, II, 960–66; Figueroa Alcocer, *Crónica*, pp. 215–16, 226; *Excélsior*, 27, 28, 29, 30 November 1923.

55. Gral. de Brigada Comicionado (*sic*) Samuel M. Santos to C. Presidente de la República, 7 July 1923, AGN, Presidentes Obregón/Calles, 106-1, 818-G-15; RDS, 812.00/26329.

56. Figueroa Uriza, *Ciudadanos en armas*, II, 960–66; *Excélsior*, 26, 27, 28, 29 October, 13, 27, 29 November 1923.

57. Figueroa Alcocer, *Crónica*, pp. 216–17; Figueroa Uriza, *Ciudadanos en armas*, II, 959. As late as November, Figueroa sent Leopoldo Carranco Cardoso to interview Calles to win his support against Neri: interview, Leopoldo Carranco Cardoso, Taxco, Guerrero, 14 June 1975.

58. Figueroa Uriza, *Ciudadanos en armas*, II, 966; Figueroa Alcocer, *Crónica*, p. 218; George T. Summerlin to Secretary of State, Mexico City, 7 December 1923, RDS 812.00/26612.

59. Figueroa Uriza, *Ciudadanos en armas*, II, 966–72; Figueroa Alcocer, *Crónica*, p. 219; *El Universal*, 1 December 1923; RDS 812.00/26612.
60. Figueroa Uriza, *Ciudadanos en armas*, II, 974; Figueroa Alcocer, *Crónica*, p. 220; *El Universal*, 2, 4 December 1923.
61. Figueroa Uriza, *Ciudadanos en armas*, II, 973–74; *El Universal*, 2, 4 December 1923.
62. Figueroa Uriza, *Ciudadanos en armas*, II, 974–75; Figueroa Alcocer, *Crónica*, pp. 220–21.
63. Figueroa Uriza, *Ciudadanos en armas*, II, 977; Figueroa Alcocer, *Crónica*, pp. 221–23; *El Universal*, 23 December 1923; *Periódico Oficial*, 29 December 1923.
64. Neri, *La rebelión delahuertista*, pp. 3–13; Fierro Armenta, *Monografía de Atoyac*, p. 179; Monroy Durán, *El último caudillo*, p. 241.
65. Figueroa Alcocer, *Crónica*, p. 224; *Periódico Oficial*, 29 December 1923.
66. On the military campaign, see Figueroa Uriza, *Ciudadanos en armas*, II, 977–80; Figueroa Alcocer, *Crónica*, pp. 223–31; *El Universal* and *Excélsior* issues from 23 December to 13 February 1923.
67. Monroy Durán, *El último caudillo*, p. 242; ASRA, 23/1247 (723.6) Toca, fol. 121, 23/1280 (723.6) Toca No. 1, fol. 164.
68. Gill, "Los Escudero," pp. 301–2; Martínez Carbajal, *Juan Escudero y Amadeo Vidales*, pp. 80–82; Figueroa Alcocer, *Crónica*, p. 226; *Excélsior*, 16 January 1924.
69. RDS, 812.00/26925.
70. RDS, 812.00/26911.
71. RDS, 812.00/27121; Figueroa Alcocer, *Crónica*, pp. 225–26.
72. *El Universal*, 10, 11, 12 March 1924.
73. Ibid., 20, 21, 27 March 1924; Figueroa Uriza, *Ciudadanos en armas*, II, 980–83; Figueroa Alcocer, *Crónica*, pp. 231–33.
74. Figueroa Uriza, *Ciudadanos en armas*, II, 933–36.
75. Ibid., pp. 963–66; *Excélsior*, 28, 30 November 1923; Gruening, *Mexico and Its Heritage*, p. 433.
76. López Mena, "Por qué y cómo," *El Nacional*, 10, 17 May 1954.
77. López Mena, "Por qué y cómo," *El Nacional*, 17 May 1954; *El Legionario*, March 1958.
78. López Mena, "Por qué y cómo," *El Nacional*, 17 May 1954; *Excélsior*, 11 November 1924; Gruening, *Mexico and Its Heritage*, p. 433.
79. On Cienfueguista unrest: López Mena, "Por qué y cómo," *El Nacional*, 17 May 1954.
80. In his inaugural address López said nothing to indicate his intentions toward agrarian reform: López Mena, "Por qué y cómo," *El Legionario*, April 1958.
81. López's opponents also included Ezequiel Padilla, José Inocente Lugo, Martín Vicario, and General José Amarillas, *jefe de las operaciones militares* in Guerrero.
82. RDS, 812.00/27201, 27349, 27400.
83. López Mena, "Por qué y cómo," *El Legionario*, June 1958.

84. *Informe* of 1 September 1925, *Periódico Oficial*, 5 September 1925.
85. de la Peña, *Guerrero económico*, I, 457.
86. Jacobs, "Revolution in Guerrero," pp. 303–4.
87. López Mena, "Por qué y cómo," *El Legionario*, April 1958; *Excélsior*, 13, 15 April 1925.
88. Martínez Carbajal, *Juan Escudero y Amadeo Vidales*, pp. 89–91.
89. Pangburn to Alexander W. Weddell, 18 May 1926, NA, RG 84—1927 (800); RDS, 812.00/27789.
90. Martínez Carbajal, *Juan Escudero y Amadeo Vidales*, p. 91.
91. Ibid., pp. 40–41.
92. Ibid., pp. 55, 57–58.
93. Ibid., pp. 59, 61–65.
94. Ibid., pp. 81–82.
95. Friedrich Katz, "Agrarian Changes in Northern Mexico," p. 272; Ankerson, "Saturnino Cedillo," p. 145–46.
96. Martínez Carbajal, *Juan Escudero y Amadeo Vidales*, pp. 110–18. It appears that the colony failed, however, due to the opposition of Spanish interests: Pangburn to Weddell, 18 May 1926, NA, RG 84—1927 (800).
97. Martínez Carbajal, *Juan Escudero y Amadeo Vidales*, pp. 154–65.
98. On the break with the Partido Obrero, see Jean Meyer, Enrique Krauze, and Cayetano Reyes, *Historia de la Revolución Mexicana: Período 1924–1928* (2 vols.; Mexico, 1977), II, 196; "The Mexican Elections for National Congressmen at Acapulco, Mexico, on July 4, 1926," NA, RG 84—1927 (800); copy of *Regeneración*, 2 May 1926, in NA, RG 84—1927 (800). On the attack on Aguas Blancas, see RDS, 812.00/27767.
99. RDS, 812.00/28620, 28737, 812.00 Guerrero/3; Pangburn to Weddell, 18 May 1926, NA, RG 84—1927 (800); Martínez Carbajal, *Juan Escudero y Amadeo Vidales*, pp. 110, 142.
100. RDS, 812.00 Guerrero/5; *El Universal*, 14, 22, 26 February 1929; Martínez Carbajal, *Juan Escudero y Amadeo Vidales*, p. 177. Amadeo Vidales was murdered in Mexico City in 1932: ibid., p. 178.
101. "The Mexican Elections for National Congressmen at Acapulco, Mexico, on July 4, 1926," NA, RG 84—1927 (800); Meyer, Krauze, and Reyes, *Historia de la Revolución Mexicana*, II, 196; also see the 2 May 1926 issue of *Regeneración*, the journal of the Partido Obrero de Acapulco, NA, RG 84—1927 (800). At the time of his rebellion, Amadeo was López's commander of the *defensas sociales* on the coast: Harry K. Pangburn to Alexander W. Weddell, 18 May 1926, in NA, RG 84—1927 (800).
102. Meyer, *La cristiada*, I, 121–23, 135, 183–84.
103. Meyer, Krauze, and Reyes, *Historia de la Revolución Mexicana*, II, 197.
104. RDS, 812.00 Guerrero/1.
105. Harry K. Pangburn to Dwight D. Morrow, 4 August 1929, NA, RG 84—1929 (350); Meyer, Krauze, and Reyes, *Historia de la Revolución Mexicana*, II, 197.
106. RDS, 812.00 Guerrero/1; *Excélsior*, 1 February 1928.

107. 812.00 Guerrero/1; *Excélsior*, 2, 7, 8, 9, 10 February 1928. For a biographical note on Martínez, see MID: 2657-G-589/30.
108. *Excélsior*, 8, 9, 11, 15 February 1928.
109. RDS, 812.00 Guerrero/8.
110. *Excélsior*, 29 November 1929.
111. *Periódico Oficial*, 7 September 1932.
112. Castrejón's *Informe*, 1 September 1931, *Periódico Oficial*, 2 September 1931.
113. See, for example, Secretario General y Secretario de Acción Social del Partido Socialista de Guerrero to Juez de la. Instancia del Distrito de Alvarez, 12 May 1931, ASRA, 23/1424 (723.6) Anexo al Local, fol. 3; Encargado del Despacho de la Liga de Comunidades Agrarias y Sindicatos de Campesinos del Estado de Guerrero to Jefe del Departmento Autónomo Agrario, 26 January 1934, ASRA, 23/10246 (723.6) Toca. *Ejidal* committees and the PSG played an important role in the anti-alcoholic campaign of 1929: *El Universal*, 8 May 1929.
114. Interviews: Pablo Alarcón, Chilpancingo, Guerrero, 24 May 1975; Ing. Manuel Mesa Andraca, Chilpancingo, Guerrero, 26 May 1975; Leopoldo Carranco Cardoso, Taxco, Guerrero, 14 June 1975; Arturo Figueroa, Tetipac, Guerrero, 8 July 1975.
115. Jacobs, "Revolution in Guerrero," pp. 303–4.
116. Meyer, *La cristiada*, III, 86–89. Note that Guerrero differed from the national pattern in that there was no perceptible increase in the rate of reform in 1927 (indeed, grants by the state executive continued to decline in that year). The rate of reform did not accelerate until 1929 (before that year the Cristero rebellion had not reached significant proportions in the state) when many of the *agraristas* of the district of Hidalgo defected to the Cristeros: Meyer, *La cristiada*, I, 311–12.
117. RDS, 812.00 Guerrero/1. This followed the declared policy of Calles.
118. *Informe*, 1 September 1931, *Periódico Oficial*, 2 September 1931.
119. "Monthly Political Report August 15, 1920," NA, RG 84—1930 (800).
120. "Minuta de Ley de Educación Pública," AGGEG, Documentos Históricos 1930 (my emphasis); "Reglamento de la Ley Federal de Tierras Ociosas Número 144," 22 March 1930, AGGEG, Leyes y Reglamentos; "Ley sobre la creación del Fundo Legal en el Estado de Guerrero Número 156," NA, RG 84—1930 (852).
121. "Quarterly Statement of Economic Conditions (October to December), 15 December 1929," NA, RG 84—1929 (610); Pangburn to Dwight W. Morrow, 4 August 1929, NA, RG 84—1929 (350); H. H. Leonard to Secretary of State, 30 November 1931, NA, RG 84—1931 (800).
122. Fierro Armenta, *Monografía de Atoyac*, pp. 188–89; Figueroa Uriza, *Ciudadanos en armas*, II, 766, 796–97, 963–65; Figueroa Alcocer, *Crónica*, p. 131; *Periódico Oficial*, 27 September 1933; Guevara to Obregón, 8 November 1924, AGN, Presidentes Obregón/Calles, 105, 818-C-191; manifesto "A los ciudadanos electores de Tasco," AMT, 1934.
123. *Periódico Oficial*, 11 July 1934.

124. Fierro Armenta, *Monografía de Atoyac*, pp. 188–89.
125. *El Universal*, 24, 31 March 1933; Joseph E. Maleady to Secretary of State, 25, 31 March 1933, NA, RG 84—1933 (800).
126. *El Universal*, 30 November, 5 December 1932.
127. *El Universal*, 9 December 1932.
128. *El Universal*, 5 March 1933.
129. *El Universal*, 23, 24, 28 March 1933; Fierro Armenta, *Monografía de Atoyac*, p. 189; Interview, Pablo Alarcón, Chilpancingo, Guerrero, 24 May 1975.
130. *El Universal*, 29, 30 March 1933.
131. *El Universal*, 9, 11, 21, 22, 23, 27 April 1933; Joseph E. Maleady to Secretary of State, NA, RG 84—1933 (800). Attacks were also launched on the PSG and the Liga de Comunidades y Sindicatos: Melesio Altamirano and Alfredo Córdoba Lara to Presidente de la Comisión Nacional Agraria, 16 June 1933, ASRA, 23/1207 (723.6) Toca, fol. 17a; Pablo Padilla to Presidente Constitucional de la República, 23 February 1934, ASRA, 23/10225 (723.6) Toca.
132. *Diario de los Debates de la Cámara de Senadores del Congreso de los Estados Unidos Mexicanos*, 5 November 1935. For a specific example, that of Tuxpan, see ASRA, 23/1318 (723.6) Toca, fol. 189.
133. Juan Arzate and Ernesto Torres to Presidente de la Comisión Nacional Agraria, 19 August 1932, ASRA, 23/10068 (723.6) Toca.
134. Francisco Casarrubias to Jefe de Procuradores Agrarios de la República, 20 June 1934, ASRA, 23/1385 (723.6) Anexo al Local.
135. *Diario de los Debates de la Cámara de Senadores*, 5 November 1935. Guevara, in fact, gave his Hacienda de Santo Tomás (42,000 hectares) to Jaleaca de Catalán to form a cooperative: *Periódico Oficial*, 27 September 1933.
136. Jacobs, "Revolution in Guerrero", pp. 303–4.
137. Frank Brandenburg, *The Making of Modern Mexico* (Englewood Cliffs, New Jersey, 1966), p. 81.
138. On the Coyuca affair, see *Excélsior*, 21, 22, 23, 25, 26, 28 September 1935; *Diario de los Debates de la Cámara de Senadores*, 5 November 1935. Ernesto Gómez was a member of the Guevarista legislature which deposed Governor Castrejón in 1933: *El Universal*, 1 March 1933.
139. *Diario de los Debates de la Cámara de Senadores*, 5 November 1935.
140. Ibid.; *Excélsior*, 6 November 1935.
141. *Periódico Oficial*, 3 March 1937.
142. MID: 2657-G-589/102.
143. *Excélsior*, 11 April 1925, 25 September 1935; *Periódico Oficial*, 5 September 1935; Figueroa Alcocer, *Crónica*, p. 127; Luis Arenal, *Estampas de Guerrero; Grabados de Luis Arenal, notas históricas de Macrina Rabadán: 1849–1949* (Mexico, 1949).
144. *El Universal*, 10 January 1939 (my emphasis), 25 January 1939.
145. *El Universal*, 4, 17 February 1941; Rafael Catalán Calvo, *Problemas del Estado de Guerrero* (Mexico, 1946), pp. 16–17.

146. *El Universal,* 15, 16, February 1941.
147. *El Universal,* 20 February 1941.
148. Catalán Calvo, *Problemas de Guerrero,* p. 17.
149. J. Brock Havron to George P. S. Shaw, 13 May 1941, NA, RG 84—1941 (800).
150. On the Zapatistas, see Womack, *Zapata.* On the Yaquis, see Hu-Dehart, "Development and Rural Rebellion."
151. Ankerson, "Saturnino Cedillo," *passim.*
152. Katz, "Agrarian Changes in Northern Mexico."
153. Knight, "Peasant and Caudillo," p. 46.
154. Figueroa Uriza, *Ciudadanos en armas,* II, 937.
155. Ibid., II, 938–52; Meyer, *La cristiada,* I, 242–45.
156. *Periódico Oficial,* 11 July 1934; *El Universal,* 15, 20 February 1941; Roderic Ai Camp, *Mexican Political Biographies: 1935–1975* (Tucson, Arizona, 1976), p. 112.
157. Gutiérrez Galindo, *Rubén Figueroa,* pp. 73–121; Ai Camp, *Mexican Political Biographies,* pp. 112–13.
158. On the kinds of political "career tracks" followed in the contemporary Mexican political system, see Peter H. Smith, *Labyrinths of Power: Political Recruitment in Twentieth-Century Mexico* (Princeton, 1979), pp. 10–11.

7. Agrarian Reform in Northern Guerrero: 1919–1940

1. The first grant of land in Guerrero was made to Pololcingo, a small town near Huitzuco, in 1919: ASRA, 23/1196 (723.6) Local, fols. 16–17. De la Peña, *Guerrero económico,* I, 456, is clearly mistaken in stating that the first grant was made to San Vicente Palapa, which received its provisional ejido five days after Pololcingo: ASRA, 23/1197 (723.6) Local, fols. 11–12.
2. Departmento de la Estadística Nacional, *Censo general de habitantes, 30 de noviembre de 1921. Estado de Guerrero* (Mexico, 1927), pp. 62, 72–73, 84, 89–90; Secretaría de la Economía Nacional, Dirección General de Estadística, *Estados Unidos Mexicanos: 6° censo de población. 1940. Guerrero* (2nd ed.; Mexico, 1948), pp. 13, 46, 75.
3. *Censo 1921. Guerrero,* pp. 56, 62, 72–73, 84, 89–90; *Censo 1940. Guerrero,* pp. 13, 46, 75, 136, 138, 141, 143–45.
4. *Censo 1940. Guerrero,* pp. 28–38, 60–71, 89–98.
5. ASRA, 23/1461 (723.6) Local, fols. 148–49.
6. ASRA, 23/1403 (723.6) Local, fols. 58–60.
7. ASRA, 23/1365 (723.6) Local, fols. 21–23.
8. Table 3.
9. ASRA, 23/10225 (723.6) Local No. 1, fols. 185–87.
10. Jacobs, "Revolution in Guerrero," pp. 298–99.
11. ASRA, 23/1361 (723.6) Local, fols. 362–69.
12. Report of Rubén Estrada M., 23 February 1935, ASRA, 23/10205 (723.6) Toca.
13. ASRA, 23/1360 (723.6) Ampliación Local, fols. 21–24.

14. ASRA, 23/1220 (723.6) Ampliación Local, fols. 32–36.

15. ASRA, 23/1361 (723.6) Local, fols. 362–69.

16. ASRA, 23/21303 (723.6) Local, fols. 27–29.

17. ASRA, 23/19284 (723.6) Local, fols. 47–49.

18. ASRA, 23/1279 (723.6) Local No. 1, fols. 38–39.

19. Jacobs, "Revolution in Guerrero," pp. 303–8.

20. Increased federal control of the reform was allowed for in the Agrarian Code of 22 March 1934: Eyler N. Simpson, *The Ejido: Mexico's Way Out* (Chapel Hill, North Carolina, 1937), pp. 456–57.

21. ASRA, 23/1199 (723.6) Toca No. 1, fols. 229–34; 23/1284 (723.6) Toca, fols. 168–73; 23/9860 (723.6) Toca, fols. 98–100.

22. ASRA, 23/1196 (723.6) Toca, fols. 68–69; 23/1233 (723.6) Toca, fols. 22–23; 23/1194 (723.6) Toca, fols. 15–16.

23. ASRA, 23/1210 (723.6) Ampliación Local, fols. 32–36.

24. ASRA, 23/1210 (723.6) Ampliación Local (1935), fols. 25–26.

25. ASRA, 23/10053 (723.6) Ampliación la. Local, fols. 65–66.

26. ASRA, 23/1385 (723.6) Local, fols. 22–24; 23/1197 (723.6) Toca, fols. 104–5; 23/1214 (723.6) Ampliación Local, fols. 36–39.

27. ASRA, 23/1383 (723.6) Restitución Toca, fol. 207; 23/17787 (723.6) Local, fol. 2; 23/1402 (723.6) Toca, fols. 39–40.

28. Iván Restrepo and José Sánchez Cortés, *La reforma agraria en cuatro regiones: El Bajío, Michoacán, La Laguna y Tlaxcala* (Mexico, 1972), pp. 111–18; Rodolfo Stavenhagen, "Aspectos sociales de la estructura agraria en México," in Rodolfo Stavenhagen et al., *Neolatifundismo y explotación, de Emiliano Zapata a Anderson Clayton & Co.* (2nd ed.; Mexico, 1971), p. 24.

29. Report of 14 November 1939, ASRA, 23/19284 (723.6) Ampliación la. Local.

30. ASRA, 23/1235 (723.6) Toca, fol. 43.

31. ASRA, 23/10068 (723.6) Local, fols. 64–65; Ampliación Local, fol. 25.

32. ASRA, 23/1360 (723.6) Ampliación Local, fols. 21–24.

33. ASRA, 23/1222 (723.6) Ampliación (1926) Local, fols. 48–54.

34. Ibid.

35. ASRA, 23/1222 (723.6) Ampliación Toca, fols. 17–18.

36. Presidential Resolution, 31 January 1940, ASRA, 23/19284 (723.6) Ampliación la. Toca.

37. ASRA, 23/1379 (723.6) Toca, fol. 66.

38. Report of Ing. José D. Novelo, 7 September 1936, ASRA, 23/1198 (723.6) Ampliación: Documentación Complementaria; 23/1224 (723.6) Ampliación Local, fols. 21–23; 23/1231 (723.6) Ampliación: Documentación Complementaria, fols. 3–4a.

39. Report of Ing. E. Sotelo Salas, 2 September 1936, ASRA, 23/8962 (723.6) Toca.

40. Report of Ing. Humberto Salas, 8 May 1936, ASRA, 23/10210 (723.6) Toca.

41. ASRA, 23/1284 (723.6) Local, fols. 19–20; Toca, fols. 204–5.

42. ASRA, 23/1360 (723.6) Ampliación Local, fols. 21–24.

43. One exception was Juchimilpa, where the *ejidatarios*, as late as 1936, still relied on the landowner for their seed maize: ASRA, 23/1422 (723.6) Ampliación Local, fol. 27.

44. ASRA, 23/1403 (723.6) Toca, fol. 71.

45. ASRA, 23/1238 (723.6) Toca, fol. 236.

46. ASRA, 23/1205 (723.6) Local, fols. 51–52.

47. For a general discussion of capital accumulation and production of a marketable surplus, see Michel Gutelman, *Réforme et mystification agraires en Amérique Latine. Le cas du Mexique* (Paris, 1971). In 1940, 35% of Guerrero's ejidos produced no marketable surplus: Secretaría de la Economía Nacional, Dirección General de Estadística, *II censo ejidal, 1940. Resumen general* (Mexico, 1942), pp. 85, 102.

48. ASRA, 23/1241 (723.6) Local, fols. 18–19.

49. ASRA, 23/1235 (723.6) Local, fol. 20.

50. ASRA, 23/1283 (723.6) Toca, fols. 81–82.

51. ASRA, 23/1223 (723.6) Toca No. 1, fols. 2–3; 23/1229 (723.6) Toca No. 1, fols. 15–18.

52. ASRA, 23/1280 (723.6) Toca No. 1, fols. 29–30, 41, 73, 85–86; AGN, Presidentes Obregón/Calles, 105, 818-C-82, 818-C-15.

53. ASRA, 23/1259 (723.6) Toca No. 1, fol. 85.

54. ASRA, 23/1211 (723.6) Ampliación Toca, fols. 7, 15, 30.

55. ASRA, 23/1211 (723.6) Ampliación Toca, fol. 34.

56. ASRA, 23/1270 (723.6) Toca No. 1, fols. 48–50, 59, 76, 129, 153–54, 163–64; AGN, Presidentes Obregón/Calles, 109, 818-R-27.

57. ASRA, 23/1199 (723.6) Toca No. 1, fols. 109, 113, 128–29b.

58. ASRA, 23/1238 (723.6) Toca, fols. 32–33, 53, 160–61, 168–70.

59. Ig. S. Figueroa et al. to Cárdenas, 12 May 1938, ASRA, 23/9749 (723.6) Toca No. 1.

60. ASRA, 23/1392 (723.6) Restitución Local No. 2, fols. 463–71.

61. ASRA, 23/1392 (723.6) Restitución: Documentación Complementaria, fols. 59–68.

62. ASRA, 23/1392 (723.6) Restitución Local No. 3, fols. 313–14, 1131; Toca, fol. 386.

63. ASRA, 23/1392 (723.6) Toca, fol. 386.

64. ASRA, 23/11996 (723.6) Local, fol. 43.

65. ASRA, 23/1459 (723.6) Local, fols. 244–56.

66. Meyer, *La cristiada*, III, 64–85.

67. ASRA, 23/13748 (723.6) Local No. 1, fols. 74–76.

68. ASRA, 23/9860 (723.6) Toca, fols. 189–93.

69. ASRA, 23/10205 (723.6) Local, fols. 14, 64; Presidential Resolution, 14 June 1939, ASRA, 23/10205 (723.6) Toca.

70. ASRA, 23/19149 (723.6) Toca, fols. 96–97.

71. Interview, Carlos Albarrán Gómez, Cocula, Guerrero, 3 July 1975.

72. ASRA, 23/1199 (723.6) Toca No. 1, fols. 291–91b, 390–93, 417–22, 452–54, 464; Luis G. Albecerra to Sadot Garcés, 6 July 1970, 23/1199 (723.6) Quejas; 23/1280 (723.6) Toca No. 3, fols. 205–6; 23/1284 (723.6) Toca, fols. 184–85.

73. Estevan Salgado et al. to Delegado del Departamento Agrario, 12 December 1935, ASRA, 23/10053 (723.6) Toca.

74. ASRA, 23/1360 (723.6) Local, fol. 17.

75. ASRA, 23/1360 (723.6) Local, fol. 54.

76. ASRA, 23/1223 (723.6) Toca No. 1, fols. 64, 105–6, 124–26, 129–34, 138–39, 158–60, 182, 186, 190–91, 211–13; AGN, Presidentes Obregón/Calles, 106-1, 818-G-15.

77. ASRA, 23/1223 (723.6) Toca No. 1, fols. 248–50, 362, 388.

78. ASRA, 23/1196 (723.6) Toca, fols. 133, 135, 139–43, 147, 151, 167, 175.

79. ASRA, 23/1318 (723.6) Toca, fol. 182.

80. ASRA, 23/1280 (723.6) Toca No. 1, fols. 258–59, 320, 367–70.

81. Juan Arzate and Ernesto Torres to Presidente de la Comisión Nacional Agraria, 19 August 1932, ASRA, 23/10068 (723.6) Toca.

82. Francisco Casarrubias to Jefe de Procuradores Agrarios, 20 June 1934, ASRA, 23/10068 (723.6) Toca.

83. Ibid.; ASRA, 23/1309 (723.6) Toca, fols. 167, 170.

84. Ronfeldt, *Atencingo*, p. 221.

85. François Chevalier, "The *Ejido* and Political Stability in Mexico," in Claudio Veliz (ed.), *The Politics of Conformity in Latin America* (Oxford, 1970), p. 190.

Epilogue

1. Jean Meyer, *Le sinarquisme: Un fascisme mexicain? 1937–1947* (Paris?, 1977), pp. 208–9.

2. Smith, *Labyrinths of Power*, p. 187.

3. López Barroso, *Diccionario geográfico, histórico y estadístico del Distrito de Abasolo*, pp. 22–35, 121–25, 249–51.

4. Meyer, Krauze, and Reyes, *Historia de la Revolución Mexicana*, II, 198.

5. *Excélsior*, 1, 3 February 1975.

References

1. Documentary Sources

Archivo de Alfredo Robles Domínguez.
Archivo de la Secretaría de la Reforma Agraria: Ramo Ejidal. Ramo Comunal.
Archivo del General Octavio Magaña.
Archivo de Madero.
Archivo de Venustiano Carranza.
Archivo General de la Nación: Ramo de los Presidentes Obregón y Calles. Ramo de Tierras.
Archivo General del Gobierno del Estado de Guerrero.
Archivo Histórico de la Defensa Nacional, annotated index of Luis Muro.
Archivo Municipal de Taxco.
Carreño, Alberto María (ed.). *Archivo del General Porfirio Díaz*. 29 vols. Mexico, 1947–1960.
Fabela, Isidro (ed.). *Documentos históricos de la Revolución Mexicana*. 27 vols. Mexico, 1960–1973.
Secretaría de la Reforma Agraria, Oficina de Estadística.
United States National Archives: Military Intelligence Division. Record Group 84, papers of the Acapulco consulate.
United States National Archives: Records of the Department of State Relating to Internal Affairs of Mexico, Microfilm No. 274.

2. Interviews

Alarcón, Pablo. Chilpancingo, Guerrero, 24 May 1975.
Albarrán Gómez, Carlos. Cocula, Guerrero, 3 July 1975.
Bahena Bahena, Zeferino. Iguala, Guerrero, 1 July 1975.
Carranco Cardoso, Leopoldo. Taxco, Guerrero, 14 June 1975.
Figueroa, Arturo. Tetipac, Guerrero, 8 July 1975.
Figueroa Alcocer, Jesús. Huitzuco, Guerrero, 1 July 1975.
Figueroa Uriza, Dr. Arturo. Chilpancingo, Guerrero, 11 June 1975.
Mesa Andraca, Ing. Manuel. Chilpancingo, Guerrero, 26 May 1975.
Téllez Peralta, Lucano. Iguala, Guerrero, 6 July 1975.
Velasco, Gabriel. Buenavista de Cuéllar, Guerrero, 9 July 1975.

3. Newspapers

El Diario del Hogar. Mexico, D.F., 1887–1912.
Diario de los Debates de la Cámara de Senadores del Congreso de los Estados Unidos Mexicanos. Mexico, D.F., 5 November 1935.
Excélsior. Mexico, D.F., 1917–1941, 1975.
La Federación. Mexico, D.F., 1893–1894.
El Imparcial. Chilpancingo, Guerrero, 1895.
El Monitor Republicano. Mexico, D.F., 1893–1901.
El País. Mexico, D.F., 1901–1913.
Periódico Oficial del Gobierno del Estado de Guerrero. Chilpancingo, Guerrero, 1870–1940.
El Universal. Mexico, D.F., 1917–1941.

4. Official Publications of the State Government of Guerrero

Guerrero. *Colección de decretos y circulares del gobierno del Estado de Guerrero.* Vol. 1. Chilpancingo, Guerrero: Imprenta del Gobierno del Estado, 1869.

———. *Memoria presentada ante la H. Legislatura del Estado de Guerrero por el C. Gobernador del mismo, General Francisco O. Arce, en cumplimiento de la fracción III del art. 57 de la Constitución.* Chilpancingo, Guerrero: Imprenta del Gobierno del Estado, 1872.

———. *Memoria presentada al IX Congreso Constitucional del Estado por el Gobernador del mismo, General Francisco O. Arce, en cumplimiento de la fracción IV del artículo 4° de la Constitución.* Chilpancingo, Guerrero: Imprenta del Gobierno del Estado, 1886.

———. *Memoria presentada al X Congreso Constitucional del Estado de Guerrero por el Gobernador del mismo, General Francisco O. Arce, en cumplimiento de la fracción IV del artículo 4° de la Constitución.* Chilpancingo, Guerrero: Imprenta del Gobierno del Estado, 1888.

———. *1894. Memoria presentada al XIV Congreso Constitucional por el Coronel Antonio Mercenario, Gobernador del Estado de Guerrero, en cumplimiento de la fracción IV del artículo 4° de la Constitución política local.* Chilpancingo, Guerrero: Tipografía del Gobierno en Palacio, 1896.

———. *Memoria presentada al XVIII Congreso Constitucional, por el ciudadano Agustín Mora, Gobernador del Estado de Guerrero, en cumplimiento de la fracción IV del artículo 4° de la Constitución política local.* Chilpancingo, Guerrero: Tipografía del Gobierno del Estado, 1903.

———. *Informe leído por el C. Damián Flores, Gobernador del Estado al abrirse el segundo período de sesiones ordinarias del XX Congreso Constitucional el día 2 de septiembre de 1907 y contestación del C. Presidente de la propia cámara.* Chilpancingo, Guerrero: Imprenta del Gobierno del Estado, 1907.

5. Statistical Publications

Departamento de la Estadística Nacional. *Censo general de habitantes, 30 de noviembre de 1921. Estado de Guerrero.* Mexico: Talleres Gráficos de la Nación, 1927.
Dirección General de Estadística. *Anuario estadístico de la República Mexicana. Formado por la Dirección General de Estadística a cargo del Dr. Antonio Peñafiel.* 15 vols. Mexico: Oficina Tip. de la Secretaría de Fomento, 1893–1912.
———. *Tercer censo de población de los Estados Unidos Mexicanos verificado el 27 de octubre de 1910.* 3 vols. Mexico: Oficina Impresora de la Secretaría de Hacienda, 1918–1920.
Secretaría de Fomento, Colonización, e Industria. *Censo general de la República Mexicana, Verificada el 28 de octubre de 1900, Conforme a las instrucciones de la Dirección General de Estadística a cargo del Dr. Antonio Peñafiel. Estado de Guerrero.* Mexico: Imprenta y Fototipia de la Secretaría de Fomento, 1905.
Secretaría de la Economía Nacional, Dirección General de Estadística. *Estados Unidos Mexicanos: 6° censo de población, 1940. Guerrero.* 2nd ed. Mexico: Publicaciones S.E.N., 1948.
———. *II censo ejidal, 1940. Resumen general.* Mexico: Talleres Gráficos de la Nación, 1942.

6. Newspaper Articles and Memoirs

Azuela, Salvador. "Un luchador de la Revolución." *El Universal,* 4 May 1957.
Barrón, Heriberto. "El tren dorado." *La Prensa,* 20 May 1934.
Chism, Richard E. "El distrito minero de Taxco." *Periódico Oficial del Gobierno del Estado de Guerrero,* 26 April 1890.
Díaz Soto y Gama, Antonio. "También en Guerrero se hizo labor agraria." *El Universal,* 15 December 1954.
Figueroa, Francisco. "Causas que motivaron la revolución de 1910 en el Estado de Guerrero." *El País.*
Gil, Miguel. "Por qué huyo de México el 12 de abril de 1920 el general Obregón." *La Prensa,* 13 April 1931.
Llano, José de. "Viñeta de la Revolución." *La Prensa,* 15 November 1931.
López Mena, Héctor F. "Campaña contra el huertismo." *El Nacional,* 25 May, 1, 8, 15, 22 June, 10, 17, 24, 31 August, 7 September 1953.
———. "Campaña contra villistas y zapatistas." *El Nacional,* 9, 16, 23, 30 November 1953.
———. "Campaña obregonista." *El Nacional,* 8, 29 March, 5, 12 April 1954.
———. "La campaña obregonista." *El Nacional,* 19 April 1954.
———. "Datos para la historia. El maderismo en Guerrero." *El Hombre Libre,* 10 September 1937.
———. "El maderismo en Guerrero." *El Hombre Libre,* 1, 3 September 1937.

————. "Por qué y cómo fuí gobernador del Estado de Guerrero." *El Legionario*, March, April, June, August 1958.

————. "Por qué y cómo fuí gobernador del Estado de Guerrero." *El Nacional*, 10, 17 May 1954.

————. "Pródromos." *El Nacional*, 6, 13 April 1953.

————. "El público dice. Datos para la historia de la Revolución. El maderismo en Guerrero." *Novedades*, 11 September 1937.

————. "Remembranzas maderistas." *Novedades*, 3 October 1938.

Millán Nava, Jesús. "Encarnizada batalla para la toma de Chilpancingo." *Jueves de Excélsior*, 27 June 1957.

————. "Hacia el ocaso." *El Universal*, 29 September 1940.

————. "La heróica defensa de Huitzuco." *Jueves de Excélsior*, 18 July 1957.

————. "Los iniciadores." *El Universal*, 18, 25 August 1940.

————. "José Inocente Lugo, el gobernador perseguido." *Jueves de Excélsior*, 7 November 1957.

————. "La Revolución en Guerrero." *El Nacional*, 28 October, 4, 18 November 1934.

Romero Flores, Jesús. "El Gral. Héctor F. López, un gran revolucionario." *El Nacional*, 21 February 1926.

7. Books, Articles, Papers, Dissertations

Aguilar Camín, Héctor. *La frontera nómada: Sonora y la revolución mexicana*. Mexico: Siglo Veintiuno Editores S.A., 1977.

————. "The Relevant Tradition: Sonoran Leaders in the Revolution." In D. A. Brading (ed.), *Caudillo and Peasant in the Mexican Revolution*, pp. 92–123. Cambridge: Cambridge University Press, 1980.

Ai Camp, Roderic. *Mexican Political Biographies: 1935–1975*. Tucson: University of Arizona Press, 1976.

Ankerson, Dudley. "Saturnino Cedillo, A Traditional Caudillo in San Luis Potosí 1890–1938." In D. A. Brading (ed.), *Caudillo and Peasant in the Mexican Revolution*, pp. 140–168. Cambridge: Cambridge University Press, 1980.

Arenal, Luis. *Estampas de Guerrero; Grabados de Luis Arenal, notas históricas de Macrina Rabadán: 1849–1949*. Mexico: Ediciones La Estampa Mexicana, 1949.

Bailey, David C. "Revisionism and the Recent Historiography of the Mexican Revolution." *Hispanic American Historical Review*, 58 (1) (February 1978), 62–79.

Barrett, Elinore M. *La cuenca del Tepalcatepec*. 2 vols. Mexico: SepSetentas, 1975.

Bartra, Roger, et al. *Caciquismo y poder político en el México rural*. Mexico: Siglo Veintiuno Editores S.A., 1975.

Bazant, Jan. *Alienation of Church Wealth in Mexico: Social and Economic Aspects of the Liberal Revolution, 1856–1875*. Cambridge: Cambridge University Press, 1971.

————. *Cinco haciendas mexicanas: Tres siglos de vida rural en San Luis Potosí.* Mexico: El Colegio de México, 1975.

————. "Peones, arrendatarios y aparceros en México: 1851–1853." *Historia Mexicana,* 23 (2) (octubre–diciembre 1973), 330–57.

Berry, Charles R. "The Fiction and Fact of the Reform: The Case of the Central District of Oaxaca, 1856–1867." *The Americas,* 26 (3) (January 1970), 277–90.

Brading, D. A. *Haciendas and Ranchos in the Mexican Bajío: León 1700–1860.* Cambridge: Cambridge University Press, 1978.

Brandenburg, Frank. *The Making of Modern Mexico.* Englewood Cliffs, New Jersey: Prentice Hall, 1966.

Bushnell, Clyde Gilbert. "The Military and Political Career of Juan Alvarez, 1790–1867." Thesis, University of Texas, Austin, 1958.

Buve, Raymond Th. J. "Patronaje en las zonas rurales de México." *Boletín de Estudios Latinoamericanos y del Caribe,* 16 (June 1974), 3–15.

————. "Peasant Movements, Caudillos and Land Reform during the Revolution (1910–1917) in Tlaxcala, Mexico." *Boletín de Estudios Latinoamericanos y del Caribe,* 18 (June 1975), 112–52.

————. "Protestas de obreros y campesinos durante el Porfiriato: Unas consideraciones sobre su desarollo e interrelaciones en el este de México central." *Boletín de Estudios Latino Americanos,* 13 (diciembre 1972), 1–20.

————. "State Governors and Peasant Mobilization in Tlaxcala." In D. A. Brading (ed.), *Caudillo and Peasant in the Mexican Revolution,* pp. 222–44. Cambridge: Cambridge University Press, 1980.

Capetillo, Alonso. *La rebelión sin cabeza. (Génesis y desarrollo del movimiento delahuertista).* Mexico: Imprenta Botas, 1925.

Carr, Barry. "Las peculiaridades del norte mexicano, 1880–1927: Ensayo de interpretación." *Historia Mexicana,* 22 (3) (enero–marzo 1973), 320–46.

————. "Recent Regional Studies of the Mexican Revolution." *Latin American Research Review,* 15 (1) (1980), 3–14.

Carranco Cardoso, Leopoldo. *Acciones militares en el Estado de Guerrero.* Mexico: Sociedad Mexicana de Geografía y Estadística, 1963.

————. *Iniciación de la Guerra de Independencia en el Territorio del hoy Estado de Guerrero.* Iguala, Guerrero: Editorial El Correo, 1967.

Carreño, Alberto María (ed.). *Archivo del General Porfirio Díaz.* 29 vols. Mexico, 1947–1960.

Catalán Calvo, Rafael. *Problemas del Estado de Guerrero.* Mexico: Editorial Cortés, 1946.

Chevalier, François. "The *Ejido* and Political Stability in Mexico." In Claudio Veliz (ed.), *The Politics of Conformity in Latin America.* Oxford: Oxford University Press, 1970.

————. *Land and Society in Colonial Mexico: The Great Hacienda.* Berkeley and Los Angeles: University of California Press, 1966.

Coatsworth, John H. "Railroads, Landholding and Agrarian Protest in the

Early Porfiriato." *Hispanic American Historical Review,* 54 (1) (February 1974), 48–71.

Córdova, Arnaldo. *La formación del poder político en México.* Mexico: Ediciones Era, 1972.

———. *La ideología de la Revolución Mexicana: Formación del nuevo régimen.* Mexico: Ediciones Era, 1973.

Cosío Villegas, Daniel. "Dónde está el villano?" *Historia Mexicana,* 1 (3) (enero–marzo 1952), 429–48.

———. (ed.). *Historia moderna de México. El Porfiriato. La vida económica.* 2 vols. Mexico: Editorial Hermes, 1965.

———. *Historia moderna de México. El Porfiriato. La vida política interior.* 2 vols. Mexico: Editorial Hermes, 1970–1972.

———. (ed.). *Historia moderna de México. El Porfiriato. La vida social.* 2 vols. Mexico: Editorial Hermes, 1956–1957.

Cumberland, Charles Curtis. *Mexican Revolution. Genesis under Madero.* Austin: University of Texas Press, 1952.

———. *Mexico: The Struggle for Modernity.* New York: Oxford University Press, 1972.

de la Peña, Moisés T. *Guerrero económico.* 2 vols. Chilpancingo, Guerrero: Gobierno del Estado de Guerrero, 1949.

Díaz Díaz, Fernando. *Caudillos y caciques: Antonio López de Santa Anna y Juan Alvarez.* Mexico: El Colegio de México, 1972.

Domínguez, Miguel. *La erección del estado de Guerrero: Antecedentes históricos.* Mexico: Secretaría de Educación Pública, 1949.

Dulles, John W. F. *Yesterday in Mexico: A Chronicle of the Revolution, 1919–1936.* Austin: University of Texas Press, 1967.

Falcón, Romana. " ¿Los origenes populares de la revolución de 1910? El caso de San Luis Potosí." *Historia Mexicana,* 29 (2) (octubre–diciembre 1979), 197–240.

———. "El surgimiento del agrarismo cardenista—Una revisión de las tesis populistas." *Historia Mexicana,* 27 (3) (enero–marzo, 1978), 338–86.

Fierro Armenta, Wilfrido. *Monografía de Atoyac.* Mexico: Imprenta Mexicana, 1973.

Figueroa Alcocer, Jesús. *Crónica de la Revolución en Guerrero.* Mexico: Impresora Galve S.A., 1971.

Figueroa Ayala, José. "Buenavista de Cuéllar, Gro.: Epopeya." Unpublished ms., n.d.

Figueroa Uriza, Arturo. *Ciudadanos en armas; Antecedencias y datos para la historia de la revolución mexicana.* 2 vols. Mexico: B. Costa-Amic Editor S.A., 1960.

Florescano, Enrique and Isabel Gil Sánchez (eds.). *Descripciones económicas regionales de Nueva España,* 2 vols. Mexico: Instituto Nacional de Antropología e Historia, 1976.

Fowler Salamini, Heather. *Agrarian Radicalism in Veracruz, 1920–1938.* Lincoln: University of Nebraska Press, 1978.

———. "Revolutionary Caudillos in the 1920s: Francisco Múgica and

Adalberto Tejeda." In D. A. Brading (ed.), *Caudillo and Peasant in the Mexican Revolution*, pp. 169–192.

Franco, Fidel. *Eusebio S. Almonte. Poeta mártir guerrerense.* Mexico: I.C.D., 1947.

Fraser, Donald J. "La política de desamortización en las comunidades indígenas, 1856–1872." *Historia Mexicana*, 21 (4) (abril–junio 1972), 615–52.

Friedrich, Paul. *Agrarian Revolt in a Mexican Village.* Chicago: University of Chicago Press, 1977.

Fuentes Díaz, Vicente. *La revolución de 1910 en el estado de Guerrero.* Mexico: Nacional Impresora, 1960.

Gadow, Hans. *Through Southern Mexico: Being an Account of the Travels of a Naturalist.* London and New York: Witherby and Co. and Charles Scribner's and Sons, 1908.

Gardiner, C. Harvey (ed.). *Mexico 1824–1828: The Journal and Correspondence of Edward Thornton Tayloe.* Chapel Hill: University of North Carolina Press, 1959.

Gerhard, Peter. *A Guide to the Historical Geography of New Spain.* Cambridge: Cambridge University Press, 1972.

Gibson, Charles. *The Aztecs under Spanish Rule: A History of the Indians of the Valley of Mexico.* Stanford, California: Stanford University Press, 1964.

Gill, Mario. "Los Escudero de Acapulco." *Historia Mexicana*, 3 (2) (octubre–diciembre 1953), 291–308.

Glade, William P., Jr. "Revolution and Economic Development." In William P. Glade, Jr., and Charles W. Anderson. *The Political Economy of Mexico. Two Studies by William P. Glade, Jr. and Charles W. Anderson.* Madison: University of Wisconsin Press, 1963.

González, Luis. *Invitación a la microhistoria.* Mexico: SepSetentas, 1973.

———. *Pueblo en vilo. Microhistoria de San José de Gracia.* 2nd ed. Mexico: El Colegio de México, 1972.

González Dávila, Amado. *Geografía del Estado de Guerrero y síntesis histórica.* Mexico: Editorial Quetzalcoatl, 1959.

Gruening, Ernest. *Mexico and Its Heritage.* London: Stanley Paul and Co., Ltd., 1928.

Guevara Ramírez, Luis. *Síntesis histórica del Estado de Guerrero.* Mexico: Colección de Estudios Históricos Guerrenses, 1959.

Gutelman, Michel. *Réforme et mystification agraires en Amérique Latine. Le cas du Mexique.* Paris: F. Maspero, 1971.

Gutiérrez Galindo, José C. *Rubén Figueroa, permanencia de una revolución en Guerrero.* Mexico: B. Costa-Amic Editor, 1975.

Hale, Charles A. *Mexican Liberalism in the Age of Mora, 1821–1853.* New Haven and London: Yale University Press, 1968.

Henderson, Peter V. "Un gobernador maderista: Benito Juárez Maza y la Revolución en Oaxaca." *Historia Mexicana*, 24 (3) (enero–marzo 1975), 372–89.

Hendrichs Pérez, Pedro. *Por tierras ignotas: Viajes y observaciones en la región del Río de las Balsas, por Pedro Hendrichs Pérez.* 2 vols. Mexico: Editorial Cultura, 1945–1946.

Hernández García, Beatriz. *Estado de Guerrero.* Mexico: Secretaría de Educación Pública, 1968.

Hu-Dehart, Evelyn. "Development and Rural Rebellion: Pacification of the Yaquis in the Late Porfiriato." *Hispanic American Historical Review,* 54 (1) (February 1974), 72–93.

Iturribarría, Jorge Fernando. "Limantour y la caída de Porfirio Díaz." *Historia Mexicana,* 10 (2) (octubre–diciembre 1960), 243–81.

Jacobs, Ian Edward. "Aspects of the History of the Mexican Revolution in the State of Guerrero up to 1940." Thesis, University of Cambridge, n.d.

Joseph, Gilbert M. "Caciquismo and the Revolution: Carrillo Puerto in Yucatán." In D. A. Brading (ed.), *Caudillo and Peasant in the Mexican Revolution,* pp. 193–221. Cambridge: Cambridge University Press, 1980.

Katz, Friedrich. "Agrarian Changes in Northern Mexico in the Period of Villista Rule, 1913–1915." In James W. Wilkie, Michael C. Meyer, and Edna Monzón de Wilkie (eds.). *Contemporary Mexico: Papers of the IV International Congress of Mexican History.* Berkeley, Los Angeles, London, and Mexico: University of California Press and El Colegio de México, 1976.

———. "Labor Conditions on Haciendas in Porifiran Mexico: Some Trends and Tendencies." *Hispanic American Historical Review,* 54 (1) (February 1974), 1–47.

———. "Pancho Villa." In George F. Wolskill and Douglas W. Richmond (eds.), *Essays on the Mexican Revolution,* pp. 26–45. Austin: University of Texas Press, 1979.

———. "Pancho Villa, Peasant Movements and Agrarian Reform in Northern Mexico." In D. A. Brading (ed.). *Caudillo and Peasant in the Mexican Revolution,* pp. 59–75. Cambridge: Cambridge University Press, 1980.

———. "Peasants in the Mexican Revolution of 1910." In Joseph Spielberg and Scott Whiteford (eds.). *Forging Nations: A Comparative View of Rural Ferment and Revolt,* pp. 61–81. East Lansing: Michigan State University Press, 1976.

———. "The Social Origins of the 1910 Revolution in Chihuahua." *Latin American Research Review,* 15 (1) (1980), 15–38.

Keith, Robert G. *Conquest and Agrarian Change: The Emergence of the Hacienda System on the Peruvian Coast.* Cambridge, Massachusetts, and London: Harvard University Press, 1976.

Knight, Alan. "Peasant and Caudillo in Revolutionary Mexico 1910–17." In D. A. Brading (ed.), *Caudillo and Peasant in the Mexican Revolution,* pp. 17–58. Cambridge: Cambridge University Press, 1980.

Knowlton, Robert J. "La individualización de la propiedad corporativa civil en el siglo XIX—Notas sobre Jalisco." *Historia Mexicana,* 28 (1) (julio-septiembre 1978), 24–61.

Lerner, Victoria. "Los fundamentos socioeconómicos del *cacicazgo* en el México postrevolucionario. El caso de Saturnino Cedillo." *Historia Mexicana*, 29 (3) (enero–marzo 1979), 375–446.

Lewis, Oscar. *Life in a Mexican Village: Tepoztlán Restudied*. Urbana: University of Illinois Press, 1972.

Lieuwen, Edwin. *Mexican Militarism: The Political Rise and Fall of the Revolutionary Army, 1910–1940*. Albuquerque: University of New Mexico Press, 1968.

López Barroso, Epigmenio. *Diccionario geográfico, histórico y estadístico del Distrito de Abasolo, del Estado de Guerrero*. Mexico: Ediciones Botas, 1967.

López [Mena], Héctor F. *Diccionario geográfico, histórico, biográfico y lingüístico del Estado de Guerrero*. Mexico: Editorial Pluma y Lápiz de México, 1942.

McBride, George M. *The Land Systems of Mexico*. New York: American Geographical Society, 1923.

Magaña, Gildardo. *Emiliano Zapata y el agrarismo en México*. 5 vols. Mexico: Editorial Ruta, 1951–1952.

Martínez Carbajal, Alejandro. *Juan Escudero y Amadeo Vidales*. Mexico: Editorial Revolución, 1961.

Martínez Saldaña, Tomás and Leticia Gándara Mendoza. *Política y sociedad en México: El caso de Los Altos de Jalisco*. Mexico: Sepinay, 1976.

Meyer, Jean. *La cristiada*. 3 vols. Mexico: Siglo Veintiuno Editores S.A., 1973.

———. "Los obreros en la Revolución Mexicana: Los Batallones Rojos." *Historia Mexicana*, 21 (1) (julio–septiembre 1971), 1–37.

———. *Problemas campesinos y revueltas agrarias (1821–1910)*. Mexico: SepSetentas, 1973.

———. *La révolution mexicaine: 1910–1940*. Paris: Calmann-Lévy, 1973.

———. *Le sinarquisme; Un fascisme mexicain? 1937–1947*. Paris?: Hachette 1977.

Meyer, Jean, Enrique Krauze, and Cayetano Reyes. *Historia de la Revolución Mexicana: Período 1924–1928*. 2 vols. Mexico: El Colegio de México, 1977.

Meyer, Michael C. *Mexican Rebel: Pascual Orozco and the Mexican Revolution, 1910–1915*. Lincoln: University of Nebraska Press, 1967.

Molina Enríquez, Andrés. *Los grandes problemas nacionales*. Mexico: Imprenta de A. Carranza e Hijos, 1909.

Monroy Durán, Luis. *El último caudillo: Apuntes para la historia de México, acerca del movimiento armado de 1923, en contra del gobierno constituído*. Mexico: José S. Rodríguez, 1924.

Muñoz, Celso. "Apuntes estadísticos del Distrito de Tasco del Estado de Guerrero." *Boletín de la Sociedad Mexicana de Geografía y Estadística*, tomo VII, época 1a. (1859), 456–58.

Muñoz y Pérez, Daniel. *El General Don Juan Alvarez: Esbozo biográfico y selección de documentos de Daniel Muñoz y Pérez*. Mexico: Editorial Academia Literaria, 1959.

Neri, Lic. Rodolfo. *La rebelión delahuertista en el Estado de Guerrero.* Chilpancingo, Guerrero: n.p., 1968.

Ochoa Campos, Moisés. *Breve historia del Estado de Guerrero.* Mexico: Librería Porrua Hnos. y Cía. S.A., 1968.

————. *Historia del Estado de Guerrero.* Mexico: Librería Porrua, Hnos. y Cía. S.A., 1968.

Orozco, Wistano Luis. *Legislación y jurisprudencia sobre terrenos baldíos por el Licenciado Don Wistano Luis Orozco.* 2 vols. Mexico: Imprenta de "El Tiempo," 1895.

Pavia, Lázaro. *Los estados y sus gobernantes.* Mexico: Tipografía de las Escalerillas Núm. 20, 1890.

Peñafiel, Dr. Antonio. *Ciudades coloniales y capitales de la república mexicana por el Dr. Antonio Peñafiel; se imprime por acuerdo del Señor general Porfirio Díaz, presidente de la república siendo secretario de fomento el Señor general Manuel González Cosío. Estado de Guerrero.* Mexico: Imprenta de la Secretaría de Fomento, 1908.

Perry, Laurens Ballard. *Juárez and Díaz: Machine Politics in Mexico.* De Kalb: North Illinois University Press, 1978.

Pi-Sunyer, Oriol. *Zamora: Change and Continuity in a Mexican Town.* New York: Holt, Rinehart, and Winston, 1973.

Powell, T. G. *El liberalismo y el campesinado en el centro de México (1750 a 1876).* Mexico: SepSetentas, 1974.

Rausch, George J., Jr. "The Early Career of Victoriano Huerta." *The Americas,* 21 (2) (October 1964), 136–45.

Restrepo, Iván and José Sánchez Cortés. *La reforma agraria en cuatro regiones: El Bajío, Michoacán, La Laguna y Tlaxcala.* Mexico: SepSetentas, 1972.

Reyes Heroles, Jesús. *El liberalismo mexicano.* 3 vols. Mexico: Universidad Nacional de México, 1957–1961.

Richmond, Douglas W. "Factional Strife in Coahuila, 1910–1920." *Hispanic American Historical Review,* 60 (1) (February 1980), 49–68.

Ronfeldt, David. *Atencingo, Politics of Agrarian Struggle in a Mexican Ejido.* Stanford, California: Stanford University Press, 1973.

Rosenzweig Hernández, Fernando. "Las exportaciones mexicanas de 1877 a 1911." *Historia Mexicana,* 9 (3) (enero–marzo 1960), 394–413.

Ross, Stanley R. *Francisco I. Madero, Apostle of Mexican Democracy.* New York: Columbia University Press, 1955.

Ruvalcaba, Luis N. (ed.). *Campaña política del C. Alvaro Obregón, candidato a la presidencia de la República 1920–1924.* 5 vols. Mexico: n.p., 1923.

Sánchez Castro, Alejandro. "La Revolución de Castillo Calderón." In Fidel Franco. *Eusebio S. Almonte. Poeta Mártir guerrerense.* Mexico: I.C.D., 1947.

Sandels, Robert. "Antecedentes de la Revolución en Chihuahua." *Historia Mexicana,* 24 (3) (enero–marzo 1975), 390–402.

Sartorius, Carl. *Mexico about 1850.* Stuttgart: Brockhaus, 1961.

Schryer, Frans J. "A Ranchero Economy in Northwestern Hidalgo, 1880–

1920." *Hispanic American Historical Review,* 59 (3) (August 1979), 418–43.

———. *The Rancheros of Pisaflores: The History of a Peasant Bourgeoisie in Twentieth Century Mexico.* Toronto: University of Toronto Press, 1980.

———. "The Role of the Rancheros of Central Mexico in the Mexican Revolution (The Case of the Sierra Alta de Hidalgo)." *Canadian Journal of Latin American Studies,* 4 (7) (1979), 21–41.

Sellerier, Carlos. "El mineral de Huitzuco." *Anales del Ministerio de Fomento,* II (1898), 69–112.

Shadow, Robert Dennis. "Land, Labor and Cattle: The Agrarian Economy of a West Mexican Municipio." Ph.D. thesis, State University of New York, Stony Brook, 1978.

Simpson, Eyler N. *The Ejido: Mexico's Way Out.* Chapel Hill: University of North Carolina Press, 1937.

Smith, Peter H. *Labyrinths of Power: Political Recruitment in Twentieth-Century Mexico.* Princeton: Princeton University Press, 1979.

Stavenhagen, Rodolfo. "Aspectos sociales de la estructura agraria en México." In Rodolfo Stavenhagen, Fernando Paz Sánchez, Cuauhtémoc Cárdenas, and Arturo Bonilla, *Neolatifundismo y explotación, de Emiliano Zapata a Anderson Clayton & Co.* 2nd ed. Mexico: Editorial Nuestro Tiempo, 1971.

Tannenbaum, Frank. *The Mexican Agrarian Revolution.* Washington, D.C.: The Brookings Institution, 1930.

Taylor, Paul S. *A Spanish-Mexican Peasant Community: Arandas in Jalisco, Mexico.* Ibero Americana: 4. Berkeley: University of California Press, 1933.

Taylor, William B. *Landlord and Peasant in Colonial Oaxaca.* Stanford, California: Stanford University Press, 1972.

Valverde, Custodio. *Julián Blanco y la revolución en el estado de Guerrero.* Mexico: Imprenta de J. Chávez y Hno., 1916.

Wasserman, Mark. "Oligarquía e intereses extranjeros en Chihuahua durante el Porfiriato." *Historia Mexicana,* 22 (3) (enero–marzo 1973), 279–319.

———. "The Social Origins of the 1910 Revolution in Chihuahua." *Latin American Research Review,* 15 (1) (1980), 17–38.

Waterbury, Ronald. "Non-revolutionary Peasants: Oaxaca Compared to Morelos in the Mexican Revolution." *Comparative Studies in Society and History,* 17 (1975), 410–42.

Whetten, Nathan L. *Rural Mexico.* Chicago: University of Chicago Press, 1948.

Wolf, Eric R. and Sidney W. Mintz. "Haciendas and Plantations in Middle America and the Antilles." *Social and Economic Studies,* 6 (3) (September 1957), 380–412.

Womack, John, Jr. *Zapata and the Mexican Revolution.* Harmondsworth: Penguin Books, 1972.

Index